Certified
MBA™
Exam Prep Guide

THOMSON
—★—
SOUTH-WESTERN

Australia · Canada · Mexico · Singapore · Spain · United Kingdom · United States

THOMSON

SOUTH-WESTERN

Certified MBA™ Exam Prep Guide

VP/Editorial Director:
Jack W. Calhoun

VP/Executive Publisher:
Dave Shaut

Director, Real Estate & Professional Certification Publishing:
Scott Person

Developmental Editor:
Sara Froelicher

Project Manager:
Susan Carson, Last Word Publishing and Communications

Production Editor:
Chris Hudson

Marketing Manager:
Mark Linton

Manufacturing Coordinator:
Charlene Taylor

Cover Designer:
Anne Marie Rekow

Printer:
West Group
Eagan, Minnesota

Contents

Introduction

The majority of the following information was reprinted with permission from the International Certification Institute (ICI).

- Do you have what you need to compete for a job? Recruitment on college campuses is down, and nearly 20 percent fewer MBAs have jobs upon graduation versus last year. Now more than ever, you'll have to rise above your competition.

- Can you prove you're worth the salary you deserve? As MBA graduates flood the market with high salary expectations, corporations are under pressure to reduce recruiting expenditures and hiring risk. Now more than ever, you'll have to prove the value of your MBA.

- Does your MBA certify your point of difference and value to a company? Probably not. And now is the time to change that. The Certified MBA™ (CMBA) is the first and only objective measure of a student's grasp of the MBA skill set. It is a distinction that inspires confidence among prospective employers.

The Certified MBA™ can enhance your value and marketability in the crowded MBA market. And the *Certified MBA™ Exam Prep Guide* can help ensure your test success.

The *Certified MBA™ Exam Prep Guide:*

- Outlines the exam structure, including the subject areas and objectives covered by the exam.

- Provides almost 1,700 sample questions for review.

- Covers all of the key components of the first-year MBA curriculum.

- Is organized so you can review by topic or by CMBA objectives.

- Features test-taking techniques and tips.

- Provides a detailed Study Inventory tool to help you track and organize your review for the exam.

WHAT IS THE CMBA?

With the increased need to differentiate yourself among the rising number of MBA graduates per year (112,258 in 1999-2000 according to the U.S. Department of Education), the International Certification Institute (ICI), in conjunction with Galton Technologies, a part of Prometric and leading provider of assessment and certification services, has developed a comprehensive certification exam to confirm your command of the business fundamentals companies expect of MBA hires.

The CMBA confirms a student's mastery of content consistent with the four core curriculum areas required across all accredited MBA programs. These areas are:

- Financial reporting, analysis, and markets
- Domestic and global economic environments of organizations
- Creation and distribution of goods and services
- Human behavior in organizations

Schools not accredited typically incorporate similar requirements into their curriculums, so enrollment in or graduation from an accredited institution is not required to be eligible to take the CMBA exam.

The explosive growth in the number of traditional and non-traditional MBA programs is also fueling your need for the CMBA. There are more than 1,200 degree granting MBA programs internationally and more than 50,000 students expected to be enrolled in online MBA programs in 2002. The CMBA can level the playing field between you and graduates who may rely on program prestige and reputation to promote their perceived difference. It can also effectively neutralize the bias of school reputation or rank in the recruiting and hiring decision.

As a further benefit, a CMBA Skills Profile™ will be provided to all students taking the CMBA exam. The CMBA Skills Profile assesses a student's performance in 10 key subject areas, enabling them to identify their strengths and pursue opportunities to improve in areas of weakness. The 10 key subject areas are:

- Financial Accounting
- Managerial Accounting
- Quantitative Methods
- Microeconomics
- Macroeconomics
- Finance
- Marketing Management
- Operations Management
- Organizational Behavior
- Strategy

The CMBA will confirm your command of these subject areas and can help you be more successful in your job search.

A Universal Measure

The Certified MBA™ (CMBA) is the only universal measure of a MBA's command of the core business fundamentals. The CMBA helps set MBAs apart in a competitive MBA job market.

The U.S. Department of Education recently reported a record 112,258 MBA degrees were granted in 1999-2000, representing a 420 percent gain in annual MBA graduates in the U.S. over a 30-year period. The competition for MBA-level jobs is more intense than ever.

For MBA employers, the CMBA will improve hiring decisions by confirming a command of the business fundamentals expected of MBA job applicants.

Recent surveys by the Graduate Management Admission Council (GMAC) reported that 40 percent of companies responding have smaller full-time campus recruiting staff. In addition, the average number of schools at which respondents recruited dropped in 2002. As recruiting resources decline and corporations continue to operate leaner organizations, recruiters are now being asked to do more with less to evaluate the growing number of MBA job applicants.

As a universal measurement of the core business fundamentals, the CMBA levels the playing field for all MBA graduates by emphasizing an individual's business education and neutralizing the influence of graduate program reputation or rank.

The CMBA inspires confidence that the candidate's skill set and performance potential will provide the greatest return on hiring investment for the company, an important advantage for any organization.

CMBA Development

The International Certification Institute (ICI) was founded to develop and deliver the CMBA exam. ICI is organized around three primary constituencies: students, businesses, and educators. Its directors facilitate advisement and product development through its Council of Academic Advisors, Council of Business Advisors, and the Association of CMBAs.

CMBA was created to satisfy two key needs – to help students stand out from the crowded MBA market and to help businesses improve their MBA hiring process by identifying the most qualified candidates. This is particularly important given current economic conditions and a record number of MBA graduates competing for fewer MBA-level jobs.

ICI partnered with the leading provider of computer-based testing services and certification development to ensure test validity. ICI also surveyed more than 100 MBA program directors to develop an exam that reflects the subject matter considered most important. More than 150 professors currently teaching in MBA programs contributed to the specific objectives and questions that make up the exam.

PREPARING FOR THE EXAM

While most traditional MBA programs incorporate the core curriculum in the first year of study, students of executive, online or accelerated MBA programs may complete core curriculum classes on alternative schedules. Whatever the case, MBA students who have completed the core curriculum of their MBA program should be prepared to take the CMBA exam.

The *Certified MBA™ Exam Prep Guide* provides everything you need to be ready for the test. You'll find

- Test-taking techniques and tips
- An outline of the exam structure, including the subject areas and objectives covered by the exam
- A Study Inventory tool to help you track and organize your review for the exam
- Nearly 1,700 test prep questions with answers

The CMBA exam is a multiple choice exam. Most questions on the exam will have four answers while some will have five answers. In some cases, you will be asked to choose multiple answers. There are no essay questions on the exam.

TAKING THE CMBA TEST

Achieving your CMBA is a straightforward process that begins online at CertifiedMBA.com and continues offline at Prometric testing centers.

APPLICATION

First, complete a five-step online application at CertifiedMBA.com. You'll create a username and password and provide personal details that will form your CMBA profile. You will also be asked to pay an application and transcript processing fee.

TRANSCRIPTS

Providing an official transcript verifies your current enrollment in a MBA program or that you have already earned your MBA degree.

Your transcript is required before you can be scheduled to take the exam. The final transcript showing that you received the degree is necessary for award of the CMBA designation.

SITTING FOR THE EXAM

After your application is submitted online, it will be reviewed. When it is accepted, you will receive both an email and hard copy letter notifying you of your acceptance and providing instructions on how to register for a date to sit for the CMBA exam through Prometric. At the time of acceptance, your credit card will be charged the exam fee.

You will take the exam on a computer at your choice of one of the 380 Prometric testing centers in the U.S. and Canada that offer the CMBA exam. The exam takes approximately six hours to complete. You are permitted to bring a Hewlett Packard 12c, 10b, 10bii or a Texas Instruments BA II Plus.

STATUS

At any time during the process, you may check on your status in the "My CMBA Account" section of this web site. You'll be able to tell at a glance if your application, transcript, or exam scores are pending, and to get the information you need to move the process toward your Certified MBA™.

HOW TO USE YOUR CMBA

Now, more than ever, your future depends on taking responsibility for your individual success. The crowded MBA market is filled with qualified job candidates. Only a select few can set themselves apart by providing assurance that they have achieved a full command of the core business fundamentals essential for success in today's challenging business environment. The Certified MBA™ clearly identifies you as "best-in-class" among MBAs. Let your employers and hiring employers see your ambition by showing them that you have achieved your CMBA.

Exam Structure

The CMBA exam tests your command of ten core subject areas consistent with accredited MBA programs. These areas are:

- Financial Accounting
- Managerial Accounting
- Quantitative Methods
- Microeconomics
- Macroeconomics
- Finance
- Marketing Management
- Operations Management
- Organizational Behavior
- Strategy

The subject area titles we have chosen are generic. The courses that you have taken may have different titles.

SUBJECT AREA DESCRIPTIONS

These subject areas are further described below:

FINANCIAL ACCOUNTING. Accounting is the language of business, with its own vocabulary and rules. This area focuses on the need for users of accounting information to understand accounting systems. Accounting is studied both as a method of communication and as a decision-making tool. Emphasis is on understanding and using the balance sheet, the income statement, and the cash flow statement.

MANAGERIAL ACCOUNTING. Managerial Accounting is the process within an organization that provides financial and other quantitative information used by managers in planning, implementing, and controlling the organization's activities. It includes cost accounting, profit planning, responsibility accounting, and capital budgeting.

QUANTITATIVE METHODS. A variety of quantitative techniques, including decision analysis, probability theory, sampling, statistical inference, time-series analysis, regression, and mathematical programming, are explored as aids in making managerial decisions in the face of varying degrees of uncertainty.

MICROECONOMICS. Microeconomics introduces the analytical skills and insights managers find useful. Recurrent themes are efficient resource allocation and value-creating marginal decisions under asymmetric information. Topics include demand and supply estimation, alternative concepts of production efficiency, competitive industry analysis, pricing techniques, rivalrous oligopoly, labor market dynamics, and managerial incentive contracts.

FINANCE. Finance applies theoretical concepts and analytical techniques to financial statement analysis, management of current assets, short-term and intermediate financing, the cost of capital, capital structure planning, and long-term financing. The stock and bond markets, including warrants, options, and other financial instruments, are major focal points.

MACROECONOMICS. Macroeconomics focuses on the role of countries in the global economy with special emphasis on world trade, the international flow of funds, monetary and fiscal policy, and the business cycle. Included are drivers of fluctuations in key features of the economies, such as gross domestic product, inflation, and exchange rates.

MARKETING MANAGEMENT. The major principles and techniques of marketing management are numerous. Buyer behavior, demand estimation, market segmentation, and brand strategy, including pricing, distribution channels, advertising, and sales force management relate to behavioral, financial, and quantitative analyses. The cultural dimensions of marketing permeate both domestic and international arenas.

OPERATIONS MANAGEMENT. Operations Management explores the relationship between the production system of the organization and the marketing, financial, and human resources systems facilitating the creation of goods and services. Content includes process analysis, work-force management, aggregate planning and scheduling, capacity and facilities planning, management of changes in process technology, and the relationship between manufacturing and corporate strategy.

ORGANIZATIONAL BEHAVIOR. Organizational Behavior focuses on understanding human behavior at the individual and group level, including the effect of organization structure, design, and culture on that behavior. Managers have traditionally been held accountable for influencing their employees' attitudes, behaviors, and performance. Study of human behavior can help managers explain and predict the actions of others inside and outside the organization. OB explores current approaches, models, and methods that managers use to influence individuals and groups.

STRATEGY. The objectives of Strategy are to instill an understanding of the viewpoints of top managers in complex organizations; major concepts and frameworks in formulating and implementing strategy, as well as the dynamics of competitive rivalry; and a comprehensive view of overall organizational functioning. Issues related to the implementation of global strategies in different cultural contexts are included.

SUBJECT AREA OBJECTIVES

The following objectives outline for you the specific areas to be covered within each area of the curriculum. These objectives will drive the specific items on the CMBA exam.

Financial Accounting

- Given a set of data, use the accounting equation to determine the amount of the missing balance sheet component.
- Select the accounting concept that applies to revenue recognition, accruals, recording of asset values, et al.
- Identify the roles of bodies with major influence on accounting standards/procedures.
- Given a scenario, determine the financial statement effects of various transactions affecting current assets.
- Given data, calculate the financial statements effects of various transactions affecting non-current assets, including depreciation, intangibles, investments, and deferred taxes.
- Given data, determine the amount of current liabilities to be recorded.
- Given financial data, determine carrying amounts of noncurrent liabilities and their disposition, including bonds payable, long-term leases, deferred taxes, et al.
- Given financial information, calculate working capital before and after specific transactions.
- Given a set of financial data, calculate the amount to be shown as contributed capital on the financial statements.
- Show the effects on financial statements of specified treasury stock transactions.
- Calculate book value with financial information provided.
- Determine retained earnings after a series of provided transactions.
- Given financial data, identify the financial statement effects of gains/losses from foreign currency translation, treatment of comprehensive income, et al.
- Given data, identify the effects of dividend actions on financial statements.
- Given data, calculate the amount to be shown as revenue for an accounting period.
- Given data, calculate the cost of sales under various alternatives.
- Given financial data, distinguish between expenses/expenditures, including accruals, R&D, stock options, et al.
- Given selected data, identify the financial statement effects of unrealized gains or losses.
- Given data, determine basic and diluted EPS.
- Given financial information, calculate cash from operations, investment, and financing.
- Given statements, calculate ratios related to liquidity, performance, investment utilization, financial condition, et al.

Managerial Accounting

- Identify examples of variable, fixed, and sunk costs.
- Given data, use the appropriate formulae to determine variable, fixed, and total costs.
- Given data, use opportunity cost concepts to enhance a management decision.
- Given selected financial data, determine appropriate cost allocations.

- Given data, calculate product and unit of service standard costs.
- With a given set of financial data concerning common costs, calculate the economic impact of processing specific products beyond split-off.
- Define target costing and contrast it with kaizen costing.
- Given data, determine activity-based costs of products.
- Given financial data, contrast income reported under various costing approaches (variable, full absorption, ABC).
- Given a scenario with financial information, calculate break-even in (units, dollars).
- Given price and cost information, use contribution margin in facilitating a specified managerial decision.
- Identify how period costs are treated in financial statements.
- Given financial data, determine the mix of planned products and activities that will generate optimum profits.
- Given data, analyze results of operations using a flexible budget.
- Given financial data, determine a company's most profitable product, customer, or division.
- Given a set of financial data, determine sales volume, efficiency, and price variances.
- Given selected financial information, identify relevant costs in new equipment, make-or-buy, and drop-or-add decisions.
- Given selected financial information, determine the minimum acceptable price for a special order.
- Given data, calculate the net present value of an investment opportunity
- Given a scenario, determine the transfer price that would maximize profits.
- Given financial data, contrast relative performance based on ROI, EVA, ROS, et al.
- Given a specified strategy, identify appropriate responsibility centers.
- Define Economic Value Added (EVA) and specify the kind of responsibility center in which it is appropriate.
- Identify the components of the Balanced Scorecard.

Finance

- Given financial and accounting information, calculate selected financial ratios.
- Given financial and accounting information, calculate the return on equity using the DuPont format.
- Differentiate the components of the extended DuPont equation.
- Given financial and accounting information, calculate or describe the common measures of investment performance.
- Differentiate between techniques used to forecast financial statements.
- Given appropriate information, calculate the future value of a present sum.
- Given appropriate information, calculate the present value of a future sum.
- Recognize the importance of annuities in the field of finance.
- Recognize the major characteristics of investment banking.
- Describe an initial public offering (IPO).
- Distinguish between the various types of bonds.
- Describe the common features of bonds.
- Describe the major characteristics of preferred and common stock.
- Distinguish between the various techniques used to make capital budgeting decisions.
- Describe the process of valuing corporate securities.

- Describe the process of forecasting cash flows in capital budgeting problems.
- Describe the implementation of risk analysis in capital budgeting problems.
- Explain the framework for understanding how the financial system works.
- Describe the meaning and determinants of rates of return on different classes of assets.
- Define working capital management.
- Describe the process of managing working capital assets and liabilities.
- Explain how to create value through financing decisions.
- Show how to relate a firm's financing mix to its investment decisions.
- Describe the corporate motives for mergers and acquisitions.
- Describe the process of evaluating mergers and acquisitions.

Macroeconomics

- Recognize how components of the economic environment (unemployment, inflation, growth, fiscal and monetary policy) affect firm actions.
- Describe the calculation and limits in use of published statistics (e.g., GDP, unemployment rate, inflation rate).
- Understand how changes in various components of aggregate demand (consumer demand, investment demand, government demand, net foreign demand) affect the macro economy.
- Explain how the money supply is expanded and contracted, and interpret the language of the Federal Reserve.
- Explain how changes in monetary policy are transmitted to changes in inflation and unemployment, and why the transmissions mechanisms may not work as predicted.
- Understand the causes of inflation, and predict how an inflationary period will affect the firm.
- Evaluate the effectiveness of policies designed to stimulate aggregate demand and those designed to stimulate aggregate supply.
- Define the yield curve and understand shifts in the curve.
- Order the components of the federal budget by size, and analyze the impact of budget items on firm decisions.
- Evaluate a macroeconomic forecast.
- Distinguish among the types of unemployment and the policies for dealing with them.
- Explain how the inequality of withdrawals and injections affect GDP changes.
- Understand the causes and cures for hyperinflation.
- Understand the causes of economic growth (more capital, more labor, more productivity), and predict the consequences of firms for each of these causes.
- Explain how international translation and transaction risk may affect firm balance sheet and income statement.
- Justify a decision to hedge international risk.
- Explain the various tools for hedging international risk (e.g., currency options, futures, and forward contracts).
- Recognize the special risks firms may face in operating in countries that use flexible exchange rates, pegged exchange rates, exchange controls, or currency boards to determine exchange rates.
- Evaluate changes in national protectionist policies.
- Show the connection between inflation rate and exchange rate.

Microeconomics

- Predict how rational and irrational decisions by consumers affect firms.
- Distinguish between cost and price.
- Explain how a firm can achieve a profit-maximizing price.
- Describe how fixed cost, marginal cost and average cost differ.
- Apply the supply and demand model to changes in price and quantity. Analyze the forces that shift supply and demand curves.
- Justify a marginal-cost pricing decision. Explain how fixed costs enter pricing decisions.
- Calculate price and income elasticity coefficients.
- Recognize the importance of cross elasticity.
- Distinguish between commodity and monopoly pricing.
- Apply elasticity concept to production and pricing decisions in firms.
- Explain how advertising should change the slope and position of the demand curve.
- Differentiate among various forms of industrial organization (pure competition, monopolistic competition, oligopoly, monopoly).
- Calculate the minimum point on an average cost function.
- Recognize how the competitive environment affects firm decisions.
- Describe a disequilibrium price, and predict market changes that result.
- Evaluate the use of antitrust laws and deregulation as methods of dealing with monopoly power.
- Apply the wage-pricing model to trade union behavior.
- Evaluate changes in the minimum wage.

Marketing

- Describe the marketing concept.
- Describe demand elasticity.
- Given a retail price and channel margin structure, calculate the manufacturer's contribution margin.
- Given a retail price, channel margin structure, market size and marketing investment, calculate a break-even market share.
- Given acquisition costs, revenue, contribution margin, discount rate, and loyalty period, calculate lifetime customer value.
- Given specific numbers of sales accounts and phone calls and visits possible per day by a sales representative, calculate the total number of sales representatives needed in a market.
- Given specific market size, purchase cycle, average retail price, and market share information, forecast annual dollar sales for a company's product/service.
- Given a sales problem faced by a company, select the appropriate course of action.
- Given certain market characteristics (size; demographic, geographic, psychographic, and/or behavioral descriptors), select the appropriate segmentation scheme for a firm.
- Given a particular product/service, identify the appropriate target market for a firm.
- Given characteristics (competitors' sizes and positions) of a particular market, select the appropriate positioning strategy for a firm.
- Describe the criteria for segmenting markets.

- Given a particular product life cycle stage (introduction, growth, maturity, or decline), identify the role played by a specific marketing mix variable (product/service, price, place, or promotion).
- Given a particular product life cycle stage (introduction, growth, maturity, or decline), select the appropriate marketing strategy (product/service, price, place, or promotion).
- Describe the marketing objective of a firm whose product/service is in a particular stage of the product life cycle (introduction, growth, maturity, or decline).
- Given a firm's particular marketing strategy (product/service, price, place, or promotion), select the appropriate corresponding marketing strategy (product/service, price, place, or promotion) for the firm.
- Given a particular market scenario, select the appropriate marketing strategy (product/service, price, place, or promotion) for a firm.
- Describe the relationship between type of decision-making (routinized, limited, extended) and marketing strategy (product/service, price, place, or promotion).
- Given a particular marketing objective for a company, select the appropriate person(s) (initiator, influencer, decider, buyer, user) at whom to direct a marketing campaign.
- Describe customer perceived value.
- Describe the differences between consumer and organizational markets.
- Given a particular problem encountered by a firm attempting to sell to an organizational buyer, infer the most likely cause.
- Describe the benefits and drawbacks of research contact methods (personal, mail, telephone, online).
- Given a firm's particular research objective, select the appropriate research approach (focus group, survey, etc)
- Describe the primary risk associated with filling a product line.
- Describe the primary rationale for brand extensions.
- Describe the differences between products and services.
- Given a firm's growth objective, select the appropriate product/service strategy.
- Explain the conditions under which a particular pricing strategy is appropriate.
- Given a particular pricing strategy, infer the assumption(s) underlying the approach.
- Describe yield management.
- Given a particular product/service type, select the appropriate distribution strategy (direct, intensive, selective, exclusive).
- Explain the role of the channel.
- Describe the difference between a channel and a supply chain.
- Given a specific promotional objective (building awareness, creating an image, reminding consumers of the product/service, generating excitement or involvement, encouraging trial, reducing post-purchase dissonance, protecting from competitive action) for a company, select the appropriate marketing communications mix variable (advertising, consumer promotions, trade promotion, event sponsorship, point-of-sale, direct mail, publicity, personal selling, public relations).
- Given a particular marketing communications execution, infer the underlying objective.

Organizational Behavior

- Analyze interpersonal relations in a work in environment based on the concept of organizational citizenship behavior.
- Analyze performance appraisals for manifestations of rating errors.
- Explain the legal basis of sexual harassment.
- Analyze employee behavior in terms of cognitive bases of motivation.
- Analyze employee behavior in terms of environmental bases of work motivation.
- Analyze group dynamics as a function of dimensions of team interaction.
- Explain the basis of the socialization process.
- Describe the basis of leadership in organizations.
- Explain the basis of organizational culture.
- Specify the benefits of various organizational structures.
- Analyze the factors that differentiate national cultures.
- Analyze the bases of social power.
- Understand issues associated with work stress in the organization.
- Analyze issues associated with justice and fairness in the workplace.
- Analyze the rationale for organizational resistance to change.
- Specify the major equal employment laws and concepts.
- Specify the legal basis of employment discrimination.
- Analyze issues associated with gender discrimination in the workplace.
- Define the concepts of job analysis and job evaluation.
- Explain the costs and benefits of various systems of employee recruitment.
- Analyze major methods of personnel selection on the basis of staffing needs.
- Explain the benefits of training needs analyses.
- Explain the benefits of performance appraisal.
- Analyze the rationale for multi-source (360-degree) assessments of performance.
- Explain the major organizational constraints on employee compensation.
- Analyze the components of a pay structure.
- Describe the administration of employee benefits systems.
- Describe the legal basis of occupational health and safety.
- Define employee rights affecting the employment relationship.
- Explain the process of unionization.

Operations

- From a list of processes, identify a process by a primary characteristic.
- Match a process to the characteristics of the markets for its products.
- Select the correct definition for an inventory management term.
- Identify the EOQ formula from a list of several similar formulas.
- Identify the nature of the basic lot-sizing trade-off made by the EOQ formula.
- Given a bill a materials, be able to identify end items or components, which characterize dependent or independent demand.
- Given a bill of materials, calculate the number of component items needed to produce an end item.
- From a list of terms, identify those which are costs or benefits associated with carrying inventory.
- Understand the relationships between activities in a critical path diagram.
- Given information about the activities that comprise a project, identify the project's critical path.
- Given information about the activities that comprise a project, calculate the amount of slack time for an activity not on the project's critical path.

- Given information about the activities that comprise a project, identify the most cost-effective way to complete the project at an earlier date than planned.
- Identify the bottleneck in a diagram of linked activities.
- Given a scenario, calculate the capacity cushion of a process.
- Given a scenario, calculate the capital costs of increasing the capacity of a process made up of a series of linked activities.
- Given several charts and a verbal description of their purpose, identify a Pareto chart.
- Understand how charting is useful in managing quality in a process.
- Understand the use of control charts.
- Understand the relationship of statistical variance to six-sigma quality measurements.
- Identify basic aggregate planning strategies.
- Describe the relationship between the degree of customer contact and the efficiency of a service.
- Identify situations where waiting line analysis can be useful.
- Identify the inputs to a waiting line problem.
- Given several call center scenarios, (in a table) rank the scenarios in terms of efficiency.
- Given a scenario, identify the job sequence resulting from a shortest operating time job priority rule.
- Identify the job priority rule that always results in the shortest average waiting time for a single-machine.
- Identify the effects of "balance delay" in assembly line layout.
- Identify the trade-offs between job enrichment, operational flexibility and workforce training.

Quantitative Methods

- Given a scenario with probabilities and quantitative outcomes, calculate the expected value.
- Given a scenario including probabilities and end values, use the principles of decision analysis to identify the range of probabilities under which a course of action would be chosen.
- Given a scenario with a historical data distribution, identify the probability of a specified event.
- Given a scenario with two small (five numbers each) sets of data (with same average and different SD's), identify the managerial impact of having the larger SD.
- Given a scenario with normal distribution (mean and SD given) and a value, calculate the probability that corresponds to the specified value.
- Given a scenario with normal distribution (mean and SD given) and the percentile, calculate the value that corresponds to the specified probability.
- Given a scenario with normal distribution (mean and SD given), calculate parameters for the aggregated (or disaggregated) normal distribution.
- Given a scenario including sample size, average and SD, differentiate SE from SD.
- Given a scenario including sample size, average and SD; calculate the 95% confidence interval for the population average.
- Given a scenario including sample size, average, and standard deviation, determine statistical significance from the average in question and managerial implications.

- Given a scenario including three groups with their averages, sample sizes, and SD's, along with the p-value of an ANOVA, determine the managerial impact if the group means are statistically significantly different.
- Given a scenario including correlation coefficient (r) and graphs, match the correlation coefficient to appropriate graphs.
- Given a scenario, determine managerial interpretation of slope and intercept coefficients.
- Given a scenario and regression output, determine how much a coefficient might vary.
- Given historical data, determine whether or not to include an outlier in generating a prediction.
- Given a scenario, regression output, and values for the independent variables, predict range of a value.
- Given a scenario and regression output, determine the significant coefficients.
- Given a scenario and regression output, determine the managerial interpretation of coefficients.
- Given a scenario and regression output, explain managerial implications of a dummy variable.
- Given a scenario with monthly data, demonstrate an understanding of the moving average method.
- Understand how to generate a forecast with data that exhibits a long-term trend and seasonal variation.
- Given a list of situations, identify those in which simulation would be a viable approach (contain random variables.)
- Given a scenario including simulation output, determine the course of action for two alternatives with means that are not significantly different.
- Given a scenario, choose appropriate distribution for a random variable.
- Given a scenario including cost and sales data, write the objective function for the appropriate Linear Programming model.
- Given a scenario including RHS and coefficients, write a constraint for the appropriate Linear Programming model.
- Given a scenario including LP Output, determine the most critical resource to relieve.

Strategy

- Identify the key elements of strategy.
- Identify the attributes of a good strategy.
- Identify the key levels of strategy.
- Distinguish between vision and mission.
- Distinguish between different perspectives on strategy.
- Describe synergy and identify examples of it.
- Distinguish between economies of scale and scope.
- Distinguish between vertical and horizontal integration.
- Distinguish between vertical and horizontal differentiation.
- Identify various levels of uncertainty and ways of dealing with the same.
- Describe the key components of a business model.
- Identify the elements of parenting advantage.
- Describe the structure-conduct-performance paradigm.
- Describe how you would use the Porter 5 forces framework to do a structural analysis of an industry.
- Define the various ways in which an industry can be defined.

- Describe strategic groups and identify how they are useful in industry analysis.
- Describe the various stages of industry evolution.
- Describe the factors that contribute to competitive advantage.
- Distinguish between core competence and distinctive competence.
- Describe the factors that affect sustainability of competitive advantage.
- Describe network effects.
- Describe various industry structures and their implications for strategy.
- Describe key components of a value chain and value system.
- Define value as commonly used in strategic management.
- Describe the various steps in the assessment of a strategy.
- Describe vulnerability analysis.
- Describe critical success factors.
- Describe Porter's generic strategies.
- Describe what is meant by "stuck in the middle."
- Describe the two-dimensional growth vector matrix.
- Distinguish between integration and diversification.
- Describe corporate motives for mergers and acquisitions.
- Describe the process for evaluating mergers and acquisitions.
- Describe different types of alliances.
- Identify the advantages and disadvantages of alliances.
- Describe forces driving globalization.
- Distinguish between multinational, global and transnational strategies.
- Describe key organizational challenges in globalization.
- Describe what factors were ignored by dot.coms in developing their strategies.
- Describe the typical factors that cause an organization to go into decline.
- Describe the process involved in the strategic transformation of an organization in decline.

Test Taking Tips

Sample test questions and hours of review are central elements in your test preparation. However, content review isn't all you need to succeed. The questions you will encounter on the Certified MBA™ Exam may be longer with more detailed graphs. Some tips that may also help for this exam:

- Carefully read through the objectives for this exam and note the formulas and calculations that may be needed.
- Always guess at an answer since a blank answer equals a wrong answer.

These test-taking tips may also help.

- Arrive for the test prepared.
- Arrive early, if possible.
- Bring everything you'll need—pencils and pens, an approved calculator, etc.
- Stay relaxed and confident.
- Remind yourself that you are well-prepared and are going to do well.
- Take several slow, deep breaths to relax.
- Don't talk to other students before a test; anxiety is contagious.
- Be comfortable but alert.
- Choose a good spot to take the test.
- Make sure you have enough room to work.
- Maintain an upright posture in your seat.
- Preview the test. Spend 5% of your time reading through the test carefully, marking key terms, deciding how to budget your time, and making brief notes for ideas you can use later.
- Answer the test questions in a strategic order. Begin by answering the easy questions you know. The last questions you answer should be the most difficult.

Once you think you are done:

- Reserve 10% of your test time to review your answers.
- Make sure you have answered all of the questions.
- Check your math answers for careless mistakes (e.g. misplaced decimals).

These tips for taking multiple choice tests may also be helpful:

- First eliminate answers you know are wrong.
- Always guess when there is no penalty for guessing or you can eliminate options.
- Since your first choice is usually correct, don't change your answers unless you are sure of the correction.

- If you are uncertain of the correct answer, cross out the options you know are definitely wrong, then mark the question so that you can reconsider it at the end of the exam.
- Read the stem of the question all the way through, then each possible answer all the way through.
- Use the options themselves to provide you with hints about things you need to know.
- "All of the above" answers are often correct. If you know two of three of options are correct, "all of the above" is a strong possibility.
- If you're not sure about a number answer, toss out the high and low and consider the middle range numbers.
- If you have no idea of the answer check for "look alike" options and check for the most inclusive option--the option that contains the most information.

Study Inventories

The following inventories are designed to help you track your study progress and organize your study plan. Use these inventories to track your review as you complete the sample test questions provided in each content area.

FINANCIAL ACCOUNTING

Content Areas	Objectives	Total Questions Missed	Review Complete	Needs Further Study
Balance Sheet	Given a set of data, use the accounting equation to determine the amount of the missing balance sheet component.			
	Given a scenario, determine the financial statement effects of various transactions affecting current assets.			
	Given financial information, calculate working capital before and after specific transactions			
	Given a set of financial data, calculate the amount to be shown as contributed capital on the financial statements.			
Income Statements	Select the accounting concept that applies to revenue recognition, accruals, recording of asset values, et al.			
	Given financial data, distinguish between expenses/expenditures, including accruals, R&D, stock options, et al.			

Content Areas	Objectives	Total Questions Missed	Review Complete	Needs Further Study
Statement of Cash Flows	Given financial information, calculate cash from operations, investment, and financing.			
Financial Statement Analysis	Given statements, calculate ratios related to liquidity, performance, investment utilization, financial condition, et al. Identify the roles of bodies with major influence on accounting standards/procedures.			
Receivables and Revenue Recognition	Given data, calculate the amount to be shown as revenue for an accounting period.			
Inventories	Given data, calculate the cost of sales under various alternatives.			
Long-Lived Tangible and Intangible Assets	Given data, calculate the financial statements effects of various transactions affecting non-current assets, including depreciation, intangibles, investments, and deferred taxes. Calculate book value with financial information provided.			
Liabilities	Given data, determine the amount of current liabilities to be recorded. Given financial data, determine carrying amounts of non-current liabilities and their disposition, including bonds payable, long-term leases, deferred taxes, et al. Given financial data, determine carrying amounts of non-current liabilities and their disposition, including bonds payable, long-term leases, deferred taxes, et al.			

Content Areas	Objectives	Total Questions Missed	Review Complete	Needs Further Study
Investments and Shareholders' equity	Given selected data, identify the financial statement effects of unrealized gains or losses. Show the effects on financial statements of specified treasury stock transactions. Determine retained earnings after a series of provided transactions. Given financial data, identify the financial statement effects of gains/losses from foreign currency translation, treatment of comprehensive income, et al. Given data, identify the effects of dividend actions on financial statements. Given data, determine basic and diluted EPS.			

MANAGERIAL ACCOUNTING

Content Areas	Objectives	Total Questions Missed	Review Complete	Needs Further Study
Measuring Costs	Given data, use the appropriate formulae to determine variable, fixed, and total costs. Given data, use opportunity cost concepts to enhance a management decision. Identify examples of variable, fixed, and sunk costs. Given data, calculate product and unit of service standard costs.			
Activity-Based Management	Given data, determine activity-based costs of products. Given financial data, contrast income reported under various costing approaches (variable, full absorption, ABC).			
Financial Modeling for Short-Term Decision Making	Given a scenario with financial information, calculate break-even in (units, dollars). Given price and cost information, use contribution margin in facilitating a specified managerial decision.			
Cost Analysis	With a given set of financial data concerning common costs, calculate the economic impact of processing specific products beyond split-off. Given selected financial information, identify relevant costs in new equipment, make-or-buy, and drop-or-add decisions. Given selected financial information, determine the minimum acceptable price for a special order. Given financial data, determine the mix of planned products and activities that will generate optimum profits.			
Capital Expenditure Decisions	Given data, calculate the net present value of an investment opportunity.			

Content Areas	Objectives	Total Questions Missed	Review Complete	Needs Further Study
Profit Planning and Budgeting	Given data, analyze results of operations using a flexible budget. Given a specified strategy, identify appropriate responsibility centers.			
Evaluating Performance	Define target costing and contrast it with kaizen costing. Given a set of financial data, determine sales volume, efficiency, and price variances. Identify the components of the Balanced Scorecard.			
Profit and Investment Center Performance	Given financial data, determine a company's most profitable product, customer, or division. Given a scenario, determine the transfer price that would maximize profits. Given financial data, contrast relative performance based on ROI, EVA, ROS, et al. Define Economic Value Added (EVA) and specify the kind of responsibility center in which it is appropriate. Identify how period costs are treated in financial statements.			
Allocating Costs to Responsibility Centers	Given selected financial data, determine appropriate cost allocations.			

QUANTITATIVE METHODS

Content Areas	Objectives	Total Questions Missed	Review Complete	Needs Further Study
Introduction to Probability	Given a scenario with a historical data distribution, identify the probability of a specified event.			
	Given a scenario with normal distribution (mean and SD given) and a value, calculate the probability that corresponds to the specified value.			
	Given a scenario with normal distribution (mean and SD given) and the percentile, calculate the value that corresponds to the specified probability.			
Probability Distributions	Given a scenario with probabilities and quantitative outcomes, calculate the expected value.			
	Given a scenario with two small (five numbers each) sets of data (with same average and different SD's), identify the managerial impact of having the larger SD.			
	Given a scenario with normal distribution (mean and SD given), calculate parameters for the aggregated (or disaggregated) normal distribution.			
	Given a scenario including sample size, average and SD, differentiate SE from SD.			
	Given a scenario, choose appropriate distribution for a random variable.			
	Given a scenario including sample size, average and SD; calculate the 95% confidence interval for the population average.			
	Given a scenario including sample size, average, and standard deviation, determine statistical significance from the average in question and managerial implications.			

Content Areas	Objectives	Total Questions Missed	Review Complete	Needs Further Study
Decision Analysis	Given a scenario including probabilities and end values, use the principles of decision analysis to identify the range of probabilities under which a course of action would be chosen.			
Forecasting	Given a scenario with monthly data, demonstrate an understanding of the moving average method. Understand how to generate a forecast with data that exhibits a long-term trend and seasonal variation. Given historical data, determine whether or not to include an outlier in generating a prediction.			
Regression Analysis	Given a scenario, regression output, and values for the independent variables, predict range of a value. Given a scenario and regression output, determine the significant coefficients. Given a scenario and regression output, determine the managerial interpretation of coefficients. Given a scenario and regression output, explain managerial implications of a dummy variable. Given a scenario and regression output, determine how much a coefficient might vary. Given a scenario including three groups with their averages, sample sizes, and SD's, along with the p-value of an ANOVA, determine the managerial impact if the group means are statistically significantly different.			

Content Areas	Objectives	Total Questions Missed	Review Complete	Needs Further Study
Linear Programming	Given a scenario including cost and sales data, write the objective function for the appropriate Linear Programming model. Given a scenario including RHS and coefficients, write a constraint for the appropriate Linear Programming model. Given a scenario including LP Output, determine the most critical resource to relieve. Given a scenario including correlation coefficient (r) and graphs, match the correlation coefficient to appropriate graphs. Given a scenario, determine managerial interpretation of slope and intercept coefficients.			
Simulation	Given a list of situations, identify those in which simulation would be a viable approach (contain random variables.) Given a scenario including simulation output, determine the course of action for two alternatives with means that are not significantly different.			

MICROECONOMICS

Content Areas	Objectives	Total Questions Missed	Review Complete	Needs Further Study
Demand and Supply	Apply the supply and demand model to changes in price and quantity. Analyze the forces that shift supply and demand curves.			
Demand Analysis	Predict how rational and irrational decisions by consumers affect firms. Distinguish between cost and price. Calculate price and income elasticity coefficients Recognize the importance of cross elasticity. Apply elasticity concept to production and pricing decisions in firms. Explain how advertising should change the slope and position of the demand curve.			
Cost Analysis and Estimation	Describe how fixed cost, marginal cost and average cost differ. Evaluate changes in the minimum wage. Calculate the minimum point on an average cost function.			
Perfect Competition and Monopoly	Distinguish between commodity and monopoly pricing. Describe a disequilibrium price, and predict market changes that result. Evaluate the use of antitrust laws and deregulation as methods of dealing with monopoly power.			
Monopolistic Competition and Oligolopy	Differentiate among various forms of industrial organization (pure competition, monopolistic competition, oligopoly, monopoly). Recognize how the competitive environment affects firm decisions.			

Content Areas	Objectives	Total Questions Missed	Review Complete	Needs Further Study
Pricing Practices	Justify a marginal-cost pricing decision. Explain how fixed costs enter pricing decisions. Apply the wage-pricing model to trade union behavior. Explain how a firm can achieve a profit-maximizing price.			

FINANCE

Content Areas	Objectives	Total Questions Missed	Review Complete	Needs Further Study
Analysis of Financial Statements	Given financial and accounting information, calculate selected financial ratios. Given financial and accounting information, calculate the return on equity using the DuPont format. Differentiate the components of the extended DuPont equation. Given financial and accounting information, calculate or describe the common measures of investment performance. Describe the meaning and determinants of rates of return on different classes of assets.			
Financial Planning and Forecasting Financial Statements	Differentiate between techniques used to forecast financial statements.			
The Financial Environment	Explain the framework for understanding how the financial system works.			
Time Value of Money	Recognize the importance of annuities in the field of finance. Given appropriate information, calculate the future value of a present sum. Given appropriate information, calculate the present value of a future sum.			
Bonds and Their Valuation	Distinguish between the various types of bonds. Describe the common features of bonds. Describe the process of valuing corporate securities.			

Content Areas	Objectives	Total Questions Missed	Review Complete	Needs Further Study
Stocks and Their Valuation	Describe the process of valuing corporate securities. Describe the major characteristics of preferred and common stock.			
Evaluating Cash Flows	Distinguish between the various techniques used to make capital budgeting decisions.			
Cash Flow Estimation and Risk Analysis	Describe the process of forecasting cash flows in capital budgeting problems. Describe the implementation of risk analysis in capital budgeting problems.			
Capital Structure Decisions	Explain how to create value through financing decisions. Show how to relate a firm's financing mix to its investment decisions.			
Initial Public Offerings and Investment Banking	Describe an initial public offering (IPO). Recognize the major characteristics of investment banking.			
Current Asset Management	Define working capital management. Describe the process of managing working capital assets and liabilities.			
Mergers and Acquisitions	Describe the corporate motives for mergers and acquisitions. Describe the process of evaluating mergers and acquisitions.			

MACROECONOMICS

Content Areas	Objectives	Total Questions Missed	Review Complete	Needs Further Study
Measuring Macroeconomic Variables	Describe the calculation and limits in use of published statistics (e.g., GDP, unemployment rate, inflation rate). Evaluate a macroeconomic forecast. Explain how the inequality of withdrawals and injections affect GDP changes.			
Classical Macroeconomic Theory	Recognize how components of the economic environment (unemployment, inflation, growth, fiscal and monetary policy) affect firm actions. Understand how changes in various components of aggregate demand (consumer demand, investment demand, government demand, net foreign demand) affect the macro economy. Evaluate the effectiveness of policies designed to stimulate aggregate demand and those designed to stimulate aggregate supply. Order the components of the federal budget by size, and analyze the impact of budget items on firm decisions.			
The Theory of Economic Growth	Understand the causes of economic growth (more capital, more labor, more productivity), and predict the consequences of firms for each of these causes. Evaluate changes in national protectionist policies.			

Content Areas	Objectives	Total Questions Missed	Review Complete	Needs Further Study
Money in the Traditional Keynesian System	Explain how the money supply is expanded and contracted, and interpret the language of the Federal Reserve. Define the yield curve and understand shifts in the curve.			
Inflation	Understand the causes of inflation, and predict how an inflationary period will affect the firm. Understand the causes and cures for hyperinflation. Distinguish among the types of unemployment and the policies for dealing with them.			
Macroeconomic Policy	Explain how changes in monetary policy are transmitted to changes in inflation and unemployment, and why the transmissions mechanisms may not work as predicted.			

Content Areas	Objectives	Total Questions Missed	Review Complete	Needs Further Study
International Dimensions of Macroeconomic Policy	Explain how international translation and transaction risk may affect firm balance sheet and income statement. Justify a decision to hedge international risk. Explain the various tools for hedging international risk (e.g., currency options, futures, and forward contracts). Recognize the special risks firms may face in operating in countries that use flexible exchange rates, pegged exchange rates, exchange controls, or currency boards to determine exchange rates. Show the connection between inflation rate and exchange rate.			

MARKETING MANAGEMENT

Content Areas	Objectives	Total Questions Missed	Review Complete	Needs Further Study
Marketing Strategy and Tactics	Given a firm's particular marketing strategy (product/service, price, place, or promotion), select the appropriate corresponding marketing strategy (product/service, price, place, or promotion) for the firm. Given a particular market scenario, select the appropriate marketing strategy (product/service, price, place, or promotion) for a firm. Describe the relationship between type of decision-making (routinized, limited, extended) and marketing strategy (product/service, price, place, or promotion).			
Marketing Research and Information Systems	Describe the benefits and drawbacks of research contact methods (personal, mail, telephone, online). Given a firm's particular research objective, select the appropriate research approach (focus group, survey, etc)			

Content Areas	Objectives	Total Questions Missed	Review Complete	Needs Further Study
Business-to-Business Marketing	Given a particular marketing objective for a company, select the appropriate person(s) (initiator, influencer, decider, buyer, user) at whom to direct a marketing campaign. Describe the differences between consumer and organizational markets. Given a particular problem encountered by a firm attempting to sell to an organizational buyer, infer the most likely cause.			
Segmenting, Targeting and Positioning Products and Services	Given certain market characteristics (size; demographic, geographic, psychographic, and/or behavioral descriptors), select the appropriate segmentation scheme for a firm. Given a particular product/service, identify the appropriate target market for a firm. Given characteristics (competitors' sizes and positions) of a particular market, select the appropriate positioning strategy for a firm. Describe the criteria for segmenting markets.			

Content Areas	Objectives	Total Questions Missed	Review Complete	Needs Further Study
Product Decisions and New Product Development	Given a particular product life cycle stage (introduction, growth, maturity, or decline), identify the role played by a specific marketing mix variable (product/service, price, place, or promotion).			
	Given a particular product life cycle stage (introduction, growth, maturity, or decline), select the appropriate marketing strategy (product/service, price, place, or promotion).			
	Describe the marketing objective of a firm whose product/service is in a particular stage of the product life cycle (introduction, growth, maturity, or decline).			
	Describe the primary risk associated with filling a product line.			
	Describe the primary rationale for brand extensions.			
	Describe the differences between products and services.			
	Given a firm's growth objective, select the appropriate product/service strategy.			
	Given acquisition costs, revenue, contribution margin, discount rate, and loyalty period, calculate lifetime customer value.			
	Describe customer perceived value.			

Content Areas	Objectives	Total Questions Missed	Review Complete	Needs Further Study
Marketing Channels and Distribution	Describe yield management. Given a particular product/service type, select the appropriate distribution strategy (direct, intensive, selective, exclusive). Explain the role of the channel. Describe the difference between a channel and a supply chain.			
Integrated Marketing Communications: Advertising, Promotions, and Other Tools	Given a specific promotional objective (building awareness, creating an image, reminding consumers of the product/service, generating excitement or involvement, encouraging trial, reducing post-purchase dissonance, protecting from competition. Given a particular marketing communications execution, infer the underlying objective.			
Personal Selling and Sales Management	Given specific numbers of sales accounts and phone calls and visits possible per day by a sales representative, calculate the total number of sales representatives needed in a market. Given a sales problem faced by a company, select the appropriate course of action.			

Content Areas	Objectives	Total Questions Missed	Review Complete	Needs Further Study
Pricing Strategies and Determination	Describe demand elasticity.			
	Given a retail price and channel margin structure, calculate the manufacturer's contribution margin.			
	Given a retail price, channel margin structure, market size and marketing investment, calculate a break-even market share.			
	Given specific market size, purchase cycle, average retail price, and market share information, forecast annual dollar sales for a company's product/service.			
	Explain the conditions under which a particular pricing strategy is appropriate.			
	Given a particular pricing strategy, infer the assumption(s) underlying the approach.			

OPERATIONS MANAGEMENT

Content Areas	Objectives	Total Questions Missed	Review Complete	Needs Further Study
Product, Process, and Service Design	From a list of processes, identify a process by a primary characteristic. Match a process to the characteristics of the markets for its products. Given several charts and a verbal description of their purpose, identify a Pareto chart.			
Facility Location, Capacity, and Layout	Given a scenario, calculate the capacity cushion of a process. Given a scenario, calculate the capital costs of increasing the capacity of a process made up of a series of linked activities.			
Service Operations Planning and Scheduling	Describe the relationship between the degree of customer contact and the efficiency of a service. Identify situations where waiting line analysis can be useful. Identify the inputs to a waiting line problem. Given several call center scenarios, (in a table) rank the scenarios in terms of efficiency.			

Content Areas	Objectives	Total Questions Missed	Review Complete	Needs Further Study
Project Management	Understand the relationships between activities in a critical path diagram. Given information about the activities that comprise a project, identify the project's critical path. Given information about the activities that comprise a project, calculate the amount of slack time for an activity not on the project's critical path. Given information about the activities that comprise a project, identify the most cost-effective way to complete the project at an earlier date than planned.			
Production Planning and Aggregate Planning	Identify basic aggregate planning strategies. Identify the bottleneck in a diagram of linked activities.			
Inventory Management	Select the correct definition for an inventory management term. Identify the EOQ formula from a list of several similar formulas. Identify the nature of the basic lot-sizing trade-off made by the EOQ formula. From a list of terms, identify those which are costs or benefits associated with carrying inventory.			
Resource Requirement Planning	Given a bill a materials, be able to identify end items or components, which characterize dependent or independent demand. Given a bill of materials, calculate the number of component items needed to produce an end item.			

Content Areas	Objectives	Total Questions Missed	Review Complete	Needs Further Study
Manufacturing Operations Scheduling	Given a scenario, identify the job sequence resulting from a shortest operating time job priority rule. Identify the job priority rule that always results in the shortest average waiting time for a single-machine. Identify the effects of "balance delay" in assembly line layout.			
Quality Control	Understand how charting is useful in managing quality in a process. Understand the use of control charts. Understand the relationship of statistical variance to six-sigma quality measurements.			
Employee Productivity	Identify the trade-offs between job enrichment, operational flexibility and workforce training.			

Content Areas	Objectives	Total Questions Missed	Review Complete	Needs Further Study
Diversity and Individual Differences	Explain the legal basis of sexual harassment. Specify the major equal employment laws and concepts. Specify the legal basis of employment discrimination. Analyze issues associated with gender discrimination in the workplace.			
Motivation and High Performance Work Systems	Analyze employee behavior in terms of cognitive bases of motivation.			
Satisfaction and Stress in the Workplace	Analyze interpersonal relations in a work environment based on the concept of organizational citizenship behavior. Understand issues associated with work stress in the organization.			
Efficiency, Motivation, and Quality in Work Design	Analyze employee behavior in terms of environmental bases of work motivation.			
Performance, Assessment, and Compensation	Analyze performance appraisals for manifestations of rating errors. Explain the benefits of performance appraisal. Analyze the rationale for multi-source (360-degree) assessments of performance. Explain the major organizational constraints on employee compensation. Analyze the components of a pay structure. Describe the administration of employee benefits systems.			

Content Areas	Objectives	Total Questions Missed	Review Complete	Needs Further Study
Managing Human Resources	Explain the costs and benefits of various systems of employee recruitment. Analyze major methods of personnel selection on the basis of staffing needs. Explain the benefits of training needs analyses. Describe the legal basis of occupational health and safety. Define employee rights affecting the employment relationship. Explain the process of unionization.			
Roles, Socialization, and Communication	Explain the basis of the socialization process. Analyze issues associated with justice and fairness in the workplace.			
Group Dynamics and Team Effectiveness	Analyze group dynamics as a function of dimensions of team interaction.			
Leadership in Groups and Organizations	Describe the basis of leadership in organizations.			
Power, Politics, and Conflict	Analyze the bases of social power.			
Structuring the Organization	Specify the benefits of various organizational structures. Define the concepts of job analysis and job evaluation.			
Culture, Change, and Organization Development	Explain the basis of organizational culture. Analyze the rationale for organizational resistance to change.			

Content Areas	Objectives	Total Questions Missed	Review Complete	Needs Further Study
The International Context	Analyze the factors that differentiate national cultures.			

STRATEGY

Content Areas	Objectives	Total Questions Missed	Review Complete	Needs Further Study
The Strategic Management Process	Identify the key elements of strategy. Identify the attributes of a good strategy. Identify the key levels of strategy. Distinguish between vision and mission. Distinguish between different perspectives on strategy. Describe the various steps in the assessment of a strategy.			
The Competitive Environment: Assessing Industry Attractiveness	Describe how you would use the Porter 5 forces framework to do a structural analysis of an industry. Define the various ways in which an industry can be defined. Describe strategic groups and identify how they are useful in industry analysis. Describe the various stages of industry evolution. Describe various industry structures and their implications for strategy. Describe Porter's generic strategies.			

Content Areas	Objectives	Total Questions Missed	Review Complete	Needs Further Study
Firm Capabilities: Assessing Strengths and Weaknesses	Distinguish between economies of scale and scope. Distinguish between core competence and distinctive competence. Describe key components of a value chain and value system. Define value as commonly used in strategic management. Describe vulnerability analysis.			
Opportunities for Distinction: Building Competitive Advantage	Distinguish between vertical and horizontal differentiation. Describe the factors that contribute to competitive advantage. Describe the factors that affect sustainability of competitive advantage. Identify various levels of uncertainty and ways of dealing with the same. Identify the elements of parenting advantage. Describe critical success factors.			
Competing on the Net: Building Virtual Advantage	Describe network effects. Describe what factors were ignored by dot.coms in developing their strategies.			

Content Areas	Objectives	Total Questions Missed	Review Complete	Needs Further Study
Corporate Strategy: Leveraging Resources to Extend Advantage	Describe synergy and identify examples of it. Distinguish between vertical and horizontal integration. Describe the key components of a business model. Distinguish between integration and diversification. Describe corporate motives for mergers and acquisitions. Describe the process for evaluating mergers and acquisitions. Describe what is meant by "stuck in the middle." Describe the typical factors that cause an organization to go into decline. Describe the process involved in the strategic transformation of an organization in decline.			
Global Strategy: Harnessing New Markets to Extend Advantage	Describe forces driving globalization. Distinguish between multinational, global and transnational strategies. Describe key organizational challenges in globalization.			
Strategic Alliances: Teaming and Allying for Advantage	Describe different types of alliances. Identify the advantages and disadvantages of alliances.			
Strategy Implementation: Organizing for Advantage	Describe the structure-conduct-performance paradigm. Describe the two-dimensional growth vector matrix.			

Resources

Need to do a little more studying? Try these MBA resources from South-Western/Thomson Learning.

ACCOUNTING

Financial Accounting: An Introduction to Concepts, Methods, and Uses, 10E
Stickney and Weil
0-324-18351-8

Management Accounting, 6E
Hansen and Mowen
0-324-06972-3

Managerial Accounting: An Introduction to Concepts, Methods, and Uses, 7E
Maher, Stickney, Weil
0-03-025963-0

DECISION SCIENCE

Quantitative Methods for Business, 8E
Anderson, Sweeney, Williams
0-324-04499-2

Operations Management, 9E
Gaither and Frazier
0-324-06685-6

ECONOMICS

The Financial System and the Economy: Principles of Money and Banking, 3E
Burton and Lombra
0-324-07182-5

Managerial Economics, 10E
Hirschey
0-324-18330-5

Macroeconomics: Theory, Policy, and International Applications, 2E
Miller and VanHoose
0-324-00717-5

FINANCE

Financial Management, 10E
Brigham and Erhardt
0-03-033561-2

Principles of Finance, 2E
Besley and Brigham
0-03-034509-X

MANAGEMENT

Strategic Management: Competitiveness and Globalization, 5E
Hitt, Ireland, Hoskisson
0-324-11479-6

Strategic Management, 3E
Pitts and Lei
0-324-00699-3

Organizational Behavior, 4E
Wagner and Hollenback
0-03-028946-7

Managing for the Future: Organizational Behavior and Processes, 3E
Ancona, et al
0-324-05575-7

MARKETING

Marketing Management, 2E
Czinkota and Kotabe
0-324-02203-4

Marketing: Best Practices, 2E
Hoffman, et al
0-03-034999-0

To find out more about these and other MBA titles, visit
http://mba.swlearning.com.

Financial Accounting

Balance Sheet

CMBA Objective Correlations

- Given a set of data, use the accounting equation to determine the amount of the missing balance sheet component.

- Given a scenario, determine the financial statement effects of various transactions affecting current assets.

- Given financial information, calculate working capital before and after specific transactions

- Given a set of financial data, calculate the amount to be shown as contributed capital on the financial statements.

Sample Questions

1. At year end, Relevance Corporation reported total assets of $22 million, total shareholders' equity of $14 million, and total contributed capital of $10 million. Total liabilities equal

    a. $1 million
    b. $6 million
    c. $7 million
    d. $8 million

ANSWER: D

2. In its first year of operations, United Universal Corporation's earnings are $2.1 million. Retained earnings at the end of the year were $1 million and contributed capital totaled $5.6 million. How much did the corporation distribute in dividends?

    a. $1.0 million
    b. $1.1 million
    c. $2.5 million
    d. $6.7 million

ANSWER: B

3. At the end of its first year, Bracket Company reported total assets of $700,000 and total liabilities of $300,000. The company earned $150,000 during the first year and distributed $30,000 in dividends. What was Bracket's contributed capital?

    a. $400,000
    b. $280,000
    c. $250,000
    d. $120,000

ANSWER: B

4. Compute the missing balance sheet amounts:

Noncurrent assets	$460,000
Shareholders' equity	A
Total assets	B
Current liabilities	270,000
Current assets	250,000
Noncurrent liabilities	100,000
Total liabilities and shareholders' equity	C
Current assets minus current liabilities	D

a. A $250,000; B $710,000; C $20,000; D $(20,000)
b. A $270,000; B $250,000; C 710,000; D $20,000
c. A $340,000; B $710,000; C $710,000; D $(20,000)
d. A $340,000; B $720,000; C $720,000; D $20,000

ANSWER: C

5. Compute the missing balance sheet amounts:

Noncurrent assets	$ 90,000
Shareholders' equity	870,000
Total assets	A
Current liabilities	20,000
Current assets	B
Noncurrent liabilities	C
Total liabilities and shareholders' equity	990,000
Current assets minus current liabilities	D

a. A $900,000; B $990,000; C $70,000; D $970,000
b. A $990,000; B $900,000; C $100,000; D $880,000
c. A $960,000; B $900,000; C $100,000; D $970,000
d. A $980,000; B $900,000; C $970,000; D $880,000

ANSWER: B

6. Compute the missing balance sheet amounts:

Noncurrent assets	$280,000
Shareholders' equity	340,000
Total assets	500,000
Current liabilities	A
Current assets	B
Noncurrent liabilities	C
Total liabilities and shareholders' equity	D
Current assets minus current liabilities	200,000

a. A $20,000; B $220,000; C $140,000; D $500,000
b. A $20,000; B $500,000; C $300,000; D $500,000
c. A $200,000; B $220,000; C $140,000; D $500,000
d. A $220,000; B $60,000; C $140,000; D $500,000

ANSWER: A

7. On January 1, Year 6, General Electric (GE) issued 1,000 shares of its common stock for a building. Real estate appraisers estimated the building to have a market value of $85,000 on the date of acquisition. The common stock of GE sold for $80 per share on the date of the acquisition. On January 1, Year 6, GE paid $560 in real estate transfer fees, $1,640 in property taxes for Year 6, and $1,200 for a two-year insurance policy beginning January 1, Year 6. At what amount should the building appear in the Building account of GE on January 1, Year 6?

    a. $80,560
    b. $81,160
    c. $82,800
    d. $85,860

ANSWER: A

8. Indicate the effects of the following transaction on the balance sheet equation, using the format:

    Assets   =   Liabilities   +   Shareholders' equity

Issued 20,000 shares of $0.10 par value common stock for $100,000.

	Assets	=	Liabilities	+	Shareholders' Equity
a.	+100,000				+100,000
b.	+100,000		+100,000		
c.	+10,000				+10,000
d.	+80,000				+80,000

ANSWER: A

9. Indicate the effects of the following transaction on the balance sheet equation, using the format:

    Assets   =   Liabilities   +   Shareholders' equity

Acquired equipment costing $7,500 for a cash payment of $700 with the balance payable over the next five years.

	Assets	=	Liabilities	+	Shareholders' Equity
a.	+7,500		+700		
b.	+7,500		+6,800		
c.	+6,800		+6,800		
d.	+700		+700		

ANSWER: C

10. Indicate the effects of the following transaction on the balance sheet equation, using the format:

    Assets   =   Liabilities   +   Shareholders' equity

Completed a consulting job and invoiced the client for $5,000, payable in 30 days.

	Assets	=	Liabilities	+	Shareholders' Equity
a.			+5,000		+5,000
b.	+5,000				+5,000
c.			+5,000		
d.	no entry				

ANSWER: B

11. Indicate the effects of the following transaction on the balance sheet equation, using the format:

Assets   =   Liabilities   +   Shareholders' equity

Ordered office supplies for the office, totaling $225.

	Assets	=	*Liabilities*	+	*Shareholders' Equity*
a.			+225		+225
b.	+225		+225		
c.			+225		
d.	no entry				

ANSWER: D

12. Indicate the effects of the following transaction on the balance sheet equation, using the format:

Assets   =   Liabilities   +   Shareholders' equity

Purchased a three-year fire insurance policy and pays in advance $3,000.

	Assets	=	*Liabilities*	+	*Shareholders' Equity*
a.			+3,000		
b.	+3,000				+5,000
c.	0				
d.	+3,000				

ANSWER: C

13. Indicate which of the following transactions that will, after the firm records the transaction and all closing entries, **increase Working Capital** = Current Assets – Current Liabilities:

a.   The record keeping system in a retail firm requires that the bookkeeper debit all wages paid to Wage Payable. The opening balance in Wages Payable was $40,000. The firm paid $185,000 in cash to employees during the period, with the debit to Wage Payable.

b.   A retail firm uses the periodic inventory method. It debits all acquisitions of merchandise to Cost of Goods Sold. Beginning Inventory was $20,000. The firm makes the required adjusting entry, if any, to recognize that the ending inventory is $25,000.

c.   The firm retires office equipment that had originally cost $10,000 and had $8,000 of accumulated depreciation at the start of the year, which was several months ago. The firm now records depreciation charges of $100 and sells the equipment for $1,000 cash.

d.   A landlord makes adjusting entries and prepares financial statements at the end of every month. During January the tenants had paid rent of $12,000 for the entire year and the fir had debited the amount to Cash and credited Rent Revenue. It makes an adjusting entry at the end of October.

e.   A customer whose account receivable for $200 had been written off as uncollectible, makes full payment of the amount previously written off. The firm decides that its original estimates of uncollectibles as a percentage of sales and of the uncollectibles balance required by an aging analysis need not be altered.

a.   b, c, d
b.   a, c, d
c.   c, d, e
d.   a, d, e

ANSWER: A

14. Indicate which of the following transactions that will, after the firm records the transaction and all closing entries, **increase Working Capital** = Current Assets – Current Liabilities:

   a. The firm undertakes an aging of the accounts receivable balances and discovers that the current uncollected accounts contain an expected $5,000 of uncollectible amounts. The Allowance for Uncollectible Accounts account has a debit balance of $6,000. The firm records the required adjusting entry, if any.

   b. The firm records depreciation of $700 on the personal computer used by the secretary of the factory supervisor.

   c. The firm uses an "allowance method" for expected costs of warranty repairs on products it has sold for many years. The opening balance in the Estimated Warranty Liability account, a current liability, was $100,000. The firm records all entries required for the following events: the firm estimates warranty costs on this period's sales to be $300,000 and pays cash for actual repairs of $280,000.

   d. The recordkeeping system in a retail firm requires that all interest paid be debited to Interest Expense. The opening balance in Interest Payable was $40,000. The firm paid $85,000 in cash for interest during the period, with the debit to Interest Expense. At the end of the period the Interest Payable is $25,000.

   e. The firm acquired an insurance policy costing $1,200 on August 1 of this year, debiting the entire amount to Insurance Expense. The firm prepares complete, correct balance sheets at the ends of March, June, September, and December. The firm makes an adjusting entry for this insurance policy in preparing its balance sheet at the end of December.

   a. b, c
   b. b, d
   c. b, d, e
   d. a, d, e

ANSWER: B

15. Indicate which of the following transactions that will, after the firm records the transaction and all closing entries, **decrease Working Capital** = Current Assets – Current Liabilities:

   a. The recordkeeping system in a retail firm requires that the bookkeeper debit all wages paid to Wages Payable. The opening balance in Wages Payable was $40,000. The firm paid $185,000 in cash to employees during the period, with the debit to Wages Payable.

   b. A retail firm uses the periodic inventory method. It debits all acquisitions of merchandise to Cost of Goods Sold. Beginning Inventory was $20,000. The firm makes the required adjusting entry, if any, to recognize that the ending inventory is $25,000.

   c. The firm retires office equipment which had originally cost $10,000 and had $8,000 of accumulated depreciation at the start of the year, which was several months ago. The firm now records depreciation charges of $100 and sell the equipment for $1,000 cash.

   d. A landlord makes adjusting entries and prepares financial statements at the end of every month. During January the tenants had paid rent of $12,000 for the entire year and the fir had debited the amount to Cash and credited Rent Revenue. It makes an adjusting entry at the end of October.

   e. A customer whose account receivable for $200 had been written off as uncollectible, makes full payment of the amount previously written off. The firm decides that its original estimates of uncollectibles as a percentage of sales and of the uncollectibles balance required by an aging analysis need not be altered.

   a. a only
   b. b only
   c. a, b
   d. b, c

ANSWER: A

16. Indicate which of the following transactions that will, after the firm records the transaction and all closing entries, **decrease Working Capital** = Current Assets – Current Liabilities:

a. The firm undertakes an aging of the accounts receivable balances and discovers that the current uncollected accounts contain an expected $5,000 of uncollectible amounts. The Allowance for Uncollectible Accounts account has a debit balance of $6,000. The firm records the required adjusting entry, if any.

b. The firm records depreciation of $700 on the personal computer used by the secretary of the factory supervisor.

c. The firm uses an "allowance method" for expected costs of warranty repairs on products it has sold for many years. The opening balance in the Estimated Warranty Liability account, a current liability, was $100,000. The firm records all entries required for the following events: the firm estimates warranty costs on this period's sales to be $300,000 and pays cash for actual repairs of $280,000.

d. The recordkeeping system in a retail firm requires that all interest paid be debited to Interest Expense. The opening balance in Interest Payable was $40,000. The firm paid $85,000 in cash for interest during the period, with the debit to Interest Expense. At the end of the period the Interest Payable is $25,000.

e. The firm acquired an insurance policy costing $1,200 on August 1 of this year, debiting the entire amount to Insurance Expense. The firm prepares complete, correct balance sheets at the ends of March, June, September, and December. The firm makes an adjusting entry for this insurance policy in preparing its balance sheet at the end of December.

a. a, b, c
b. c only
c. a, e
d. a, c, e

ANSWER: D

17. Indicate which of the following transactions that will, after the firm records the transaction and all closing entries, **leave Working Capital** = Current Assets – Current Liabilities **unchanged**:

a. The recordkeeping system in a retail firm requires that the bookkeeper debit all wages paid to Wages Payable. The opening balance in Wages Payable was $40,000. The firm paid $185,000 in cash to employees during the period, with the debit to Wages Payable.

b. A retail firm uses the periodic inventory method. It debits all acquisitions of merchandise to Cost of Goods Sold. Beginning Inventory was $20,000. The firm makes the required adjusting entry, if any, to recognize that the ending inventory is $25,000.

c. The firm retires office equipment that had originally cost $10,000 and had $8,000 of accumulated depreciation at the start of the year, which was several months ago. The firm now records depreciation charges of $100 and sell the equipment for $1,000 cash.

d. A landlord makes adjusting entries and prepares financial statements at the end of every month. During January the tenants had paid rent of $12,000 for the entire year and the fir had debited the amount to Cash and credited Rent Revenue. It makes an adjusting entry at the end of October.

e. A customer whose account receivable for $200 had been written off as uncollectible, makes full payment of the amount previously written off. The firm decides that its original estimates of uncollectibles as a percentage of sales and of the uncollectibles balance required by an aging analysis need not be altered.

a. a, d, e
b. c only
c. e only
d. a, b, e

ANSWER: C

Income Statements

CMBA Objective Correlations

- Select the accounting concept that applies to revenue recognition, accruals, recording of asset values, et al.

- Given financial data, distinguish between expenses/expenditures, including accruals, R&D, stock options, et al.

Sample Questions

1. Which of the following concepts best characterizes the accrual basis of accounting?

    a. Conservatism
    b. Matching
    c. Understandability
    d. Going concern

ANSWER: B

2. Under accrual accounting, which principles must the accountant consider in order to record revenue?

    a. Timing and recognition
    b. Recognition and substantiation
    c. Amount and measurement
    d. Timing and measurement

ANSWER: D

3. Under the accrual method, the timing of revenue recognition is influenced by

    a. where the purchaser gets funds to pay the seller
    b. whether the buyer pays with cash or a promise
    c. when the services or product are provided
    d. when the seller has received a form of payment

ANSWER: C

4. The accrual basis of accounting recognizes expenses when:

	Related revenues are recognized	The expense is incurred	The service/product is received
a.	Yes	Yes	No
b.	Yes	No	No
c.	No	Yes	Yes
d.	No	No	Yes

ANSWER: A

5. The accrual basis of accounting is often contrasted with the cash basis of accounting. Which of the following is true of the cash basis of accounting?

    a. the cash basis is not subject to manipulation
    b. most larger companies use the cash basis of accounting
    c. the cash basis of accounting provides a strong basis to determine the total assets of the company
    d. the cash basis provides an inferior picture of operating performance

ANSWER: A

6. The amount of revenue recognized may need to be adjusted to recognize

	Delayed receipt of payments	Sales discounts and allowances	Uncollectible accounts	Sales returns
a.	Yes	Yes	Yes	Yes
b.	Yes	No	No	No
c.	No	Yes	No	Yes
d.	No	No	Yes	No

ANSWER: D

7. Electra Company purchased $50,000 worth of office supplies on January 1. Electra expects to use 60 percent of the supplies in the first year and the remainder in the second year. After adjusting entries (and before closing entries), how much should Electra show in its Supplies Expense account?

    a. $50,000
    b. $30,000
    c. $25,000
    d. $0

ANSWER: B

8. WKS Manufacuturing Corp. purchased a new cutting machine for its manufacturing plant on January 1. The machine cost $250,000 and is expected to be used in production for 4 years at which time its estimated salvage value will be $10,000. The yearly straight-line depreciation for this asset would be

    a. $60,000
    b. $50,000
    c. $25,000
    d. $2,500

ANSWER: A

9. On July 1, Year 1, University Bagels bought an insurance policy costing $600 that would insure the retail building for two years against fire loss. What asset account and what amount are recorded on the balance sheet at December 31, Year 1?

    a. Prepaid Insurance, $450
    b. Insurance Expense, $300
    c. Prepaid Insurance, $300
    d. Insurance Expense, $150

ANSWER: A

10. On October 1, Year 1, Word-of-Mouth Catering accepted a $10,000, 120-day note from a customer. The note earns 10% interest per year. What is the amount of interest receivable recorded at December 31, Year 1? (Assume no other entries to record interest have been made.)

  a. $333
  b. $250
  c. $83
  d. $0, because interest is not due until January 31 of Year 2

ANSWER: B

11. Assume that a firm uses the accrual basis of accounting. How much revenue will the firm recognize for the month of August if it collects $800 in August for merchandise sold and delivered in July?

  a. $800
  b. $400
  c. $200
  d. $0

ANSWER: D

12. Assume that a firm uses the accrual basis of accounting. How much revenue will the firm recognize for the month of August if it collects $2,400 interest on a 6-month certificate of deposit, which matures on August 15th?

  a. $2,400
  b. $1,200
  c. $200
  d. $400

ANSWER: C

13. Assume that a firm uses the accrual basis of accounting. How much revenue will the firm recognize for the month of August if it sells $3,000 of merchandise on account in August. The firm allows a 2% discount for payment prior to 30 days and customers take the discount.

  a. $2,940
  b. $3,000
  c. $60
  d. $0

ANSWER: A

14. In the income statement, expenses are generally classified by the
  a. nature of the good or service sold
  b. department in the firm that carried out the activity
  c. nature of the related revenue
  d. type of customer

ANSWER: B

15. Expenses measure

    a.   the outflows of assets from selling goods and providing services to customers
    b.   the increase of liabilities from selling goods and providing services to customers
    c.   all sources of cash received by a firm
    d.   both (a) and (b)

ANSWER: D

16. The Purple Company spent $300,000 on research and development during Year 8 to generate new product lines. One of the three projects resulted in a successful patented product while the other two projects resulted in unsuccessful efforts. How much of the $300,000 should be recognized as an expense in Year 8?

    a. $300,000
    b. $200,000
    c. $100,000
    d. $0

ANSWER: A

17. The Purple Company spent $300,000 on research and development during Year 8 to generate new product lines. One of the three projects resulted in a successful patented product while the other two projects resulted in unsuccessful efforts. For the successful project, $50,000 was spent before technological feasibility, and $75,000 was incurred afterwards. Under international accounting standards, how much of the $300,000 should be recognized as an expense in Year 8?

    a. $300,000
    b. $225,000
    c. $175,000
    d. $50,000

ANSWER: B

Statement of Cash Flows

CMBA Objective Correlations

- Given financial information, calculate cash from operations, investment, and financing.

Sample Questions

1. If cash decreases by $10,000 during the year, liabilities decrease by $5,000, and shareholders' equity increases by $5,000, what is the total change in noncash assets for the year?

    a. a decrease of $5,000
    b. an increase of $10,000
    c. a decrease of $10,000
    d. an increase of $5,000

ANSWER: B

2. Which is a source of cash?

    a. increase in inventory
    b. decrease in bonds payable
    c. decrease in accounts payable
    d. decrease in accounts receivable

ANSWER: D

3. Which is a use of cash?

    a. an increase in inventory
    b. a decrease in accounts receivable
    c. a decrease in equipment
    d. an increase in accounts payable

ANSWER: A

4. In a statement of cash flows, interest payments to lenders should be classified as cash outflows for

    a. operating activities
    b. financing activities
    c. investing activities
    d. lending activities

ANSWER: A

5. In a statement of cash flows, payments to acquire long-term bonds or other debt instruments with maturities greater than one year of other entities should be classified as cash outflows for

    a. operating activities
    b. financing activities
    c. investing activities
    d. lending activities

ANSWER: C

6. In a statement of cash flows, proceeds from the issuance of common stock should be classified as cash outflows for

    a. operating activities
    b. financing activities
    c. investing activities
    d. lending activities

ANSWER: B

7. The Flatiron Company had retained earnings at the beginning of the year totaling $10,000. At the end of the year retained earnings totaled $20,000. Depreciation was $5,000 for the year and the company paid dividends of $15,000. What is the amount recorded as Net Income in the operating activities section of the statement of cash flows prepared using the indirect method?

    a. a net loss of $15,000
    b. a net income of $15,000
    c. a net income of $0
    d. a net income of $25,000

ANSWER: D

8. At the end of the first year of operations the Avalanche Company had ending inventory totaling $20,000. The company sold goods at a cost of $240,000. Purchases of goods for the year totaled $220,000. What is the effect of inventory on the statement of cash flows for year 1?

    a. an outflow of $220,000
    b. an inflow of $220,000
    c. an outflow of $20,000
    d. an inflow of $240,000

ANSWER: C

9. The following information is available from Zak Corporation's accounting records for the year ended December 31, Year 4:

Cash received from customers	$550,000
Rents received	65,000
Cash paid for purchase of supplies	325,000
Income taxes paid	45,000
Cash dividends paid to shareholders	25,000

Net cash flow from operating activities for Year 4 totaled

a. $180,000
b. $220,000
c. $245,000
d. $290,000

ANSWER: C

Items 10-12 are based on the following:

Royce Company had the following transactions during the fiscal year ended December 31, Year 4.

- Accounts receivable decreased from $115,000 on December 31, Year 3, to $100,000 on December 31, Year 4.
- Royce's Board of Directors declared dividends on December 31, Year 4, of $.05 per share on the 2.8 million shares outstanding, payable to shareholders of record on January 31, Year 5. The company did not declare or pay dividends for fiscal year, Year 3.
- Sold a truck with a net book value of $7,000 for $5,000 cash, reporting a loss of $2,000.
- Paid interest to bondholders of $780,000.
- Cash increased from $106,000 on December 31, Year 3, to $284,000 on December 31, Year 4.

10. Royce Company uses the direct method to prepare its Statement of Cash Flows at December 31, Year 4. The interest that is paid to bondholders would

a. be reported in the Financing Section, as a use or outflow of cash
b. be reported in the Operating Section, as a use or outflow of cash
c. be reported in the Investing Section, as a use or outflow of cash
d. be reported in the Debt Section, as a use or outflow of cash

ANSWER: B

11. Royce Company uses the indirect method to prepare its Year 4 Statement of Cash Flows, and would show a(n)

a. source or inflow of funds of $5,000 from the sale of the truck in the Financing Section
b. deduction of $15,000 in the Operating Section, representing the decrease in year-end accounts receivable
c. source or inflow of funds of $7,000 from the sale of the truck in the Financing Section
d. addition of $2,000 in the Operating Section for the $2,000 loss on the sale of the truck

ANSWER: D

12. The total of cash provided (used) by operating activities plus cash provided (used) by investing activities plus cash provided (used) by financing activities is

   a. cash provided of $284,000
   b. cash provided of $178,000
   c. cash used of $178,000
   d. cash used of $582,000

ANSWER: B

13. Liabilities increased by $20,000 during the year. All other accounts, except cash, in total remained the same. What is the net increase or decrease in cash during the year?

   a. $0
   b. $20,000 decrease
   c. $20,000 increase
   d. cannot be determined from information given

ANSWER: C

14. If cash decreases by $20,000, liabilities increase by $5,000, and shareholders' equity increases by $10,000, what is the change in noncash assets for the year?

   a. $35,000 decrease
   b. $5,000 decrease
   c. $35,000 increase
   d. $5,000 increase

ANSWER: C

15. The net income for Cypress Inc. was $3,000,000 for the year ended December 31, Year 3. Additional information is as follows.

Depreciation on fixed assets	*$1,500,000*
Proceeds from sale of land	200,000
Increase in accounts payable	300,000
Dividends on preferred stock	400,000

   The net cash provided by operating activities in the statement of cash flows for the year ended December 31, Year 3, should be

   a. $4,200,000
   b. $4,500,000
   c. $4,600,000
   d. $4,800,000

ANSWER: D

Financial Statement Analysis

CMBA Objective Correlations

- Given statements, calculate ratios related to liquidity, performance, investment utilization, financial condition, et al.

- Identify the roles of bodies with major influence on accounting standards/procedures.

Sample Questions

1. If the rate of return on assets for the year is 15%, a general interpretation of the ratio would be

    a.   the assets generated $0.15 cash per dollar of cash invested
    b.   15% of the assets produced income while the remainder were at break-even for the year
    c.   before payment for use of capital, $0.15 was earned for each dollar of assets used by the company
    d.   dividends of $0.15 per share were paid

ANSWER: C

2. The accounts payable turnover ratio can reveal

    a.   the result of sales divided by average working capital
    b.   the number of days in the operating cycle
    c.   the length of the operating cycle in order to compare it with industry averages
    d.   the number of days that a firm's accounts payable remain outstanding

ANSWER: D

3. The ratio that measures a firm's ability to generate earnings from its resources is

    a.   days' sales in inventory
    b.   asset turnover
    c.   sales to working capital
    d.   days' sales in receivables

ANSWER: B

4. The following information pertains to the Hamilton Company for the year ended June 30, Year 2:

Common shares outstanding	750,000
Stated value per share	$15.00
Market price per share	$45.00
Year 1 dividends paid per share	$4.50
Year 2 dividends paid per share	$7.50
Earnings per share	$9.00

The price-earnings ratio for Hamilton's common stock is

a. 3.0 times
b. 4.0 times
c. 5.0 times
d. 6.0 times

ANSWER: C

Items 5 and 6 are based on the following:

Assume the following information for Ramer Company, Matson Company, and for their common industry for a recent year.

	Ramer	*Matson*	*Industry Average*
Current ratio	3.50	2.80	3.00
Accounts receivable turnover	5.00	8.10	6.00
Inventory turnover	6.20	8.00	6.10
Interest coverage ratio	9.00	12.30	10.40
Debt/equity ratio	0.70	0.40	0.55
Return on investment	0.15	0.12	0.15
Dividend payout ratio	0.80	0.60	0.55
Earnings per share	$3.00	$2.00	—

5. Which one of the following is correct if both companies have the same total assets and the same sales?

a. Ramer has more cash than Matson.
b. Ramer has fewer current liabilities than Matson.
c. Matson has less shareholders' equity than Ramer.
d. Matson has a shorter operating cycle than Ramer.

ANSWER: D

6. The attitudes of both Ramer and Matson concerning risk are **best** explained by the

a. current ratio, accounts receivable turnover, and inventory turnover
b. return on investment and dividend payout ratio
c. current ratio and earnings per share
d. debt/equity ratio and interest coverage ratio

ANSWER: D

7.   Windham Company has current assets of $400,000 and current liabilities of $500,000. Windham Company's current ratio would be increased by

   a.   the purchase of $100,000 of inventory on account
   b.   the collection of $100,000 of accounts receivable
   c.   the purchase of temporary investments for $100,000 cash
   d.   the payment of $100,000 of accounts payable

ANSWER: A

Items 8 through 10 are based on the following:

King Products Corporation
Statement of Financial Position
(in thousands)

| | June 30 | |
	Year 6	Year 5
Cash	$ 60	$ 50
Marketable securities (at market)	40	30
Accounts receivable (net)	90	60
Inventories (at lower of cost or market)	120	100
Prepaid items	30	40
Total current assets	$ 340	$280
Long-term investments (at cost)	50	40
Land (at cost)	150	150
Building (net)	160	180
Equipment (net)	190	200
Patents (net)	70	34
Goodwill (net)	40	26
Total long-term assets	$ 660	$630
Total assets	$1,000	$910
Notes payable	$ 46	$ 24
Accounts payable	94	56
Accrued interest	30	30
Total current liabilities	$ 170	$110
Notes payable, 10% due 12/31/Year 12	20	20
Bonds payable, 12% due 6/30/Year 15	30	30
Total long-term debt	$ 50	$ 50
Total liabilities	$ 220	$160
Preferred stock–5% cumulative, $100 par, non-participating, authorized, issued and outstanding, 2,000 shares	200	200
Common stock–$10 par, 40,000 shares authorized, 30,000 shares issued and outstanding	300	300
Additional paid-in capital–common	150	150
Retained earnings	130	100
Total shareholders' equity	$ 780	$750
Total liabilities and shareholders' equity	$1,000	$910

King Products Corporation

Income Statement
For the year ended June 30
(in thousands)

	Year 6
Net sales	$600
Costs and expenses	
Cost of goods sold	440
Selling, general, and administrative	60
Interest expense	10
Income before taxes	$ 90
Income taxes	45
Net income	$ 45

8.   King Products Corporation's inventory turnover for the fiscal year ended at June 30, Year 6, was

    a.   3.7
    b.   4.0
    c.   4.4
    d.   5.0

ANSWER: B

9.   King Products Corporation's accounts receivable turnover for the fiscal year ended at June 30, Year 6, was

    a.   4.9
    b.   5.9
    c.   6.7
    d.   8.0

ANSWER: D

10.   King Products Corporation's quick (acid test) ratio at June 30, Year 6, was

    a.   0.6
    b.   1.1
    c.   1.8
    d.   2.0

ANSWER: B

Items 11 through 16 are based on the following:

Devlin Company
Statement of Financial Position
as of May 31

(in thousands)Assets	Year 7	Year 6
Current assets		
Cash	$ 45	$ 38
Trading securities	30	20
Accounts receivable (net)	68	48
Inventories	90	80
Prepaid expenses	22	30
Total current assets	$255	$216
Investments, at equity	38	30
Property, plant, and equipment (net)	375	400
Intangible assets (net)	80	45
Total assets	$748	$691
Liabilities and shareholders' equity		
Current liabilities		
Notes payable	$ 35	$ 18
Accounts payable	70	42
Accrued expenses	5	4
Income taxes payable	15	16
Total current liabilities	125	80
Long-term debt	35	35
Deferred taxes	3	2
Total liabilities	$163	$117
Shareholders' equity		
Preferred stock, 6%, $100 par value, cumulative	150	150
Common stock, $10 par value	225	195
Additional paid-in capital–common stock	114	100
Retained earnings	96	129
Total shareholders' equity	$585	$574
Total liabilities and shareholders' equity	$748	$691

Devlin Company
Income Statement
For the year ended May 31
(in thousands)

	Year 7	Year 6
Net sales	$480	$460
Costs and expenses		
Cost of goods sold	330	315
Selling, general, and administrative	52	51
Interest expense	8	9
Income before taxes	$ 90	$ 85
Income taxes	36	34
Net income	$ 54	$ 51

11. Devlin Company's acid-test ratio at May 31, Year 7, was

   a. 0.60 to 1
   b. 0.90 to 1
   c. 1.14 to 1
   d. 1.86 to 1

ANSWER: C

12. Assuming there are no preferred stock dividends in arrears, Devlin Company's return on common shareholders' equity for the year ended May 31, Year 7, was

   a. 6.3 percent
   b. 7.5 percent
   c. 7.8 percent
   d. 10.5 percent

ANSWER: D

13. Devlin Company's inventory turnover for the year ended May 31, Year 7, was

   a. 3.67 times
   b. 3.88 times
   c. 5.33 times
   d. 5.65 times

ANSWER: B

14. Devlin Company's asset turnover for the year ended May 31, Year 7, was

   a. 0.08 times
   b. 0.46 times
   c. 0.67 times
   d. 0.73 times

ANSWER: C

15. Devlin Company's rate of return on assets for the year ended May 31, Year 7, was

   a. 7.2 percent
   b. 7.5 percent
   c. 8.2 percent
   d. 11.2 percent

ANSWER: C

16. Devlin Company's times interest earned for the year ended May 31, Year 7, was

   a. 6.75 times
   b. 11.25 times
   c. 12.25 times
   d. 18.75 times

ANSWER: C

17. The acronym for the agency authorized by the U.S. Congress to regulate, among other things, the financial reporting practices of most public corporations is:
    a. SEC
    b. IASB
    c. FASB
    d. None of the above

ANSWER: A

18. The acronym for an organization that promotes the international harmonization of accounting standards is:
    a. SEC
    b. IASB
    c. FASB
    d. None of the above

ANSWER: B

19. The acronym for an independent board responsible, since 1973, for establishing generally accepted accounting principles is:
    a. SEC
    b. IASB
    c. FASB
    d. None of the above

ANSWER: C

Receivables and Revenue Recognition

CMBA Objective Correlations

- Given data, calculate the amount to be shown as revenue for an accounting period.

Sample Questions

1. Income from the contract for Year 5 under the percentage-of-completion method is:

   a. $1,400,000
   b. $2,800,000
   c. $3,360,000
   d. None of the above

ANSWER: B

2. Income from the contract for Year 5 under the cost-recovery-first method is:

   a. $1,400,000
   b. $2,800,000
   c. $4,200,000
   d. None of the above

ANSWER: D

3. Income from the contract for Year 5 under the installment method is:

   a. $1,400,000
   b. $2,800,000
   c. $3,360,000
   d. None of the above

ANSWER: A

4. Income from the contract for Year 5 under the completed contract method is:

   a. $1,400,000
   b. $2,800,000
   c. $3,360,000
   d. None of the above

ANSWER: D

5. In year 1, Southern Construction agrees to construct a school building for $12,000,000, receiving payments for the work of $6,000,000 in both year 1 and year 2. Southern estimates that the costs will be $4,000,000 in Year 1 and $6,000,000 in Year 2. If Southern uses the percentage-of-completion method (based on total costs), what amount of profit is recognized in each year of the contract?

	Year 1	Year 2
a.	$0	$2,000,000
b.	$2,000,000	$0
c.	$1,000,000	$1,000,000
d.	$800,000	$1,200,000

ANSWER: D

6. In year 1, Northern Construction agrees to build a fire station that will be completed in year 2. Construction starts in year 1. The station will have costs of $2,000,000 in year 1 and $2,000,000 in year 2. Northern receives payment for the station of $5,000,000 in advance, in year 1. If Northern uses the completed contract method, what net profit is recognized by Northern in each year?

	Year 1	Year 2
a.	$0	$1,000,000
b.	$1,000,000	$0
c.	$3,000,000	($2,000,000)
d.	$500,000	$500,000

ANSWER: A

7. The mining industry frequently recognizes revenue using the completion of production method. This method is acceptable under the revenue recognition principle because

	Sales prices are reasonably assured	Assets are readily realizable	Production cost can be readily determined
a.	Yes	Yes	No
b.	Yes	No	Yes
c.	No	Yes	No
d.	Yes	No	Yes

ANSWER: A

8. Recognizing income after the time of sale is

   a. never appropriate
   b. always appropriate
   c. never in accordance with GAAP
   d. appropriate for some specific circumstances

ANSWER: D

9. Which methods of revenue recognition are acceptable for use in recognizing revenue from service transactions?

	Installment method	Percentage of completion method	Completed contract method
a.	Yes	Yes	Yes
b.	Yes	Yes	No
c.	No	No	No
d.	Yes	No	Yes

ANSWER: A

10. Stuart Manufacturing sells an old machine to KSS Corp. which is having financial difficulty. Stuart agrees to accept payment over 3 years. The adjusted basis of the machine to the seller is $5,000 and the buyer is expected to make payments of $2,000 per year for 3 years. What amount of net profit is recognized by the seller in year 3 if the seller uses the installment method? (Assume that the buyer makes the payments.)

    a. $2,000
    b. $1,000
    c. $333.33
    d. $0

ANSWER: C

11. Ullrich Co. sells an asset to a buyer for a total sales price of $6,000 with a payment schedule of $2,000 in year 1, $2,000 in year 2, and $2,000 in year 3. The cost of the asset is $5,000. Under the cost-recovery-first method, how much revenue is recognized in year 3?

    a. $2,000
    b. $1,000
    c. $333.33
    d. $0

ANSWER: B

12. Revenues measure

    a.   the inflows of assets from selling goods and providing services to customers
    b.   the reduction of liabilities from selling goods and providing services to customers
    c.   all sources of cash received by a firm
    d.   both (a) and (b)

ANSWER: D

Cost of Sales

CMBA Objective Correlations

- Given data, calculate the cost of sales under various alternatives.

Sample Questions

1. Value Company's beginning and ending inventories for the fiscal year ended September 30, Year 5, are

	October 1, Year 4	September 30, Year 5
Raw materials	$15,000	$22,000
Work-in-process	40,000	35,000
Finished goods	8,000	12,000

Production data for the fiscal year ended September 30, Year 5, are

Raw materials purchased	$ 80,000
Purchase discounts	1,000
Direct labor	100,000
Manufacturing overhead	75,000

Cost of goods sold for the year ended September 30, Year 5, for Value Company is

   a. $262,000
   b. $252,000
   c. $260,000
   d. $248,000

ANSWER: D

2. Western Inc. uses a periodic inventory system. Beginning inventory is $20,000 and purchases for the year are $80,000. A physical inventory shows that $15,000 of the inventory remains. How much is recorded as cost of goods sold for the year?

   a. $75,000
   b. $80,000
   c. $85,000
   d. $95,000

ANSWER: C

Items 3 and 4 are based on the following:

	Date	Units	$/unit
Beginning inventory, Year 1	January	10	1.00
Purchases	January	15	1.10
	February	20	1.20
	June	15	1.30
	September	15	1.25
Ending inventory, Year 1	December	30	

3. Under a periodic inventory system, what is the cost of goods sold reported in the Year 1 income statement using the FIFO cost flow assumption?

    a. $38.25
    b. $50.50
    c. $53.25
    d. $56.25

ANSWER: B

4. Under a periodic inventory system, what is the cost of goods sold reported in the Year 1 income statement using the weighted-average cost flow assumption?

    a. $32.73
    b. $49.80
    c. $51.40
    d. $53.25

ANSWER: D

Items 5 through 7 are based on the following:

The inventory record for a particular item for Year 2 appears below. The firm uses a periodic inventory system.

Inventory, January 1, Year 2	20,000	$0.20	$4,000
Purchases:			
March 2	4,000	.24	$ 960
April 30	3,000	.28	840
June 15	6,000	.32	1,920
September 30	2,000	.26	520
December 15	1,000	.20	200
Total purchases	16,000		$4,440
Total available for sale	36,000		$8,440
Units sold	28,000		

5. The cost of goods sold for year 2 under FIFO is:

    a. $6,120
    b. $6,320
    c. $6,520
    d. $6,840

ANSWER: A

6. The cost of goods sold for year 2 under LIFO is:

    a. $6,120
    b. $6,320
    c. $6,520
    d. $6,840

ANSWER: D

7. The cost of goods sold for year 2 under weighted-average cost-flow assumption is (rounded to the nearest dollar):

    a. $7,772
    b. $6,972
    c. $6,564
    d. $6,220

ANSWER: C

8. Using the data presented below, calculate the cost of sales for the Beta Corporation for Year 2:

Current ratio	3.5
Quick ratio	3.0
Current liabilities, December 31, Year 2	$600,000
Inventory, December 31, Year 1	$500,000
Inventory turnover	8.0

    a. $1,600,000
    b. $2,400,000
    c. $3,200,000
    d. $6,400,000

ANSWER: C

Long-Lived Tangible and Intangible Assets

CMBA Objective Correlations

- Given data, calculate the financial statements effects of various transactions affecting non-current assets, including depreciation, intangibles, investments, and deferred taxes.

- Calculate book value with financial information provided.

Sample Questions

Items 1 through 5 are based on the following.

Warren Corporation acquired a new office machine on January 2, Year 2, for $120,000. The machine has a 10-year life and a $10,000 estimated salvage value.

1. Depreciation for Year 2 using the double-declining-balance method is:

    a. $26,000
    b. $24,000
    c. $22,000
    d. $20,000

ANSWER: B

2. Depreciation for Year 3 using the double-declining-balance method is:

    a. $19,600
    b. $19,200
    c. $17,600
    d. $17,200

ANSWER: B

3. Depreciation for Year 2 using the sum-of-the-years'-digits method is:

    a. $24,000
    b. $22,000
    c. $20,000
    d. $18,000

ANSWER: C

4. Depreciation for Year 3 using the sum-of-the-years'-digits method is (to the nearest dollar):

    a. $19,636
    b. $18,000
    c. $16,066
    d. $14,727

ANSWER: B

5. On December 31, Year 6, before making adjusting entries for the year, the book value of the machine using the straight-line method is $76,000. Warren Corporation estimates at this date that the machine will have a remaining useful life of three years, or eight years in total. Salvage is now estimated to be zero. Depreciation expense for Year 6 (to the nearest dollar) is therefore:

    a. $25,330
    b. $19,000
    c. $15,000
    d. $13,750

ANSWER: B

6. On January 1, Year 4, a company purchased a new machine for $360,000. The machine has an estimated useful life of eight years and depreciation is computed by the sum-of-the-years'-digits method. The accumulated depreciation at December 31, Year 7, should be

    a. $50,000
    b. $100,000
    c. $180,000
    d. $260,000

ANSWER: D

7. Which method of depreciation will result in the greatest depreciation charge in the last year of the asset's life?

    a.   MACRS
    b.   straight-line
    c.   150% declining balance
    d.   sum-of-the-years' digits

ANSWER: B

8. When a fixed plant asset with a five-year estimated useful life is sold during the second year, how would the use of a decreasing charge method of depreciation instead of the straight-line method affect the gain or loss on the sale of the fixed plant asset?

	Gain	Loss
a.	Increase	Increase
b.	Increase	Decrease
c.	Decrease	Increase
d.	Decrease	Decrease

ANSWER: B

Items 9 through 13 are based on the following.

In Year 1, the Miller Company acquired equipment for $15,000 with an estimated salvage value of $3,000. The economic life of the equipment is 6 years or 12,000 hours. The MACRS life is 5 years. The property was disposed of in Year 7 for $4,000. The firm used the equipment according to the following schedule:

Year 1	500 hours
Year 2	2,500 hours
Year 3	3,000 hours
Year 4	2,000 hours
Year 5	2,000 hours
Year 6	2,000 hours

9.   What is the depreciation expense for Year 4 using the straight-line method?

    a. $2,500
    b. $2,000
    c. $1,833
    d. $1,571

ANSWER: A

10.   What is the depreciation expense for Year 3 using the production method?

    a. $3,000
    b. $2,750
    c. $2,400
    d. $2,200

ANSWER: C

11.   What is the depreciation expense for Year 2 using the 150% declining balance method.

    a. $2,813
    b. $2,500
    c. $2,109
    d. $2,083

ANSWER: A

12.   What is the depreciation expense for Year 2 using the sum-of-the-years'-digits method?

    a. $4,285
    b. $3,571
    c. $3,428
    d. $2,857

ANSWER: D

13.   What is the depreciation expense for Year 1 using the modified accelerated cost recovery system?

    a. $3,000
    b. $2,800
    c. $2,400
    d. $2,200

ANSWER: A

14. Boulder Company purchased equipment that was installed and put into service January 2, Year 6, at a total cost of $128,000. Salvage value was estimated at $8,000. The equipment is being depreciated over eight years by the double declining balance method. For Year 7, how much depreciation expense should Boulder Company record on this equipment?

    a. $22,500
    b. $24,000
    c. $30,000
    d. $32,000

ANSWER: B

15. In Year 1, a firm purchased a truck for $12,000. The estimated salvage value was $2,000 and the estimated useful life was 10 years. In Year 4, it was determined that the salvage value would only be $1,000 and that the truck would have a total estimated useful life of 7 years rather than 10. Assuming the straight-line method is used, what is the depreciation expense for Year 4 of the truck?

    a. $1,000
    b. $1,750
    c. $1,950
    d. $2,000

ANSWER: D

16. Pareto Corporation owns 40% of Spring Corporation. During Year 3, Spring has net income of $60,000. What entry should Pareto record related to its investment in Spring during Year 3?

a.	Investment in Spring Corp.	24,000	
	Equity in Earnings of Affiliate		24,000
b.	Dividend Receivable	24,000	
	Dividend Income		24,000
c.	Investment Receivable	24,000	
	Investment Income		24,000
d.	Investment in Spring Corp.	24,000	
	Investment Income		24,000

ANSWER: A

17. InvestCo purchases 30% of NewCo's stock on January 1, Year 1, for $100,000. In Year 1, NewCo paid total dividends of $30,000 and had a net income of $70,000. In Year 2, NewCo suffered a loss of $20,000 and paid no dividends. On January 1, Year 3, InvestCo sells its investment in NewCo for $105,000. How is the sale recorded?

a.	Cash	105,000	
	Loss on Sale	1,000	
	Investment in NewCo		106,000
b.	Cash	105,000	
	Loss on Sale	4,000	
	Investment in NewCo		109,000
c.	Cash	105,000	
	Loss on Sale	10,000	
	Investment in NewCo		115,000
d.	Cash	105,000	
	Gain on Sale		14,000
	Investment in NewCo		91,000

ANSWER: A

Liabilities

CMBA Objective Correlations

- Given data, determine the amount of current liabilities to be recorded.

- Given financial data, determine carrying amounts of non-current liabilities and their disposition, including bonds payable, long-term leases, deferred taxes, et al.

- Given financial data, determine carrying amounts of non-current liabilities and their disposition, including bonds payable, long-term leases, deferred taxes, et al.

Sample Questions

1. An event that does not result in the recording of a liability is

   a. the sale of an automobile for cash by a manufacturer that provides free maintenance for 2 years
   b. the sale of Colorado Rockies' season tickets during the month of January
   c. the declaration of cash dividends to be paid in 4 weeks
   d. the purchase of land for common stock when the land is to be stated at more than the par value of the stock

ANSWER: D

2. Which of the following is **not** a current liability?

   a. liabilities due within the current operating cycle
   b. accounts payable to creditors
   c. short-term notes payable
   d. accumulated depreciation

ANSWER: D

3. The EMB Company requires advance payments for custom orders made to customer's specifications. Information concerning for Year 2's entries include:

Customer advances, balance, beg. of Year 2	$295,000
Advances received with orders in Year 2	460,000
Advances applied to orders shipped in Year 2	410,000
Nonrefundable advances received on orders canceled in Year 2	125,000

   At the end of the fiscal year, what amount should EMB report as current liability for customer advances?

   a. $0
   b. $220,000
   c. $345,000
   d. $370,000

ANSWER: B

4. On January 2, Year 12, 10 years after issue, the market prices these bonds to yield 12 percent. The amount at which Harris Corporation shows these bonds on its books at this date is equal to:

    a. the present value of $2,000,000 at 4 percent for 20 periods, plus the present value of an annuity of $100,000 at 4 percent for 20 periods
    b. the present value of $2,000,000 at 5 percent for 20 periods, plus the present value of an annuity of $100,000 at 5 percent for 20 periods
    c. the present value of $2,000,000 at 6 percent for 20 periods, plus the present value of an annuity of $100,000 at 6 percent for 20 periods
    d   the present value of $2,000,000 at 12 percent for 10 periods, plus the present value of an annuity of $100,000 at 6 percent for 20 periods

ANSWER: A

5. On January 2, Year 18, when the book value of the bonds is $2,538,618, Harris Corporation redeems the bonds on the open market for $2,400,000. Which of the following statements best describes the reporting of this item on the income statement for Year 18? (Ignore income tax effects.)

    a. Gain of $138,618 reported in the section "Income from Continuing Operations."
    b. Gain of $138,618 reported in the section "Income from Discontinued Operations."
    c. Gain of $138,618 reported in the section "Extraordinary Gains and Losses."
    d. Gain of $138,618 credited directly to Retained Earnings.

ANSWER: C

6. Marquette, Inc. issued $6,000,000 of 12% bonds on December 1, Year 1, due on December 1, Year 6, with interest payable each December 1 and June 1. The bonds sold for $5,194,770 to yield 16%. If the discount is amortized by the effective interest method, Marquette, Inc.'s interest expense for the fiscal year ended November 30, Year 2 related to its $6,000,000 bond issue will be

    a. $623,372
    b. $720,000
    c. $835,610
    d. $881,046

ANSWER: C

7. When the bond indenture provides that stated amounts of principal will become due during the term of the bond, the bond is called a

    a. sinking fund bond
    b. serial bond
    c. callable bond
    d. refunded bond

ANSWER: B

8. A callable bond

    a. must be retired from a sinking fund maintained by the bond issuer
    b. may be retired at a specified price at the option of the bond purchaser
    c. may be reacquired by the issuing company at a specified price
    d. are registered with an agent to insure correct payment of bond interest amounts

ANSWER: C

9. A bond sinking fund is recorded on the balance sheet as

    a.   a current liability
    b.   a long-term liability
    c.   a noncurrent asset
    d.   part of shareholders' equity

ANSWER: C

Items 10 and 11 are based on the following.

On January 1, Year 7, Plantation Restaurant is planning to enter as the lessee into the two lease agreements described below. Each lease is noncancelable, and Plantation does not receive title to either leased property during or at the end of the lease term. All payments required trader these agreements are due on January 1 each year.

Lessor	*Hadaway Inc.*	*Cutter Electronics*
Type of property	**Oven**	**Computer**
Yearly rental	$15,000	$4,000
Lease term	10 years	3 years
Economic life	15 years	5 years
Purchase option	None	$3,000
Renewal option	None	None
Fair market value at inception of lease	$125,000	$10,200
Unguaranteed residual value	None	$2,000
Lessee's incremental borrowing rate	10%	10%
Executory costs paid by	Lessee	Lessor
Annual executory costs	$800	$500
Present value factor at 10% (of an annuity due)	6.76	2.74

10. Plantation Restaurant should treat the lease agreement with Hadaway Inc. as a(n)

    a.   capital lease with an initial asset value of $101,400
    b.   operating lease, charging $14,200 in rental expense and $800 in executory costs to annual operations
    c.   operating lease, charging the present value of the yearly rental expense to annual operations
    d.   operating lease, charging $15,000 in rental expense and $800 in executory costs to annual operations

ANSWER: D

11. Plantation Restaurant should treat the lease agreement with Cutter Electronics as a(n)

    a.   capital lease with an initial asset value of $10,960
    b.   capital lease with an initial asset value of $10,200
    c.   operating lease, charging $3,500 in rental expense and $500 in executory costs to annual operations
    d.   capital lease with an initial asset value of $9,590

ANSWER: D

Items 12 and 13 are based on the following.

Bearings Manufacturing Company Inc. purchased a new machine on January 1, Year 5, for $100,000. The company uses the straight-line depreciation method with an estimated equipment life of five years and a zero salvage value for financial statement purposes, and uses the three-year. Modified Accelerated Cost Recovery System (MACRS) with an estimated equipment life of three years for income tax reporting purposes. Bearings is subject to a 35 percent marginal income tax rate. Assume that the deferred tax liability at the beginning of the year is zero, and that Bearings has a positive earnings tax position, The MACRS tax rates for three-year equipment are shown below.

Year	Rate
1	33.33%
2	44.45
3	14.81
4	7.41

12. What is the deferred tax liability at December Year 5 (rounded to the nearest whole dollar)?

   a. $7,000
   b. $33,330
   c. $11,666
   d. $4,666

ANSWER: D

13. For Bearings Manufacturing Company Inc., assume that the following new corporate income tax rates will go into effect.

        Year 6- Year 8   40%
        Year 9   45%

What is the amount of the deferred tax asset/liability at December 31, Year 5 (rounded to the nearest whole dollar)?

   a. $16,112
   b. $10,997
   c. $7,000
   d. $6,332

ANSWER: D

14. Which one of the following temporary differences will result in a deferred tax asset?

   a.   Use of the straight-line depreciation method for financial statement purposes and the Modified Accelerated Cost Recovery System (MACRS) for income tax purposes.
   b.   Installment sale profits accounted for on the accrual basis for financial statement purposes and on a cash basis for income tax purposes.
   c.   Advance rental receipts accounted for on the accrual basis for financial statement purposes and on a cash basis for tax purposes.
   d.   Investment gains accounted for under the equity method for financial statement purposes and under the cost method for income tax purposes.
   e.   Prepaid expenses accounted for on the accrual basis for financial statement purposes and on a cash basis for income tax purposes.

ANSWER: C

Investments and Shareholder Equity

CMBA Objective Correlations

- Given selected data, identify the financial statement effects of unrealized gains or losses.

- Show the effects on financial statements of specified treasury stock transactions.

- Determine retained earnings after a series of provided transactions.

- Given financial data, identify the financial statement effects of gains/losses from foreign currency translation, treatment of comprehensive income, et al.

- Given data, identify the effects of dividend actions on financial statements.

- Given data, determine basic and diluted EPS.

Sample Questions

1. Short-term marketable equity securities were acquired on July 1, Year 1 for $23,000, and classified as available-for-sale. On December 31, Year 1, the securities had a market value of $24,000, determined as follows:

	Cost *July 1, Year 1*	Fair Market Value *December 31, Year 1*
Security AA	**$ 9,000**	**$ 7,000**
Security BB	5,000	10,000
Security CC	9,000	7,000
Total	$23,000	$24,000

What adjustment is required to reflect December 31, Year 1 fair value?

a. unrealized holding gain on available-for-sale securities of $1,000, reported in other comprehensive income
b. unrealized holding gain on available-for-sale securities of $1,000, reported in the income statement
c. realized holding gain on available-for-sale securities available for sale of $1,000, reported in the income statement
d. realized holding gain on available-for-sale securities available for sale of $1,000, reported in other comprehensive income

ANSWER: A

Items 2 and 3 are based on the following:

Information concerning Monahan Company's portfolio of debt securities at May 31, Year 6, and May 31, Year 7, is presented below. All of the debt securities were purchased by Monahan during June, Year 5. Prior to June, Year 5, Monahan had no investments in debt or equity securities.

As of May 31, Year 6	_Amortized Cost_	_Fair Value_
Cleary Company bonds	$164,526	$168,300
Beauchamp Industry bonds	204,964	205,200
Morrow Inc. bonds	305,785	285,200
	$675,275	$658,700

As of May 31, Year 7	_Amortized Cost_	_Fair Value_
Cleary Company bonds	$152,565	$147,600
Beauchamp Industry bonds	193,800	204,500
Morrow Inc. bonds	289,130	291,400
	$635,495	$643,500

2.   Assuming that the above securities are properly classified as available-for-sale securities under Statement of Financial Accounting Standards #115, "Accounting for Certain Investments in Debt and Equity Securities," the unrealized holding gain or loss as of May 31, Year 7, would be

   a.   recognized as a $8,005 unrealized holding gain on the income statement
   b.   recognized as other comprehensive income with a year-end credit balance of $8,005 in the Unrealized Holding Gain/Loss account
   c.   recognized as a $24,580 unrealized holding loss on the income statement
   d.   not recognized

ANSWER: B

3.   Assuming that the above securities are properly classified as held-to-maturity securities under Statement of Financial Accounting Standards #115, "Accounting for Certain Investments in Debt and Equity Securities," the unrealized holding gain or loss as of May 31, Year 7, would be

   a.   recognized as a $8,005 unrealized holding gain on the income statement
   b.   recognized as other comprehensive income with a year-end credit balance of $8,005 in the Unrealized Holding Gain/Loss account
   c.   recognized as a $24,580 unrealized holding loss on the income statement
   d.   not recognized

ANSWER: D

4.   Doug's Discount Furniture discovered that its merchandise inventory was $100,000 less than reported at the end of the previous period when cost of goods sold was computed using a periodic method. The correcting entry is:

a.	Cost of Goods Sold	100,000	
	Retained Earnings		100,000
b.	Merchandise Inventory	100,000	
	Retained Earnings		100,000
c.	No entry necessary		
d.	Retained Earnings	100,000	
	Merchandise Inventory		100,000

ANSWER: D

5. Other comprehensive income includes

   a. changes in the market value of marketable equity securities
   b. changes in the market value of derivatives used as cash-flow hedges
   c. unrealized translation gains and losses from translating the foreign statements of foreign units into U.S. dollars
   d. all of the above

ANSWER: D

6. Other comprehensive income includes

   a. changes in the market value of held to maturity debt securities
   b. changes in the market value of derivatives used as cash-flow hedges
   c. realized gains and losses from marketable equity securities
   d. all of the above

ANSWER: B

7. Treasury stock can be defined as

   a. unissued stock, that is shares that have never been sold by the corporation
   b. designated stock, that is shares used for the specific purpose of converting preferred stock to common stock
   c. investment stock, that is shares acquired from a subsidiary company
   d. reacquired stock, that is outstanding shares purchased on the open market by the issuing corporation

ANSWER: D

8. A firm owns 1,000 treasury shares which it acquired for $15 per share (par value $1). The firm sells 500 of the treasury shares for $20 per share. Using the cost method, what is the entry to record the purchase using the cost method?

a.	Cash	10,000	
	Common Stock—Treasury Shares		10,000
b.	Cash	10,000	
	Common Stock—Treasury Shares		7,500
	Additional Paid-in Capital—Treasury Stock		2,500
c.	Cash	10,000	
	Common Stock—Treasury Shares		500
	Additional Paid-in Capital—Treasury Stock		9,500
d.	Cash	10,000	
	Common Stock—Par	1,000	
	Common Stock—Treasury Shares		11,000

ANSWER: B

9. The major segments of the statement of retained earnings for a period are

   a. dividends declared, prior period adjustments, and changes due to treasury stock transactions
   b. prior period adjustments, before tax income or loss, income tax, and dividends paid
   c. net income or loss from operations, dividends paid, and extraordinary gains and losses
   d. net income or loss, prior period adjustments, and dividends paid and/or declared

ANSWER: D

10. What is the accounting effect if the board of directors declares a dividend on December 15 and states that it will be payable on January 15?

    a. No liability is reported at December 31 because the dividend is not yet payable.
    b. A liability is recorded as of December 15 because the shareholders could actually demand payment prior to January 15.
    c. A liability is recorded only if the date of record is prior to December 31.
    d. No entry is required until January 15.

ANSWER: B

11. What limits the dividends that may be paid to corporate shareholders?

    a. Nothing as long as sufficient earnings support the payment.
    b. Creditors only if the firm is in default on debt payments.
    c. Statutory factors only.
    d. Statutory and contractual requirements.

ANSWER: D

12. On December 1, Charles Company's Board of Directors declared a cash dividend of $1.00 per share on the 50,000 shares of common stock outstanding. The company also has 5,000 shares of treasury stock. Shareholders of record on December 15 are eligible for the dividend which is to be paid on January 1. On December 1, the company should

    a. make no accounting entry
    b. debit retained earnings for $50,000
    c. debit retained earnings for $55,000
    d. debit retained earnings for $50,000 and paid-in-capital for $5,000
    e. debit dividends payable and credit cash

ANSWER: B

Items 13 through 15 are based on the following.

Excerpts from the Statement of Financial Position for Landau Corporation as of September 30, Year 5, are presented below.

Cash	$ 950,000
Accounts receivable (net)	1,675,000
Inventories 2,806,000	
Total current assets	$5,431,000
Accounts payable	$1,004,000
Accrued liabilities	785,000
Total current liabilities	$1,789,000

The Board of directors of Landau Corporation met on October 4, Year 5, and declared regular quarterly cash dividends amounting to $750,000 ($0.60 per share). The dividend is payable on October 25, Year 5, to all shareholders of record as of October 12, Year 5.

Assume that the only transactions to affect Landau Corporation during October Year 5 are the dividend transactions and that the closing entries have been made.

13. Landau's total shareholders' equity would be

    a. unchanged by the dividend declaration and decreased by the dividend payment
    b. decreased by the dividend declaration and increased by the dividend payment
    c. unchanged by either the dividend declaration or the dividend payment
    d. decreased by the dividend declaration and unchanged by the dividend payment

ANSWER: D

14. If the dividend declared by Landau Corporation had been a ten percent stock dividend instead of a cash dividend, Landau's current liabilities would have been

    a. decreased by the dividend declaration and increased by the dividend distribution
    b. unchanged by the dividend declaration and increased by the dividend distribution
    c. unchanged by the dividend declaration and decreased by the dividend distribution
    d. unchanged by either the dividend declaration or the dividend distribution

ANSWER: D

15. If the dividend declared by Landau Corporation had been a ten percent stock dividend instead of a cash dividend, Landau's total shareholders' equity would have been
    a. decreased by the dividend declaration and increased by the dividend distribution
    b. unchanged by the dividend declaration and increased by the dividend distribution
    c. increased by the dividend declaration and unchanged by the dividend distribution
    d. unchanged by either the dividend declaration or the dividend distribution

ANSWER: D

16. A stock dividend indicates

    a. a permanent commitment of assets generated by reinvested earnings
    b. an increase to total owner's equity
    c. an attempt to shift the control of the company by diluting ownership
    d. A transfer of corporate assets to shareholders without using cash

ANSWER: A

17. The actual total amount of a cash dividend to be paid is determined on the date of

    a. payment
    b. declaration
    c. record
    d. clearing

ANSWER: B

18. Earnings per share tells the shareholder the amount of

    a. cash generated per share of common stock
    b. dividends earned by the common shareholder
    c. dividend per share of common stock
    d. income per share as if preferred stock dividends had been paid

ANSWER: D

19. On January 1, Year 5, Toga Corporation granted stock options to top management. The options were exercisable within 4 years from the date of grant only if the employee was still in Toga's employ. When computing year-end earnings per share at December 31, Year 1, Toga should

  a. exclude the options until the year they are exercisable
  b. include the options in diluted earnings per share if they are dilutive
  c. include the options in diluted earnings per share if they are antidilutive
  d. ignore the options because they are not considered common stock equivalents

ANSWER: B

20. Earnings per share is a measure of

  a. cash income earned by the common shareholder
  b. profitability
  c. the financial viability of a firm
  d. the amount of dividends that will be paid by the firm

ANSWER: B

21. Earnings per share tells the shareholder the amount of

  a. cash generated per share of common stock
  b. dividends earned by the common shareholder
  c. dividend per share of common stock
  d. income per share as if preferred stock dividends had been paid

ANSWER: D

Managerial Accounting

Measuring Costs

CMBA Objective Correlations

- Given data, use the appropriate formulae to determine variable, fixed, and total costs.

- Given data, use opportunity cost concepts to enhance a management decision.

- Identify examples of variable, fixed, and sunk costs.

- Given data, calculate product and unit of service standard costs.

Sample Questions

1. The fundamental relationship among total costs, fixed costs, and variable costs can be explained as follows:
   a. Total Costs + Fixed Costs = Variable Costs
   b. Total Costs + Variable Costs = Fixed Costs
   c. Total Costs = Fixed Costs − Variable Costs
   d. Total Costs = Fixed Costs + Variable Costs

ANSWER: D

2. Fixed cost per unit
   a. increases as activity increases.
   b. decreases as activity increases.
   c. stays the same.
   d. first increases, then decreases.

ANSWER: B

3. If revenues are $20 per unit, variable costs are $10 per unit, and fixed costs are $150, what is the operating profit when 100 units are sold?
   a. $850
   b. $1,740
   c. ($16,000)
   d. ($140)

ANSWER: A

4. The major purpose of cost estimation is to break down total cost into
    a. short-run and long-run components.
    b. fixed and variable components.
    c. controllable and noncontrollable components.
    d. direct and indirect components.

ANSWER: B

5. Valley Company incurred a total cost of $5,000 to produce 300 units of output. A total of 450 hours was incurred for this effort. If the variable cost was $10 per direct labor hour, then the fixed cost was
    a. a.$4,500.
    b. $3,000.
    c. $2,000.
    d. $ 500.

ANSWER: D

6. Which of the following cost estimation methods is based on studies of what future costs should be rather than what past costs have been?
    a. Engineering method
    b. Account analysis
    c. Visual curve-fitting
    d. Regression

ANSWER: A

7. Columbia Hospital for Women is planning to expand its labor and delivery room facilities. Although variable costs per patient will remain unchanged, fixed costs will increase by 20 percent. Last year's costs are below.

Variable costs $50 per patient
Fixed costs $20,000 per month

Calculate the future total cost assuming 100 patients are expected each month.
    a. $25,000
    b. $29,000
    c. $20,500
    d. $20,000

ANSWER: B

Julianna Company

Data from the duplicating department of Julianna Company for the last six months are as follows:

	Duplicating Dept.'s Costs	Number of Copies Made
January	$18,000	22,000
February	$19,000	24,000
March	$21,000	27,000
April	$17,000	20,000
May	$19,500	25,000
June	$24,000	30,000

Regression output from the above data is given below:

Constant	2807.895
Std Err of Y Est	499.3417
R Squared	0.967696
No. of Observations	6
Degrees of Freedom	4
X Coefficients	0.686842
Std Err of Coef.	0.062745

8. Refer to the regression output for Julianna Company; what is the variable rate per copy?
    a. .97
    b. .69
    c. .06
    d. 4.99

ANSWER: B

9. Refer to the regression output for Julianna Company; what is the fixed cost?
    a. $499.34
    b. $2807.90
    c. $96.77
    d. $68.68

ANSWER: B

10. Based on the regression output for Julianna Company, which of the following equations should be used to compute an estimate of future total costs?
    a. TC= $499.34 + .687(X)
    b. TC= $499.34 + .062(X)
    c. TC= $2807.90 + .687(X)
    d. TC= $2807.90 + .062(X)

ANSWER: C

11. Refer to the regression output for Julianna Company; if 22,000 copies are made next month, what total cost should be incurred?
    a. $15,631.34
    b. $ 1863.34
    c. $17,921.90
    d. $ 1651.90

ANSWER: C

12. Capacity costs:
    a. are certain fixed costs that provide a firm with the capacity to produce or sell or both
    b. need not be incurred in the short run to conduct business
    c. are uncontrollable in the long run
    d. are always non-value added

ANSWER: A

13. Fixed costs expressed on a per unit basis
    a. will react directly with changes in activity.
    b. will react inversely with changes in activity.
    c. are not affected by activity.
    d. should be ignored in making decisions since they cannot change.

ANSWER: B

14. Julia Mining Company spent $25 million four years ago to develop Gold mining operations in a remote area of Alaska. Gold prices have since declined dramatically and the company is considering abandoning the operation. The term that would best describe the $25 million expenditure regarding the abandonment decision is
    a. noncontrollable cost.
    b. sunk cost.
    c. nonvalue-added cost.
    d. opportunity cost.

ANSWER: B

15. When cost relationships are linear, total variable costs will vary in proportion to changes in
    a. direct labor hours.
    b. total material costs.
    c. total overhead costs.
    d. volume of production.

ANSWER: D

16. When the number of units manufactured increases, the most significant change in average unit cost will be reflected as
    a. an increase in the nonvariable component.
    b. a decrease in the variable component.
    c. a decrease in the nonvariable component.
    d. an increase in the variable component.

ANSWER: C

17. Unit fixed costs
    a. are constant per unit regardless of units produced or sold.
    b. are determined by dividing total fixed costs by a denominator such as production or sales volume.
    c. vary directly with the activity level when stated on a per unit basis.
    d. include a fixed and variable component.

ANSWER: B

18. Total variable costs
    a. do not vary in total within the relevant range.
    b. vary in total in proportion to the activity level.
    c. vary in total in an inverse relationship with production.
    d. vary in total, but not in proportion to changes in the activity level.

ANSWER: B

19. Unit variable costs
    a. do not vary in total within the relevant range.
    b. vary in total in an inverse relationship with production.
    c. are not relevant for decision-making
    d. are total variable costs divided by the activity level.

ANSWER: D

20. Income forgone from not using an asset in its best economic alternative is an example of a(n):
    a. outlay cost
    b. direct cost
    c. indirect cost
    d. opportunity cost

ANSWER: D

21. A cost that does not relate directly to a cost object is a(n):
    a. outlay cost
    b. direct cost
    c. indirect cost
    d. opportunity cost

ANSWER: C

22. A cost that changes in total as the level of activity changes is a(n):
    a. fixed cost
    b. direct cost
    c. indirect cost
    d. variable cost

ANSWER: D

Activity-Based Management

CMBA Test Correlations

- Given data, determine activity-based costs of products.

- Given financial data, contrast income reported under various costing approaches (variable, full absorption, ABC).

Sample Questions

1. Under activity-based costing, overhead costs are accumulated
    a. in a single, plant-wide pool.
    b. by departments.
    c. in pools established by identified cost drivers.
    d. in facility-level activities.

ANSWER: C

2. Activity-based costing
    a. can only be used in manufacturing.
    b. can be used for manufacturing, marketing, or administrative activities.
    c. should only be used for service companies.
    d. can be used only for manufacturing and administrative, but not for marketing activities.

ANSWER: B

3. Companies are likely to benefit from activity-based accounting systems if:
    a. they have had few changes in activities over time and few corresponding changes have been made in the accounting system.
    b. they have low overhead costs.
    c. they have a narrow range of products.
    d. they have wide variations in the volume of individual production runs and setups are costly (i.e., complex production methods).

ANSWER: D

4. Which company is *not* likely to benefit from activity-based costing?
    a. A manufacturer of one product
    b. A manufacturer or one high volume product and one low volume product
    c. A university with three schools: Science, Law, and Business
    d. A bank with multiple product lines

ANSWER: A

5. Activity-based management treats fixed costs as
    a. costs which vary directly with volume.
    b. costs which cannot be controlled over the long-run.
    c. costs which may vary for reasons other than volume.
    d. sunk costs which have no future economic benefit.

ANSWER: C

6. Which costs are often not assigned to product lines using activity-based management?
    a. unit
    b. batch
    c. product/process
    d. organizational or facility

ANSWER: D

7. Studies have shown that after activity-based costing has been implemented, the costs of
    a. high-volume, standard products have declined significantly.
    b. high-volume, specialty products have increased significantly.
    c. low-volume, standard products have declined significantly.
    d. all products have increased significantly.

ANSWER: A

8. Activity-based costing improves cost assignment because
    a. management is provided with true costs.
    b. it uses a greater number of cost pools and cost drivers than traditional overhead allocation techniques.
    c. it follows generally accepted accounting principles more closely.
    d. it is easier to use than traditional overhead allocation techniques.

ANSWER: B

9. Which of the following is likely to indicate a need for activity-based costing?
    a. a low variety of products or services.
    b. an extensive use of common processes.
    c. diversity in product volumes.
    d. a high level of effectiveness of current overhead allocations.

ANSWER: C

10. Activity-based management can be used to reduce customer response time by
    a. identifying value-added activities and eliminating them.
    b. identifying and eliminating activities which consume the most resources.
    c. minimizing the time the product is in the value-chain.
    d. identifying marketing expenses which relate directly to customer complaints.

ANSWER: B

11. Which of the following is *not* a step accountants must follow in activity-based costing?
   a. Identify the activities that consume resources and assign costs to them.
   b. Identify the cost drivers associated with each activity.
   c. Compute a cost rate per cost driver
   d. Compute the variance between the estimated cost driver and the actual cost driver.

ANSWER: D

Marshall Manufacturing Co.

Marshall Manufacturing Co. uses an activity-based costing system. The company has gathered the following information concerning various cost pools and activity drivers;

Activity cost pool	Normal Cost	Activity cost driver	Activity level
Material Handling	$10,000	Number of moves	5,000
Machine setups	$40,000	Number of setups	2,000
Inspections	$ 2,500	Number of Inspections	500
Electricity Costs	$20,000	Kilowatt Hours	10,000

The following data was collected and is specific to Item No. 824.

Direct Material Cost	$15,000
Direct Labor Cost	5,000 (@ $10 per hour)
Number of machine setups	100
Number of material moves	250
Number of inspections	50
Kilowatt hours of electricity used	500
Units produced	1,000

12. What would be the amount of allocated power cost to Item No. 824?
   a. $1,000
   b. $1,500
   c. $ 500
   d. $5,000

ANSWER: A

13. What would be the amount of quality inspection cost allocated to Item No. 824?
   a. $2,500
   b. $ 125
   c. $1,000
   d. $ 250

ANSWER: D

14. What would be the amount of setup cost allocated to Item No. 824?
   a. $40,000
   b. $ 8,000
   c. $ 2,500
   d. $ 2,000

ANSWER: D

15. What would be the unit cost for the inspection activity on Item No. 824?
   a. $ 4.00
   b. $80.00
   c. $ 5.00
   d. $ 1.00

ANSWER: C

16. What would be the unit cost for the materials handling activity at Marshall Manufacturing Co.?
   a. $ 4.00
   b. $80.00
   c. $ 2.00
   d. $ 1.00

ANSWER: C

17. What would be the unit cost for the machine setup activity at Marshall Manufacturing Co.?
   a. $ 4.00
   b. $80.00
   c. $ 2.00
   d. $20.00

ANSWER: D

18. The cost-volume-profit model is consistent with
   a. variable costing.
   b. full absorption costing.
   c. normal costing.
   d. all of the above.

ANSWER: A

Financial Modeling for Short-Term Decision Making

CMBA Objective Correlations

- Given a scenario with financial information, calculate break-even in (units, dollars).

- Given price and cost information, use contribution margin in facilitating a specified managerial decision.

Sample Questions

1. The breakeven point can be determined by
    a. fixed costs/selling price per unit.
    b. fixed costs/variable costs per unit.
    c. variable costs/selling price per unit.
    d. fixed costs/contribution margin per unit.

ANSWER: D

2. The breakeven point would be increased by
    a. a decrease in fixed costs.
    b. an increase in the contribution margin ratio.
    c. an increase in variable costs.
    d. a decrease in variable costs.

ANSWER: C

3. If a company's sales price per unit is $100, variable costs per unit are $60, and fixed costs for the year are $600,000. How many units must the company sell to break even?
    a. 36,000
    b. 22,500
    c. 15,000
    d. 9,000

ANSWER: C

4. If a company has variable costs of $20 per unit, fixed costs of $3,000 per month and sells its product for $50, how many units must it sell to earn a profit of $4,500?
    a. 300
    b. 250
    c. 100
    d. 50

ANSWER: B

5. If a company's selling price per unit is $15, variable costs per unit are $8, fixed costs for the year are $90,750, how many units must it sell to earn a 10 percent return on sales?
   a. 21,000
   b. 19,091
   c. 16,500
   d. 15,000

ANSWER: C

6. A company currently breaks even at 1,000 units. Its fixed costs are $40,000 and its variable costs are $10 per unit. What is the product's selling price per unit?
   a. $100
   b. $ 50
   c. $ 35
   d. $ 25

ANSWER: B

7. A company's selling price is $12 per unit, variable cost is $3 per unit, and fixed costs are $25,000. What is the breakeven point in sales dollars?
   a. $53,333
   b. $44,444
   c. $33,333
   d. $1,333

ANSWER: C

8. A company's selling price is $18 per unit, variable cost is $6 per unit, and fixed costs are $36,000. If fixed costs increased by $6,000, how many additional units must be sold to break even?
   a. 5,000
   b. 1,000
   c. 500
   d. 250

ANSWER: C

TopSail Company

TopSail Company produces one type of machine with the following costs and revenues for the year:

Total revenues	$5,600,000
Total fixed costs	$2,700,000
Total variable costs	$1,400,000
Total units produced and sold	700,000

9. Refer to the TopSail Company; what is the selling price per unit?
   a. $ 8
   b. $ 6
   c. $ 2
   d. $12

ANSWER: A

10. Refer to the TopSail Company; what is the variable cost per unit?
    a. $ 6
    b. $ 2
    c. $ 4
    d. $12

ANSWER: B

11. Refer to the TopSail Company; what is the contribution margin per unit?
    a. $ 6
    b. $ 2
    c. $ 4
    d. $12

ANSWER: A

12. Refer to the TopSail Company; what is the breakeven point in units?
    a. 700,000
    b. 2,100,000
    c. 1,400,000
    d. 450,000

ANSWER: D

13. Refer to the TopSail Company; how many units must be sold to make an operating profit of $300,000 for the year?
    a. 500,000
    b. 1,000,000
    c. 1,500,000
    d. 2,000,000

ANSWER: A

Sun Devil, Inc.

Sun Devil, Inc. is considering the introduction of a new product with the following price and cost characteristics:

Sales price	$75 each
Variable cost	$25 each
Fixed cost	$300,000 per year

It expects to sell 70,000 units for the year.

14. Refer to Sun Devil, Inc; how many units must be sold to break even?
    a. 4,000
    b. 6,000
    c. 12,000
    d. 3,000

ANSWER: B

15. Refer to Sun Devil, Inc; how many units must be sold to make an operating profit of $15,000?
    a. 4,200
    b. 12,600
    c. 6,300
    d. 3,150

ANSWER: C

16. Refer to Sun Devil, Inc; if 7,000 units are sold, what operating profit is expected?
    a. 225,000
    b. 50,000
    c. 525,000
    d. 350,000

ANSWER: B

17. Refer to Sun Devil, Inc; what would be the breakeven point in units if the sales price decreased by 20%?
    a. 5,000
    b. 7,500
    c. 20,000
    d. 8,571

ANSWER: D

18. Refer to Sun Devil, Inc; what would be the breakeven point in units if variable costs per unit decreased by 40%?
    a. 10,000
    b. 5,000
    c. 6,667
    d. 3,600

ANSWER: B

19. Refer to Sun Devil, Inc; what would be the breakeven point in units if fixed costs were increased by $50,000?
    a. 7,000
    b. 4,667
    c. 14,000
    d. 3,500

ANSWER: A

Cost Analysis

CMBA Objective Correlations

- With a given set of financial data concerning common costs, calculate the economic impact of processing specific products beyond split-off.

- Given selected financial information, identify relevant costs in new equipment, make-or-buy, and drop-or-add decisions.

- Given selected financial information, determine the minimum acceptable price for a special order.

- Given financial data, determine the mix of planned products and activities that will generate optimum profits.

Sample Questions

1. The short-run differential costs of a product are $25. Fixed costs are $5 per unit based on 10,000 units produced during this period. The company has adequate capacity to accept a special order of 1,000 units. What is the minimum price that could be charged using the differential approach to pricing?
    a. $ 5.00
    b. $20.00
    c. $25.00
    d. $30.00

ANSWER: C

2. The Correct Balance Company manufactures adding machines. The company's capacity is 5,000 units per month; however, it currently is selling only 3,000 units per month. Company X has asked Correct Balance to sell 1,000 adding machines at $25 each. Normally, Correct Balance sells its product for $35. The company records report each adding machine's full absorption costs are $30 which includes fixed costs of $20. If Correct Balance was to accept Company X's offer, what would be the impact on Correct Balance's operating income?
    a. Additional profit of $15,000
    b. Additional profit of $25,000
    c. A loss of $5,000 on this order
    d. A loss of $10,000 on this order

ANSWER: A

3. San Juan Corporation sells a product for $25 per unit and has the following costs for the product:

Direct Materials	$10
Direct Labor	5
Variable Overhead	3
Fixed Overhead	2
Total	$20

San Juan received a special order for 100 units of the product. The order would require rental of a special tool which costs $200. What is the minimum price per unit S should charge for this special order if they wish to earn a $300 profit on this order? Assume there is sufficient idle capacity to accept this order.
    a. $18
    b. $20
    c. $23
    d. $25

ANSWER: C

4. Kandy Corporation sells a product for $25 per unit and has the following costs for the product:

Direct Materials	$10
Direct Labor	5
Variable Overhead	3
Fixed Overhead	2
Total	$20

Kandy received a special order for 100 units of the product. The order would require rental of a special tool which costs $200. What is the minimum price per unit K should charge for this special order if they wish to earn a $600 profit? Assume K is currently producing and selling at maximum capacity.
    a. $23
    b. $24
    c. $26
    d. $28

ANSWER: D

5. Production of a special order will increase gross profit when the additional revenue from the special order is greater than
    a. the nonvariable costs incurred in producing the order
    b. the direct material and labor costs in producing the order
    c. the fixed costs incurred in producing the order
    d. the marginal cost of producing the order

ANSWER: D

6. In considering a special order that will enable a company to make use of presently idle capacity, which of the following costs would be irrelevant?
    a. Materials
    b. Depreciation
    c. Direct Labor
    d. Variable Overhead

ANSWER: B

Managerial Accounting

Grizzly Company

Grizzly Company manufactures footballs. The forecasted income statement for the year before any special orders is as follows:

	Amount	Per Unit
Sales	4,000,000	$10.00
Manufacturing CGS	3,200,000	8.00
Gross Profit	800,000	2.00
Selling Expenses	300,000	.75
Operating Income	$ 500,000	$ 1.25

7. Fixed costs included in the above forecasted income statement are $1,200,000 in manufacturing CGS and $100,000 in selling expenses. Grizzly received a special order offering to buy 50,000 footballs for $7.50 each. There will be no additional selling expenses if Grizzly accepts. Assume Grizzly has sufficient capacity to manufacture 50,000 more footballs. The unit relevant cost for Grizzly's decision is
    a. $8.00
    b. $5.00
    c. $8.75
    d. $5.75

ANSWER: B

8. By what amount would operating income of Grizzly be increased or decreased as a result of accepting the special order?
    a. $25,000 decrease
    b. $62,500 decrease
    c. $100,000 increase
    d. $125,000 increase

ANSWER: D

Clear Sailing Lifeboats

Clear Sailing Lifeboats uses 12,000 units of a certain component in production each year. Presently, this component is purchased from an outside supplier at $9.50 per unit. For some time now there has been idle capacity in the factory that could be utilized to make this component. The costs associated with manufacturing the component internally rather than buying it from the outside supplier are:

Direct materials	$3 per unit
Direct Labor	$3 per unit
Variable Overhead	$2 per unit
Fixed Overhead (based on production of 8,000 units per month)	$2 per unit
Annual salary of new supervisor	$12,000

9. Refer to Clear Sailing Lifeboats. Assuming other things stay the same, at what price per unit from the outside supplier would Mandy be indifferent (on economic grounds) to buying or making the components?
    a. $9.50
    b. $9.00
    c. $8.50
    d. $8.00

ANSWER: B

10. Refer to Clear Sailing Lifeboats. If Mandy chooses to make the component instead of buying it outside the changes in the company's net income per year would be a:
   a. $6,000 decrease
   b. $6,000 increase
   c. $8,400 decrease
   d. $8,400 increase

ANSWER: B

11. In the decision to replace an obsolete piece of manufacturing equipment with a state of the art model, which of the following would be considered a relevant cost?
   a. The book value of the old equipment
   b. Depreciation expense on the old equipment.
   c. The loss on sale (or disposal) of the old equipment.
   d. The current sale (disposal) price of the old equipment

ANSWER: D

12. Which of the following is an example of a make-or-buy decision?
   a. Adding a product line
   b. Dropping a segment
   c. Subcontracting work in place of using the company's own employees
   d. Hiring skilled labor in place of unskilled labor

ANSWER: C

13. ABC Company has three products that use common facilities. The relevant data concerning these three products follows:

Product	A	B	C	Total
Sales	$10,000	$30,000	$40,000	$80,000
Variable costs	5,000	20,000	25,000	50,000
Contribution Margin	5,000	10,000	15,000	30,000
Fixed cost	5,000	15,000	30,000	50,000
Operating loss	0	-$ 5,000	-$15,000	-$20,000

Fixed costs are allocated common costs. If product line C is dropped, what will be the impact on operating profits?
   a. Operating loss will decrease to ($15,000)
   b. Operating loss will decrease to ($5,000)
   c. Operating loss will increase to ($35,000)
   d. There would be no change in operating profits

ANSWER: C

14. Mother's Products makes cups and plates. It can sell all of either product it can make. The relevant data for these two products follows:

	Cups	Plates
Machine time per unit	.5 Hour	2 Hours
Selling price per unit	$10	$20
Variable costs per unit	$ 2	$ 4

Total fixed overhead is $240,000. The company has 100,000 machine hours available for production. The company should select which product to maximize operating profits?
   a. Plates because its contribution margin per unit is $16
   b. Plates because its contribution margin per hour is $8
   c. Cups because its contribution margin per hour is $16
   d. Cups because its contribution margin per unit is $8

ANSWER: C

15. McDowel and Company has two sales offices: East and West. The company's records report the following information:

	East	West
Sales	$40,000	$50,000
Direct Costs:		
Variable	$15,000	$25,000
Fixed	$15,000	$10,000
Allocated common costs	$20,000	$10,000

Management is considering dropping the East office. What will happen to operating income if East is eliminated?
   a. Profit of $10,000
   b. Profit of $5,000
   c. Loss of $10,000
   d. Company would be at breakeven

ANSWER: C

16. Nifty Toys manufactured 500 dolls that were defective. The manufacturing costs of the dolls follow:

Direct Materials	$30
Direct Labor	$24
Variable Overhead	$10
Fixed Overhead	$12

The dolls normally sell for $100. The company can rework the dolls which will cost $3 for direct materials, $20 for direct labor, and $2 for variable overhead. In addition, fixed overhead will be applied at the rate of 75 percent of direct labor cost. Alternatively, the company could sell the dolls "as is" for a selling price of $70. What should management do to maximize profits?
   a. Sell the dolls as is
   b. Rework the dolls
   c. Sell half of the dolls as is and rework the other half
   d. Scrap the dolls to minimize losses

ANSWER: B

17. M Corporation makes automobile engines. The company's records show the following costs to manufacture part #308FD:

Direct Materials	$13
Direct Labor	$15
Variable Overhead	$20
Fixed Overhead	$10

Another manufacturer has offered to supply M Corporation with part #308FD for a cost of $50 per unit. M Corporation uses 1,000 units annually. If M Corporation accepts the offer, what will be the short-run impact on operating income?
   a. Decrease in profits equal to $8,000
   b. Decrease in profits equal to $2,000
   c. Increase in profits equal to $8,000
   d. Increase in profits equal to $2,000

ANSWER: B

BLUE Company

The following questions are based on BLUE Company, which needs 10,000 units a certain part to be used in production. If BLUE buys the part from RED Company instead of making it, BLUE could not use the present facilities for another manufacturing activity. Sixty percent (60%) of the fixed overhead applied will continue regardless of what decision is made.

The following quantitative information is available regarding the situation presented:
Cost to BLUE to make the part:

Direct materials	$7
Direct labor	24
Variable overhead	12
Fixed overhead applied	15
	$58
	===

Cost to buy the part from	
RED Company	$53
	===

18. In deciding whether to make or buy the part, BLUE's total relevant cost to make the part is
   a. $352,000
   b. $490,000
   c. $540,000
   d. $580,000

ANSWER: B

19. Which alternative is more desirable for BLUE and by what amount?
   a. Buy, $40,000
   b. Make, $40,000
   c. Buy, $50,000
   d. Make, $50,000

ANSWER: B

Capital Expenditure Decisions

CMBA Objective Correlations

- Given data, calculate the net present value of an investment opportunity.

Sample Questions

1. The internal rate of return equates the net present value
   a. to a positive number.
   b. to a negative number.
   c. to zero.
   d. all of the above.

   ANSWER: C

2. Projects are accepted if the internal rate of return
   a. is less than the cutoff or hurdle rate.
   b. exceeds the cutoff or hurdle rate.
   c. is less than the incremental borrowing rate.
   d. exceeds the incremental borrowing rate.

   ANSWER: B

3. For the internal rate of return to rank projects the same way as the net present value rule, which condition must exist?
   a. The cutoff rate used for the internal rate equals the cost of capital.
   b. Projects are mutually exclusive.
   c. Projects have different lives.
   d. There must be more than one internal rate of return.

   ANSWER: A

4. The Wealthy Club, Inc. is considering an investment that requires $20,000 and promises to return $28,090 is 3 years. The company's income tax rate is 40 percent. What is the approximate internal rate of return?
   a. 8 percent
   b. 10 percent
   c. 12 percent
   d. 15 percent

   ANSWER: C

5. A project requires an initial investment of $43,000 and has the following expected stream of cash flows:
   Year 1 $20,000
   Year 2 $30,000
   The internal rate of return for the project is closest to
   a. 0 percent
   b. 10 percent
   c. 15 percent
   d. 20 percent

ANSWER: B

6. If the net present value of a proposed project is positive, then the actual rate of return
   a. is higher than the cost of capital.
   b. is lower than the cost of capital.
   c. is equal to the cost of capital.
   d. is negative.

ANSWER: A

7. Project A has an expected cash flow of $500,000 at the end of year 5. Project B has an expected cash flow of $100,000 to be received at the end of each year for the next five years. What can be said of the net present value of project A compared to project B?
   a. They are the same because both cash flows total $500,000 over the lives of the projects.
   b. Project A is preferred because of the largest lump-sum payment in year 5.
   c. Project B is preferred because of the periodic payments made consistently throughout the years.
   d. The both have the same internal rate of return and either should be accepted.

ANSWER: C

8. A company purchased an asset at a cost of $80,000. Annual operating cash flows are expected to be $30,000 each year for 4 years. At the end of the asset life, there will be no residual (salvage) value. What is the net present value if the cost of capital is 12 percent (Ignore income taxes)?
   a. $40,000
   b. $24,400
   c. $11,120
   d. $5,650

ANSWER: C

9. A company purchased an asset at a cost of $80,000. Annual operating cash flows are expected to be $30,000 each year for 4 years. At the end of the asset life, the salvage value is expected to be $5,000. What is the net present value if the cost of capital is 15 percent (ignore income taxes)?
   a. $40,000
   b. $14,298
   c. $8,510
   d. $5,650

ANSWER: C

10. A not-for-profit company purchased an asset at a cost of $60,000. Annual operating cash flows are expected to be $20,000 each year for 4 years. At the end of the asset life, there will be no residual (salvage) value. Ignore income taxes. What is the net present value if the cost of capital is 10 percent?
    a. $(1,960)
    b. $3,397
    c. $12,400
    d. $23,400

ANSWER: B

11. Softglow Company invested $180,000 in a new machine. The machine will generate cash flows before taxes at year-end of $90,000, $80,000, and $70,000 for the next three years. The company uses a 15 percent cost of capital. What is the net present value of purchasing the machine?
    a. $4,778
    b. $9,230
    c. $25,826
    d. $60,000

ANSWER: A

Profit Planning and Budgeting

CMBA Objective Correlations

- Given data, analyze results of operations using a flexible budget.

- Given a specified strategy, identify appropriate responsibility centers.

Sample Questions

1. Which of the following is a basic purpose of a budget?
    a. Forecasts the result of operations
    b. Provides a basis for performance measurement
    c. Communicates
    d. All of the above

ANSWER: D

2. The key idea in a flexible budget is
    a. the budget formula.
    b. the forecasting of a specific volume of activity.
    c. the exclusion of variable factory overhead costs.
    d. the inclusion of fixed costs.

ANSWER: A

3. If management desires finished goods inventory to decrease over the period, what can be said about the relationship between units produced and units sold?
    a. Units produces > units sold
    b. Units produced < units sold
    c. Units produced = units sold
    d. Nothing can be said without more information.

ANSWER: B

4. An example of a discretionary fixed cost is
    a. rent.
    b. advertising.
    c. shipping costs.
    d. depreciation.

ANSWER: B

5. A distinction between forecasting and planning
    a. arises because they are based upon different assumptions about economic events.
    b. presents the plan for a range of activity so that the plan can be adjusted for changes in activity level.
    c. classifies budget requests by activity and estimates the benefits arising from each activity.
    d. divides the activities of individual responsibility centers into a series of packages, which are ranked ordinally.

ANSWER: B

6. Ineffective budgets and/or control systems are characterized by
    a. the use of budgets as a planning tool only and disregarding them for control purposes.
    b. the lack of timely feedback in the use of the budget.
    c. the use of budgets for harassment of individuals as opposed to motivation.
    d. All of the above.

ANSWER: D

7. The primary difference between a fixed budget and a flexible budget is that a fixed budget
    a. includes only fixed costs, while a flexible budget includes only variable costs.
    b. is concerned only with future acquisitions of fixed assets, while a flexible budget is concerned with expenses, which vary with sales.
    c. cannot be changed after the period begins, while a flexible budget can be changed after the period begins.
    d. is a plan for a single level of sales (or other measure of activity), while a flexible budget consists of several plans, one for each of several levels of sales (or other measure of activity).

ANSWER: D

8. The basic difference between a fixed budget and a flexible budget is that a
    a. flexible budget considers only variable costs but a fixed budget considers all costs.
    b. flexible budget allows management latitude in meeting goals whereas a fixed budget is based on a fixed standard.
    c. fixed budget is for an entire production facility but a flexible budget is applicable to single departments only.
    d. fixed budget is based on one specific level of production and a flexible budget can be prepared for any production level within a relevant range.

ANSWER: D

9. When production levels are expected to increase within a relevant range, and a flexible budget is used, what effects would be anticipated with respect to each of the following?

	Fixed Costs Per Unit	Variable Costs Per Unit
a.	Decrease	Increase
b.	Decrease	No Change
c.	No Change	No Change
d.	No Change	Increase

ANSWER: B

10. A flexible budget is
    a. not appropriate when costs and expenses are affected by fluctuations in volume limits.
    b. appropriate for any relevant level of activity.
    c. appropriate for control of factory overhead but not for control of direct materials and direct labor.
    d. appropriate for control of direct materials and direct labor but not for control of factory overhead.

ANSWER: B

11. A flexible budget is appropriate for a

Direct-Labor Budget	Marketing Budget
a. No	No
b. No	Yes
c. Yes	No
d. Yes	Yes

ANSWER: D

12. If a company wishes to establish a factory overhead budget system in which estimated costs can be derived directly from estimates of activity levels, it should prepare a
    a. zero-based budget.
    b. flexible budget.
    c. discretionary budget.
    d. fixed budget.

ANSWER: B

13. Herring Company is preparing a flexible budget for the coming year and the following maximum capacity estimates for the furniture division are available:

Direct labor hours   60,000
Variable factory overhead $150,000
Fixed factory overhead $240,000

Assume that Herring's normal capacity is 80% of maximum capacity. What would be the total factory overhead rate, based on direct labor hours, in a flexible budget at normal capacity?
    a. $6.00
    b. $6.50
    c. $7.50
    d. $8.13

ANSWER: C

14. In what type of responsibility centers are the managers responsible for costs, only?
    a. cost
    b. revenue
    c. profit
    d. investment

ANSWER: A

15. In what type of responsibility centers are the managers responsible for revenues, only?
    a. cost
    b. revenue
    c. profit
    d. investment

ANSWER: B

16. In what type of responsibility centers are the managers responsible for both costs and revenues?
    a. cost
    b. revenue
    c. profit
    d. investment

ANSWER: C

17. In what type of responsibility centers are the managers responsible for revenues, costs, and assets?
    a. cost
    b. revenue
    c. profit
    d. investment

ANSWER: D

Evaluating Performance

CMBA Objective Correlations

- Define target costing and contrast it with kaizen costing.

- Given a set of financial data, determine sales volume, efficiency, and price variances.

- Identify the components of the Balanced Scorecard.

Sample Questions

1. An important point in variance analysis is that
   a. every variance must be investigated.
   b. a responsibility center's variances are calculated holding all other things constant.
   c. often price and usage variances cannot be separated.
   d. all of the above.

   ANSWER: B

2. Which function is normally responsible for sales price variances?
   a. marketing
   b. administration
   c. production
   d. purchasing

   ANSWER: A

3. Price variance is calculated as follows:
   a. actual quantity x (actual price - standard price).
   b. standard quantity x (actual price - standard price).
   c. actual price x (actual quantity - standard allowed quantity).
   d. standard price x (actual quantity - standard allowed quantity).

   ANSWER: A

4. Efficiency variance is calculated as follows:
   a. actual quantity x (actual price - standard price).
   b. standard quantity x (actual price - standard price).
   c. actual price x (actual quantity - standard allowed quantity).
   d. standard price x (actual quantity - standard allowed quantity).

ANSWER: D

5. The sum of the price and efficiency variances
   a. always equals the difference between budgeted and actual.
   b. always equals the difference between the flexible budget and actual.
   c. is always positive.
   d. is always negative.

ANSWER: B

6. If variable overhead is applied on the basis of direct labor hours and there is an unfavorable direct labor price variance, the variable overhead price variance
   a. will always be unfavorable.
   b. will always be favorable.
   c. will always be zero.
   d. there is no relationship between the two variances.

ANSWER: D

7. The total fixed overhead variance is
   a. the difference between the fixed overhead budgeted for a period and the amount of fixed overhead applied to the units produced.
   b. the predetermined fixed overhead rate multiplied by the budgeted activity.
   c. the predetermined fixed overhead rate multiplied by the standard allowed activity.
   d. the difference between actual fixed overhead and the budgeted fixed overhead.

ANSWER: D

The Julia Company

The Julia Company established standard costs as follows:

Materials: 5 pieces @ $1.00 per piece
Labor: 2 hours @ $7.00 per hour

In October, 1,000 units were completed. During the month, 5,200 pieces were purchased at $1.10 per piece. Labor costs were $14,175 for 2,100 hours.
(U denotes unfavorable, F denotes favorable)

8. Refer to the Julia Company; what is the material price variance?
   (U denotes unfavorable, F denotes favorable)
   a. $100F
   b. $100U
   c. $520f
   d. $520U

ANSWER: D

9. Refer to the Julia Company; what is the material efficiency variance?
   (U denotes unfavorable, F denotes favorable)
   a. $200F
   b. $200U
   c. $400U
   d. None of the above

ANSWER: B

10. Refer to the Julia Company; what is the labor price variance?
    (U denotes unfavorable, F denotes favorable)
    a. $525F
    b. $525U
    c. $1050U
    d. None of the above

ANSWER: A

11. Refer to the Julia Company; what is the labor efficiency variance?
    (U denotes unfavorable, F denotes favorable)
    a. $350U
    b. $700F
    c. $700U
    d. None of the above

ANSWER: C

12. In target costing,
    a. selling price is estimated, product is designed, and actual cost is estimated.
    b. product is designed, allowable cost is determined, and selling price is estimated.
    c. selling price is estimated, allowable cost is determined, and product is designed.
    d. actual cost is estimated, product is designed, and selling price is estimated.

ANSWER: C

13. Usage variances focus on
    a. efficiency of the results.
    b. effectiveness of the results.
    c. prices of resources.
    d. the length of the production process.

ANSWER: A

14. To exercise effective control, managers must
    a.   introduce kaizen costing concepts into the production area.
    b.   prepare cost tables for all products the company regularly produces.
    c.   capture and report variances as early as possible.
    d.   use automated production facilities.

ANSWER: C

15. In analyzing factory overhead variances, a volume variance is the difference between the
    a.   amount shown in the flexible budget and the amount shown in the master budget.
    b.   master budget application rate and the flexible budget application rate times actual hours worked.
    c.   budget allowance based on standard hours allowed for actual production for the period and the amount budgeted to be applied during the period.
    d.   actual amount spent for overhead items during the period and the amount applied during the period

ANSWER: C

16. The planned activity level for the assembly department of Guice Manufacturing during the month of December was 10,000 direct labor hours. The actual number of direct labor hours worked during December was 9,000. Overhead is allocated on the basis of actual direct labor hours. What kind of variance occurred?
    a.   A favorable labor rate variance.
    b.   An unfavorable labor rate variance.
    c.   A favorable overhead volume variance.
    d.   An unfavorable overhead volume variance.

ANSWER: D

17. The balanced scorecard is:
    a.   a management method that focuses attention on achieving organizational objectives.
    b.   a set of performance targets and results that show an organization's performance in meeting its objectives relating to its stakeholders.
    c.   both a) and b).
    d.   none of the above

ANSWER: C

18. The _____ is a management method that focuses attention on achieving
    a.   organizational objectives.
    b.   mission statement.
    c.   balanced scorecard.
    d.   code of conduct.
    e.   customer satisfaction assessment.

ANSWER: B

Profit and Investment Center Performance

CMBA Objective Correlations

- Given financial data, determine a company's most profitable product, customer, or division.

- Given a scenario, determine the transfer price that would maximize profits.

- Given financial data, contrast relative performance based on ROI, EVA, ROS, et al.

- Define Economic Value Added (EVA) and specify the kind of responsibility center in which it is appropriate.

- Identify how period costs are treated in financial statements.

Sample Questions

1. Other factors remaining the same, the rate of return on investment may be improved by
   a. increasing investment in assets.
   b. increasing expenses.
   c. reducing sales.
   d. decreasing investment in assets.

ANSWER: D

2. Transfer prices are
   a. charges for transportation of goods outside units of an organization.
   b. charges for goods sold by subunits to outside customers.
   c. charges for goods exchanged among subunits.
   d. charges for goods stored within a subunit.

ANSWER: C

3. Disadvantages of transfer prices based on actual cost include
   a. reducing the incentive of managers of supplying divisions to control their costs.
   b. passing on efficiencies or inefficiencies of supplying divisions to receiving divisions.
   c. both a and b.
   d. none of the above.

ANSWER: C

4. Return on investment for divisions and other company segments is a function of
   a. assets employed and expected future cash flows.
   b. contributed margin and invested capital.
   c. investment turnover and profit margin on sales.
   d. physical sales volume, prices, variable costs, and fixed costs.

ANSWER: C

5. The Samantha Division reported in 2001 sales of $150,000, an asset turnover ratio of 3.0, and a rate of return on average assets of 15 percent. The percentage of net income to sales is
   a. 6 percent.
   b. 12 percent.
   c. 3 percent.
   d. 5 percent.

ANSWER: D

6. A division has sales of $4,000,000, operating profit of $400,000 and investment of $1,000,000. What is the ROI for the division?
   a. 10 percent
   b. 40 percent
   c. 4 percent
   d. 400 percent

ANSWER: B

7. A division has sales of $1,500,000, operating profit of $150,000 and investment of $1,200,000. What is the asset turnover for the division?
   a. 10 percent
   b. 25 percent
   c. 125 percent
   d. 400 percent

ANSWER: C

8. A division has sales of $2,500,000, operating profit of $125,000 and investment of $1,500,000. What is the profit margin for the division?
   a. 60 percent
   b. 3 percent
   c. 5 percent
   d. 200 percent

ANSWER: C

9. If a firm operates at capacity, the transfer price should be the
   a. external market price.
   b. differential cost.
   c. actual cost.
   d. standard cost.

ANSWER: A

10. Negotiated transfer prices are appropriate when
    a. there are cost savings to the selling division.
    b. there is no external market price.
    c. the internal market price reflects a bargain price.
    d. all of the above.

ANSWER: D

11. The Newton Company has two divisions, X and Y. Division X has a total cost of $30 per unit for its product of which $20 is fixed. Division X is at full capacity. Division Y would like to purchase 20,000 units from Division X, but thinks the $35 price Division X normally charges on the outside is too high. At what price should Division X sell to Division Y in order to suffer no additional losses?
    a. $35
    b. $30
    c. $20
    d. $10

ANSWER: A

A company purchased assets costing $400,000 which will be depreciated over 4 years with no salvage value. The company started the year with nondepreciable assets of $100,000. Annual cash profits are expected to be $200,000. For ROI computation, the company uses end-of-year asset values.

12. Refer to the above data. What is the ROI for year 1 using net book value?
    a. 12.5%
    b. 25%
    c. 30%
    d. 16.67%

ANSWER: B

13. Refer to the above data. What is the ROI for year 1 using gross book value?
    a. 30%
    b. 25%
    c. 20%
    d. 12.5%

ANSWER: C

14. If sales for year 1 totaled $700,000, what was the profit margin?
    a. 21%
    b. 14%
    c. 7%
    d. 3.5%

ANSWER: B

15. The return on investment (ROI) ratio measures
    a. Only asset turnover.
    b. Only earnings as a percent of sales.
    c. Both asset turnover and earnings as a percent of sales.
    d. Asset turnover and earnings as a percent of sales, correcting for the effects of differing depreciation methods.

ANSWER: C

16. Which of the following will *not* improve return on investment if other factors are constant?
    a. Increasing sales volume while holding fixed expenses constant.
    b. Decreasing assets.
    c. Increasing selling prices.
    d. None of the above.

ANSWER: D

17. A company proposed a transfer price based upon the full cost price. Full cost price is
    a. the retail price.
    b. the price representing the cash outflows of the supplying division plus the contribution to the supplying division from an outside sale.
    c. the price usually set by an absorption costing calculation.
    d. the price set by charging for variable costs plus a lump-sum or an additional markup, but less than full markup.

ANSWER: C

18. Which of the following is the most valid reason for using other than a full-cost based transfer price between decentralized units of a company? A full-cost price
    a. is typically more costly to implement.
    b. does not ensure the control of costs of a supplying unit.
    c. is not available unless market based prices are available.
    d. does not reflect the excess capacity of the supplying unit.

ANSWER: B

19. To avoid waste and maximize efficiency when transferring products among divisions in a competitive economy, a large diversified corporation should base transfer prices on
    a. variable costs.
    b. market price.
    c. full cost
    d. production cost.

ANSWER: B

20. Miller company has two divisions, B and S, each operated as a profit center. S charges S $35 per unit for each unit transferred to B. Other data are as follows:

S's variable cost per unit	$ 30
S's fixed costs	$10,000
S's annual sales to S	5,000 units
S's sales to outsiders	50,000 units

S is planning to raise its transfer price to $50 per unit. Division B can purchase units at $40 each from outside vendors, but doing so would idle S's facilities now committed to producing units for B. Division S cannot increase its sales to outsiders. From the perspective of the company as a whole, from whom should Division B acquire the units, assuming B's market is unaffected?

    a. Outside vendors.
    b. Division S, but only at the variable cost per unit.
    c. Division S, but only until fixed costs are covered, then should purchase from outside vendors.
    d. Division S, in spite of the increased transfer price.

ANSWER: D

21. What measurement methodology alleviates the shortcoming of the return on investment measurement?
    a. zero-based budgeting
    b. planning programming and budgeting
    c. economic value added
    d. program evaluation and review technique

ANSWER: C

22. What measurement methodology results from calculating the Divisions After-Tax Operating Profit- [(Division's Total Assets – Divisions Current Liabilities) x Weighted Average Cost of Capital].
    a. return on investment (total assets base)
    b. return on investment (shareholders' equity)
    c. economic value added
    d. number of times interest earned

ANSWER: C

The following data is for the PT Division of Concept Cars for the year ended December 31, 2001:

After-Tax Operating Profit	$300,000
Total Assets	2,000,000
Current Liabilities	1,000,000
Long Term Liabilities	800,000
Shareholders Equity	200,000
Weighted Average Cost of Capital	10%

23. What is the Economic Value Added?
    a. 70,000
    b. 100,000
    c. 150,000
    d. 200,000

ANSWER: D

The following data is for the Toothpaste Division of Happy Smiles Are US as of September 30, 2001:

After-Tax Operating Profit	$200,000
Total Assets	1,300,000
Current Liabilities	300,000
Long Term Liabilities	800,000
Shareholders Equity	200,000
Weighted Average Cost of Capital	10%

24. What is the Economic Value Added?
    a. 70,000
    b. 100,000
    c. 150,000
    d. 200,000

ANSWER: B

Allocating Costs to Responsibility Centers

CMBA Objective Correlations

- Given selected financial data, determine appropriate cost allocations.

Sample Questions

1. Big Farm, Inc. has two production departments (Planting and Harvesting) and two service departments (Cafeteria and Repairs). The service department costs must be allocated to production departments. Management has decided to allocate the cost of the cafeteria to other departments based upon the average number of employees and the cost of the Repairs Department based upon the number of machine hours used.

Departments	Pre-Allocation Costs	Number of Employees	Machine Hours
Cafeteria	$43,200	5	100
Repairs	60,000	12	12,000
Planting	350,000	20	40,000
Harvesting	700,000	40	20,000

Regardless of the allocation method used, Big Farm always starts the allocation process with the Cafeteria Department.

If Big Farm distributes costs directly (direct method) from service departments to productions departments, what additional overhead costs should be allocated from the service departments to the Planting Department?

   a. $56,800
   b. $54,400
   c. $35,940
   d. $67,200

ANSWER: B

2. Diverse Company allocates telephone expenses based on a variable rate of $1 per phone call. It allocates the fixed monthly charge equally over its budgeted usage. Division A expected to make 300 telephone calls, but actually made 350. Division B expected to make 300 telephone calls, but actually made 250. Actual fixed costs for the month totaled $3,000. What are the amounts allocated to the two divisions using a dual rate of allocation?

   a. Division A = $2,259 Division B = $1,291
   b. Division A = $2,209 Division B = $1,391
   c. Division A = $1,850 Division B = $1,750
   d. Division A = $1,800 Division B = $1,800

ANSWER: C

3. Peters Retail, Inc. utilizes 8,000 square feet of floor space in departments A, B, and C. Rental of $30,000 is incurred annually for this space. Department A occupied 1,000 square feet, Department B occupied 3,000 square feet, and Department C occupied 4,000 square feet. How much of the rent expense is allocated to Department A?
   a. $30,000
   b. $15,000
   c. $11,250
   d. $3,750

ANSWER: D

4. Peters Retail, Inc. utilizes 8,000 square feet of floor space in departments A, B, and C. Rental of $30,000 is incurred annually for this space. Department A occupied 1,000 square feet, Department B occupied 3,000 square feet, and Department C occupied 4,000 square feet. How much of the rent expense is allocated to Department B?
   a. $30,000
   b. $15,000
   c. $11,250
   d. $3,750

ANSWER: C

5. Columbia Hospital for Women charges for labor and delivery room overhead based on hours of use. The following data represents the annual budget for the labor and delivery room:

Nurses compensation	$2,000,000
Supplies	600,000
Allocated rent	300,000
Allocated utilities	100,000
Total budgeted cost	$3,000,000

The total hours of labor and delivery room care expected for the year is 300,000 hours. If a patient spends 4 hours in the labor and delivery room, what is the total overhead costs that would be charged?
   a. $80.00
   b. $40.00
   c. $20.00
   d. $4.00

ANSWER: C

6. Which of the following statements best describes cost allocation?
   a. A company can maximize or minimize total company income by selecting different bases on which to allocate indirect costs.
   b. A company should select an allocation base to raise or lower reported income on given products.
   c. A company's total income will remain unchanged no matter how indirect costs are allocated.
   d. A company, as a general rule, should allocate indirect costs randomly or based on an "ability-to-bear" criterion.

ANSWER: C

7. Cost allocation concepts are appropriate
   a. only as management deems appropriate.
   b. in manufacturing, nonmanufacturing, and service organizations.
   c. in allocating costs to production departments, but not from one service department to another.
   d. None of the above.

ANSWER: B

8. In order to identify costs that relate to a specific product, an allocation base should be chosen that
   a. does not have a cause and effect relationship.
   b. has a causal relationship.
   c. considers variable costs but not fixed costs.
   d. considers direct materials and direct labor but not factory overhead.

ANSWER: B

9. What is the function of a cost allocation base?
   a. To accumulate costs.
   b. To allocate costs.
   c. To establish a cost objective.
   d. To disaggregate costs.

ANSWER: B

10. The overhead allocation method that allocates service department costs with consideration of services rendered to other service departments is the
    a. step method.
    b. direct method.
    c. an arbitrary method.
    d. none of the above.

ANSWER: A

11. In which of the following cost allocation methods may no other service department costs be charged back to a particular service department after the first service department's cost has been allocated?
    a. the direct method.
    b. the step method.
    c. the direct method and the step method.
    d. None of the above.

ANSWER: C

12. The fixed costs of service departments should be allocated to production departments based on
    a. actual short-run utilization based on predetermined rates.
    b. actual short-run units based on actual rates.
    c. the service department's expected costs of long-run capacity.
    d. the service department's actual costs based on actual utilization of services.

ANSWER: C

13. Stephanie Company has two production departments: D and J. Stephanie also has 3 service departments: Personnel, Administration, and Shipping. Shipping costs are allocated on the basis of number of packages, while Personnel and Administration costs are allocated using number of employees. Assume that the benefits provided ranking for the service is in the order listed below.

Department	Costs	Employees	# of Packages
Personnel	$600,000	25	7,000
Administration	800,000	20	9,000
Shipping	700,000	12	27,500
D	500,000	10	5,000
J	400,000	15	6,000

Using the direct method, what amount of personnel costs is allocated to Department J (rounded to the nearest $)?

   a. $120,000
   b. $240,000
   c. $300,000
   d. $360,000

ANSWER: D

Finance

Analysis of Financial Statements

CMBA Objective Correlations

- Given financial and accounting information, calculate selected financial ratios.

- Given financial and accounting information, calculate the return on equity using the DuPont format.

- Differentiate the components of the extended DuPont equation.

- Given financial and accounting information, calculate or describe the common measures of investment performance.

- Describe the meaning and determinants of rates of return on different classes of assets.

Sample Questions

1. You have collected the following information regarding Companies C and D:

   - The two companies have the same total assets.
   - The two companies have the same operating income (EBIT).
   - The two companies have the same tax rate.
   - Company C has a higher debt ratio and a higher interest expense than Company D.
   - Company C has a lower profit margin than Company D.

   Based on this information, which of the following statements is most correct?

   a. Company C must have a higher level of sales.
   b. Company C must have a lower ROE.
   c. Company C must have a higher times-interest-earned (TIE) ratio.
   d. Company C must have a lower ROA.
   e. Company C must have a higher basic earning power (BEP) ratio.

   ANSWER: D

2. Van Buren Company has a current ratio = 1.9. Which of the following actions will increase the company's current ratio?

   a. Use cash to reduce short-term notes payable.
   b. Use cash to reduce accounts payable.
   c. Issue long-term bonds to repay short-term notes payable.
   d. All of the answers above are correct.
   e. Answers b and c are correct.

   ANSWER: D

3.   Which of the following statements is most correct?

    a.   If a company uses cash to buy inventory, its current ratio will decline.
    b.   If a company uses some of its cash to pay off short-term debt, then its current ratio will always decline, given the way the ratio is calculated, other things held constant.
    c.   During a recession, it is reasonable to think that most companies' inventory turnover ratios will change while their fixed asset turnover ratios will remain fairly constant.
    d.   During a recession, we can be confident that most companies' DSOs (or ACPs) will decline because their sales will probably decline.
    e.   Each of the statements above is false.

ANSWER: E

4.   Which of the following statements is most correct?

    a.   If two companies have the same return on equity, they should have the same stock price.
    b.   If Company A has a higher profit margin and higher total assets turnover relative to Company B, then Company A must have a higher return on assets.
    c.   If Company A and Company B have the same debt ratio, they must have the same times interest earned (TIE) ratio.
    d.   Answers b and c are correct.
    e.   None of the answers above is correct.

ANSWER: B

5.   Last year Thatcher Industries had a current ratio of 1.2, a quick ratio of 0.8, and current liabilities of $500,000. Which of the following statements is most correct?

    a.   If the company obtained a short-term bank loan for $500,000 and used the proceeds to purchase inventory, its current ratio would fall.
    b.   Last year Thatcher industries had $200,000 in inventories.
    c.   Last year Thatcher industries had $416,667 in current assets.
    d.   All of the answers above are correct.
    e.   Answers a and b are correct.

ANSWER: E

6.   You observe that a firm's profit margin is below the industry average, its debt ratio is below the industry average, and its return on equity exceeds the industry average. What can you conclude?

    a.   Return on assets is above the industry average.
    b.   Total assets turnover is above the industry average.
    c.   Total assets turnover is below the industry average.
    d.   Both statements a and b are correct.
    e.   None of the statements above is correct.

ANSWER: B

7.   Your company had the following balance sheet and income statement information for 1998:

Balance sheet:

Cash	$ 20		
A/R	1,000		
Inventories	5,000		
Total C.A.	$ 6,020	Debt	$ 4,000
Net F.A.	2,980	Equity	5,000
Total Assets	$ 9,000	Total claims	$ 9,000

Income statement:

Sales	$10,000
Cost of goods sold	9,200
EBIT	$ 800
Interest (10%)	400
EBT	$ 400
Taxes (40%)	160
Net Income	$ 240

The industry average inventory turnover is 5. You think you can change your inventory control system so as to cause your turnover to equal the industry average, and this change is expected to have no effect on either sales or cost of goods sold. The cash generated from reducing inventories will be used to buy tax-exempt securities which have a 7 percent rate of return. What will your profit margin be after the change in inventories is reflected in the income statement?

a.   2.1%
b.   2.4%
c.   4.5%
d.   5.3%
e.   6.7%

ANSWER: C

8.   The Wilson Corporation has the following relationships:

Sales/Total assets	2.0
Return on assets (ROA)	4%
Return on equity (ROE)	6%

What is Wilson's profit margin and debt ratio?

a.   2% and 0.33
b.   4% and 0.33
c.   4% and 0.67
d.   2% and 0.67
e.   4% and 0.50

ANSWER: A

9.　A fire has destroyed a large percentage of the financial records of the Carter Company. You have the task of piecing together information in order to release a financial report. You have found the return on equity to be 18 percent. If sales were $4 million, the debt ratio was 0.40, and total liabilities were $2 million, what was the return on assets (ROA)?

a.　10.80%
b.　0.80%
c.　1.25%
d.　12.60%
e.　Insufficient information.

ANSWER:　A

10.　Selzer Inc. sells all its merchandise on credit. It has a profit margin of 4 percent, days sales outstanding equal to 60 days, receivables of $150,000, total assets of $3 million, and a debt ratio of 0.64. What is the firm's return on equity (ROE)?

a.　7.1%
b.　33.3%
c.　3.3%
d.　71.0%
e.　8.1%

ANSWER:　C

11.　Alumbat Corporation has $800,000 of debt outstanding, and it pays an interest rate of 10 percent annually on its bank loan. Alumbat's annual sales are $3,200,000; its average tax rate is 40 percent; and its net profit margin on sales is 6 percent. If the company does not maintain a TIE ratio of at least 4 times, its bank will refuse to renew its loan, and bankruptcy will result. What is Alumbat's current TIE ratio?

a.　2.4
b.　3.4
c.　3.6
d.　4.0
e.　5.0

ANSWER:　E

12.　Kansas Office Supply had $24,000,000 in sales last year. The company's net income was $400,000. Its total assets turnover was 6.0. The company's ROE was 15 percent. The company is financed entirely with debt and common equity. What is the company's debt ratio?

a.　0.20
b.　0.30
c.　0.33
d.　0.60
e.　0.66

ANSWER:　C

13.   Thomas Corp. has the following simplified balance sheet:

Cash	$ 50,000	Current liabilities	$125,000
Inventory	150,000		
Accounts receivable	100,000	Long-term debt	175,000
Net fixed assets	200,000	Common equity	200,000
Total	$500,000	Total	$500,000

Sales for the year totaled $600,000. The company president believes the company carries excess inventory. She would like the inventory turnover ratio to be 8x and would use the freed up cash to reduce current liabilities. If the company follows the president's recommendation and sales remain the same, the new quick ratio would be:

a. 2.4
b. 4.0
c. 4.5
d. 1.2
e. 3.0

ANSWER: E

14.   Taft Technologies has the following relationships:

Annual sales	$1,200,000
Current liabilities	$ 375,000
Days sales outstanding (DSO) (360-day year)	40
Inventory Turnover ratio	4.8
Current ratio	1.2

The company's current assets consist of cash, inventories, and accounts receivable. How much cash does Taft have on its balance sheet?

a. -$ 8,333
b. $ 66,667
c. $125,000
d. $200,000
e. $316,667

ANSWER: B

15. Collins Company had the following partial balance sheet and complete income statement information for 1998:

Partial Balance Sheet:

Cash		$ 20
A/R		1,000
Inventories		2,000
Total current assets	$ 3,020	
Net fixed assets	2,980	
Total assets	$ 6,000	

Income Statement:

Sales		$10,000
Cost of goods sold	9,200	
EBIT		$ 800
Interest (10%)	400	
EBT		$ 400
Taxes (40%)		160
Net Income		$ 240

The industry average DSO is 30 (360-day year). Collins plans to change its credit policy so as to cause its DSO to equal the industry average, and this change is expected to have no effect on either sales or cost of goods sold. If the cash generated from reducing receivables is used to retire debt (which was outstanding all last year and which has a 10 percent interest rate), what will Collins' debt ratio (Total debt/Total assets) be after the change in DSO is reflected in the balance sheet?

a. 33.33%
b. 45.28%
c. 52.75%
d. 60.00%
e. 65.71%

ANSWER: E

Financial Planning and Forecasting Financial Statements

CMBA Objective Correlations

- Differentiate between techniques used to forecast financial statements.

Sample Questions

1. The percentage of sales method is based on which of the following assumptions?

    a. All balance sheet accounts are tied directly to sales.
    b. Most balance sheet accounts are tied directly to sales.
    c. The current level of total assets is optimal for the current sales level.
    d. Answers a and c above.
    e. Answers b and c above.

    ANSWER: E

2. Jefferson City Computers has developed a forecasting model to determine the additional funds it needs in the upcoming year. All else being equal, which of the following factors is likely to increase its additional funds needed (AFN)?

    a. A sharp increase in its forecasted sales and the company's fixed assets are at full capacity.
    b. A reduction in its dividend payout ratio.
    c. The company reduces its reliance on trade credit that sharply reduces its accounts payable.
    d. Statements a and b are correct.
    e. Statements a and c are correct.

    ANSWER: E

3. The percentage of sales method produces accurate results unless which of the following conditions is (are) present?

    a. Fixed assets are "lumpy."
    b. Strong economies of scale are present.
    c. Excess capacity exists because of a temporary recession.
    d. Answers a, b, and c all make the percentage of sales method inaccurate.
    e. Answers a and c make the percentage of sales method inaccurate, but, as the text explains, the assumption of increasing economies of scale is built into the percentage of sales method.

    ANSWER: D

4.   A company is forecasting an increase in sales and is using the AFN model to forecast the additional capital that they need to raise. Which of the following factors are likely to increase the additional funds needed (AFN)?

   a. The company has a lot of excess capacity.
   b. The company has a high dividend payout ratio.
   c. The company has a lot of spontaneous liabilities that increase as sales increase.
   d. The company has a high profit margin.
   e. All of the answers above are correct.

   ANSWER: B

5.   Which of the following statements is most correct?

   a. The AFN formula method assumes that the balance sheet ratios of assets and liabilities to sales ($A*/S_0$ and $L*/S_0$) remain constant over time, while the percentage of sales method does not.
   b. When assets are added in large, discrete units as a company grows, then the assumption of constant ratios and steady growth rates is most appropriate.
   c. Temporary excess capacity can be characteristic of a firm that adds lumpy assets as it grows or one that experiences cyclical changes.
   d. For a firm that has lumpy assets, small increases in sales can be accommodated without expanding fixed assets, even when the firm is at capacity.
   e. The graphical relationship between assets and sales where economies of scale are present is always linear.

   ANSWER: C

6.   On the basis of historical relationships between its balance sheet items and its sales, profit margin, and dividend policy, Thode Corporation's analysts have graphed the relationship of additional funds needed (on the Y-axis) to possible growth rates in sales (on the X-axis). If Thode decides to _increase_ the percentage of earnings paid out as dividends, which of the following changes would occur in the graph?

   a. The line would shift to the right.
   b. The line would pass through the origin.
   c. The line would shift to the left.
   d. The slope coefficient would fall.
   e. The slope coefficient would increase.

   ANSWER: C

7.   Which of the following statements is most correct?

   a.   Any forecast of financial requirements involves determining how much money the firm will need and is obtained by adding together increases in assets and spontaneous liabilities and subtracting operating income.
   b.   The percentage of sales method of forecasting financial needs requires only a forecast of the firm's balance sheet. Although a forecasted income statement helps clarify the need, it is not essential to the percentage of sales method.
   c.   Because dividends are paid after taxes from retained earnings, dividends are not included in the percentage of sales method of forecasting.
   d.   Financing feedbacks describe the fact that interest must be paid on the debt used to help finance AFN and dividends must be paid on the shares issued to raise the equity part of the AFN. These payments would lower the net income and retained earnings shown in the projected financial statements.
   e.   All of the statements above are false.

   ANSWER: D

8.   Which of the following statements is most correct?

   a.   Inherent in the AFN formula is the assumption that each asset item must increase in direct proportion to sales increases and that spontaneous liability accounts also grow at the same rate as sales.
   b.   If a firm has positive growth in its assets, but has no increase in retained earnings, AFN for the firm must be positive.
   c.   Using the AFN formula, if a firm increases its dividend payout ratio in anticipation of higher earnings, but sales actually decrease, the firm will automatically experience an increase in additional funds needed.
   d.   Higher sales usually require higher asset levels. Some of the increase in assets can be supported by spontaneous increases in accounts payable and accruals, and by increases in certain current asset accounts and retained earnings.
   e.   Dividend policy does not affect requirements for external capital under the AFN formula method.

   ANSWER: A

9. Gemini Beverage has the following historical balance sheet:

Cash	$20	Accounts payable	$200
Accounts receivable	240	Notes payable	130
Inventory	320	Accruals	30
Total current assets	$580	Current liabilities	$360
Net plant & equipment	$420	Long-term bonds	$260
		Common stock	270
		Retained earnings	110
Total assets	$1,000	Total liab. & equity	$1,000

Over the next year Gemini's current assets, accounts payable, and accruals will grow in proportion to sales. Last year's sales were $800 and this year's sales are expected to increase by 40 percent. The firm will retain $58 in earnings to fund current asset growth, and the rest of the increase will be funded entirely with notes payable. The net plant and equipment account will increase to $500 and will be funded directly by a new equity issue. What will Gemini's new current ratio be after the changes in the firm's financial picture are complete?

a. 1.52
b. 1.61
c. 1.26
d. 1.21
e. 1.37

ANSWER: A

The Financial Environment

CMBA Objective Correlations

- Explain the framework for understanding how the financial system works.

Sample Questions

1. The New York Stock Exchange is primarily

   a. A secondary market.
   b. An organized auction market.
   c. An over-the-counter market.
   d. Answers a and b are correct.
   e. Answers b and c are correct.

   ANSWER: D

2. Which of the following statements is most correct?

   a. The NYSE does not exist as a physical location; rather it represents a loose collection of dealers who trade stock electronically.
   b. An example of a primary market transaction is buying 100 shares of Wal-Mart stock from your uncle.
   c. Capital market instruments include long-term debt and common stock.
   d. Statements b and c are correct.
   e. Statements a, b, and c are correct.

   ANSWER: C

3. Which of the following statements is most correct?

   a. If an investor sells 100 shares of Microsoft to his brother-in-law, this is a primary market transaction.
   b. Private securities are generally less liquid than publicly traded securities.
   c. Money markets are where short-term, liquid securities are traded, whereas capital markets represent the markets for long-term debt and common stock.
   d. Statements b and c are correct.
   e. All of the statements above are correct.

   ANSWER: D

4. Money markets are markets for

   a. Foreign currency exchange.
   b. Consumer automobile loans.
   c. Corporate stocks.
   d. Long-term bonds.
   e. Short-term debt securities.

   ANSWER: E

5.   Which of the following statements is correct?

a.   The New York Stock Exchange is an organized auction market.
b.   Money markets include markets for consumer automobile loans.
c.   If an investor sells shares of stock through a broker, then it would be a primary market transaction.
d.   Capital market transactions involve only the purchase and sale of equity securities.
e.   None of the answers above is correct.

ANSWER: A

6.   If the Federal Reserve sells $50 billion of short-term U.S. Treasury securities to the public, other things held constant, what will this tend to do to short-term security prices and interest rates?

a.   Prices and interest rates will both rise.
b.   Prices will rise and interest rates will decline.
c.   Prices and interest rates will both decline.
d.   Prices will decline and interest rates will rise.
e.   There will be no changes in either prices or interest rates.

ANSWER: D

7.   Assume interest rates on long-term government and corporate bonds were as follows:

T-bond = 7.72%   A = 9.64%
AAA   = 8.72%   BBB = 10.18%

The differences in rates among these issues were caused primarily by

a.   Tax effects.
b.   Default risk differences.
c.   Maturity risk differences.
d.   Inflation differences.
e.   Answers b and d are correct.

ANSWER: B

8.   Which of the following statements is most correct?

a.   The yield on a 2-year corporate bond will always exceed the yield on a 2-year Treasury bond.
b.   The yield on a 3-year corporate bond will always exceed the yield on a 2-year corporate bond.
c.   The yield on a 3-year Treasury bond will always exceed the yield on a 2-year Treasury bond.
d.   All of the answers above are correct.
e.   Statements a and c are correct.

ANSWER: A

Time Value of Money

CMBA Objective Correlations

- Recognize the importance of annuities in the field of finance.

- Given appropriate information, calculate the future value of a present sum.

- Given appropriate information, calculate the present value of a future sum.

Sample Questions

1. Suppose someone offered you the choice of two equally risky annuities, each paying $10,000 per year for five years. One is an ordinary (or deferred) annuity, the other is an annuity due. Which of the following statements is most correct?

    a. The present value of the ordinary annuity must exceed the present value of the annuity due, but the future value of an ordinary annuity may be less than the future value of the annuity due.
    b. The present value of the annuity due exceeds the present value of the ordinary annuity, while the future value of the annuity due is less than the future value of the ordinary annuity.
    c. The present value of the annuity due exceeds the present value of the ordinary annuity, and the future value of the annuity due also exceeds the future value of the ordinary annuity.
    d. If interest rates increase, the difference between the present value of the ordinary annuity and the present value of the annuity due remains the same.
    e. Answers a and d are correct.

    ANSWER: C

2. You deposited $1,000 in a savings account that pays 8 percent interest, compounded quarterly, planning to use it to finish your last year in college. Eighteen months later, you decide to go to the Rocky Mountains to become a ski instructor rather than continue in school, so you close out your account. How much money will you receive?

    a. $1,171
    b. $1,126
    c. $1,082
    d. $1,163
    e. $1,008

    ANSWER: B

3. What is the *future value* of a 5-year ordinary annuity with annual payments of $200, evaluated at a 15 percent interest rate?

   a. $ 670.44
   b. $ 842.91
   c. $1,169.56
   d. $1,522.64
   e. $1,348.48

   ANSWER: E

4. What is the *present value* of a 5-year ordinary annuity with annual payments of $200, evaluated at a 15 percent interest rate?

   a. $ 670.43
   b. $ 842.91
   c. $1,169.56
   d. $1,348.48
   e. $1,522.64

   ANSWER: A

5. Assume that you will receive $2,000 a year in Years 1 through 5, $3,000 a year in Years 6 through 8, and $4,000 in Year 9, with all cash flows to be received at the end of the year. If you require a 14 percent rate of return, what is the present value of these cash flows?

   a. $ 9,851
   b. $13,250
   c. $11,714
   d. $15,129
   e. $17,353

   ANSWER: C

6. If a 5-year ordinary annuity has a present value of $1,000, and if the interest rate is 10 percent, what is the amount of each annuity payment?

   a. $240.42
   b. $263.80
   c. $300.20
   d. $315.38
   e. $346.87

   ANSWER: B

7.　　Your uncle has agreed to deposit $3,000 in your brokerage account at the beginning of each of the next five years (t = 0, t = 1, t = 2, t = 3 and t = 4). You estimate that you can earn 9 percent a year on your investments. How much will you have in your account four years from now (at t = 4)? (Assume that no money is withdrawn from the account until t = 4.)

    a.　$13,719.39
    b.　$17,954.13
    c.　$19,570.00
    d.　$21,430.45
    e.　$22,436.12

    ANSWER:　　　B

8.　　You just put $1,000 in a bank account which pays 6 percent nominal annual interest, compounded monthly. How much will you have in your account after 3 years?

    a.　$1,006.00
    b.　$1,056.45
    c.　$1,180.32
    d.　$1,191.00
    e.　$1,196.68

    ANSWER:　　　E

9.　　You are given the following cash flows. What is the present value (t = 0) if the discount rate is 12 percent?

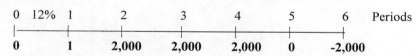

    a.　$3,277
    b.　$4,804
    c.　$5,302
    d.　$4,289
    e.　$2,804

    ANSWER:　　　A

10. A project with a 3-year life has the following probability distributions for possible end-of-year cash flows in each of the next three years:

Year 1		Year 2		Year 3	
Prob	Cash Flow	Prob	Cash Flow	Prob	Cash Flow
0.30	$300	0.15	$100	0.25	$200
0.40	500	0.35	200	0.75	800
0.30	700	0.35	600		
		0.15	900		

Using an interest rate of 8 percent, find the expected present value of these uncertain cash flows. (Hint: Find the expected cash flow in each year, then evaluate those cash flows.)

a. $1,204.95
b. $ 835.42
c. $1,519.21
d. $1,580.00
e. $1,347.61

ANSWER: E

11. Find the present value of an income stream which has a negative flow of $100 per year for 3 years, a positive flow of $200 in the 4th year, and a positive flow of $300 per year in Years 5 through 8. The appropriate discount rate is 4 percent for each of the first 3 years and 5 percent for each of the later years. Thus, a cash flow accruing in Year 8 should be discounted at 5 percent for some years and 4 percent in other years. All payments occur at year-end.

a. $ 528.21
b. $1,329.00
c. $ 792.49
d. $1,046.41
e. $ 875.18

ANSWER: C

12. You are saving for the college education of your two children. One child will enter college in 5 years, while the other child will enter college in 7 years. College costs are currently $10,000 per year and are expected to grow at a rate of 5 percent per year. All college costs are paid at the beginning of the year. You assume that each child will be in college for four years.

You currently have $50,000 in your educational fund. Your plan is to contribute a fixed amount to the fund over each of the next 5 years. Your first contribution will come at the end of this year, and your final contribution will come at the date at which you make the first tuition payment for your oldest child. You expect to invest your contributions into various investments which are expected to earn 8 percent per year. How much should you contribute each year in order to meet the expected cost of your children's education?

a. $2,894
b. $3,712
c. $4,125
d. $5,343
e. $6,750

ANSWER: B

13. A young couple is planning for the education of their two children. They plan to invest the same amount of money at the end of each of the next 16 years, i.e., the first contribution will be made at the end of the year and the final contribution will be made at the time the oldest child enters college.

The money will be invested in securities that are certain to earn a return of 8 percent each year. The oldest child will begin college in 16 years and the second child will begin college in 18 years. The parents anticipate college costs of $25,000 a year (per child). These costs must be paid at the end of each year. If each child takes four years to complete their college degrees, then how much money must the couple save each year?

    a. $ 9,612.10
    b. $ 5,071.63
    c. $12,507.29
    d. $ 5,329.45
    e. $ 4,944.84

ANSWER: B

14. Today is Rachel's 30th birthday. Five years ago, Rachel opened a brokerage account when her grandmother gave her $25,000 for her 25th birthday. Rachel added $2,000 to this account on her 26th birthday, $3,000 on her 27th birthday, $4,000 on her 28th birthday, and $5,000 on her 29th birthday. Rachel's goal is to have $400,000 in the account by her 40th birthday.

Starting today, she plans to contribute a fixed amount to the account each year on her birthday. She will make 11 contributions, the first one will occur today, and the final contribution will occur on her 40th birthday. Complicating things somewhat is the fact that Rachel plans to withdraw $20,000 from the account on her 35th birthday to finance the down payment on a home. How large does each of these 11 contributions have to be for Rachel to reach her goal? Assume that the account has earned (and will continue to earn) an effective return of 12 percent a year.

    a. $11,743.95
    b. $10,037.46
    c. $11,950.22
    d. $14,783.64
    e. $ 9,485.67

ANSWER: A

Bonds and Their Valuation

CMBA Objective Correlations

- Distinguish between the various types of bonds.

- Describe the common features of bonds.

- Describe the process of valuing corporate securities.

Sample Questions

1. Which of the following events would make it more likely that a company would choose to call its outstanding callable bonds?

    a. A reduction in market interest rates.
    b. The company's bonds are downgraded.
    c. An increase in the call premium.
    d. Answers a and b are correct.
    e. Answers a, b, and c are correct.

    ANSWER: A

2. Other things held constant, if a bond indenture contains a call provision, the yield to maturity that would exist without such a call provision will generally be _____ the YTM with it.

    a. higher than
    b. lower than
    c. the same as
    d. either higher or lower, depending on the level of call premium, than
    e. unrelated to

    ANSWER: B

3. All of the following may serve to _reduce_ the coupon rate that would otherwise be required on a bond issued at par, except a

    a. Sinking fund.
    b. Restrictive covenant.
    c. Call provision.
    d. Change in rating from Aa to Aaa.
    e. None of the answers above (all may reduce the required coupon rate).

    ANSWER: C

4.   Which of the following statements is most correct?

a.   All else equal, if a bond's yield to maturity increases, its price will fall.
b.   All else equal, if a bond's yield to maturity increases, its current yield will fall.
c.   If a bond's yield to maturity exceeds the coupon rate, the bond will sell at a premium over par.
d.   All of the answers above are correct.
e.   None of the answers above is correct.

ANSWER: A

5.   Which of the following statements is most correct?

a.   If a bond's yield to maturity exceeds its annual coupon, then the bond will be trading at a premium.
b.   If interest rates increase, the relative price change of a 10-year coupon bond will be greater than the relative price change of a 10-year zero coupon bond.
c.   If a coupon bond is selling at par, its current yield equals its yield to maturity.
d.   Both a and c are correct.
e. None of the answers above is correct.

ANSWER: C

6.   A 10-year corporate bond has an annual coupon payment of 9 percent. The bond is currently selling at par ($1,000). Which of the following statements is most correct?

a.   The bond's yield to maturity is 9 percent.
b.   The bond's current yield is 9 percent.
c.   If the bond's yield to maturity remains constant, the bond's price will remain at par.
d.   Both answers a and c are correct.
e.   All of the answers above are correct.

ANSWER: E

7.   Which of the following statements is most correct?

a.   Other things held constant, a callable bond would have a *lower* required rate of return than a noncallable bond.
b.   Other things held constant, a corporation would rather issue noncallable bonds than callable bonds.
c.   Reinvestment rate risk is worse from a typical investor's standpoint than interest rate risk.
d.   If a 10-year, $1,000 par, zero coupon bond were issued at a price which gave investors a 10 percent rate of return, and if interest rates then dropped to the point where k_d = YTM = 5%, we could be sure that the bond would sell at a *premium* over its $1,000 par value.
e.   If a 10-year, $1,000 par, zero coupon bond were issued at a price which gave investors a 10 percent rate of return, and if interest rates then dropped to the point where k_d = YTM = 5%, we could be sure that the bond would sell at a *discount* below its $1,000 par value.

ANSWER: E

8. Which of the following statements is most correct?

a. The market value of a bond will always approach its par value as its maturity date approaches, provided the issuer of the bond does not go bankrupt.
b. If the Federal Reserve unexpectedly announces that it expects inflation to increase, then we would probably observe an immediate increase in bond prices.
c. The total yield on a bond is derived from interest payments and changes in the price of the bond.
d. Statements a and c are correct.
e. All of the statements above are correct.

ANSWER: D

9. Which of the following statements is most correct?

a. If a bond is selling for a premium, this implies that the bond's yield to maturity exceeds its coupon rate.
b. If a coupon bond is selling at par, its current yield equals its yield to maturity.
c. If rates fall after its issue, a zero coupon bond could trade for an amount above its par value.
d. Statements b and c are correct.
e. None of the statements above is correct.

ANSWER: B

10. Which of the following statements is most correct?

a. All else equal, a bond that has a coupon rate of 10 percent will sell at a discount if the required return for a bond of similar risk is 8 percent.
b. The price of a discount bond will increase over time, assuming that the bond's yield to maturity remains constant over time.
c. The total return on a bond for a given year consists only of the coupon interest payments received.
d. Both b and c are correct.
e. All of the statements above are correct.

ANSWER: B

11. Which of the following statements is most correct?

a. All else equal, a bond that has a coupon rate of 10 percent will sell at a discount if the required return for a bond of similar risk is 8 percent.
b. Debentures generally have a higher yield to maturity relative to mortgage bonds.
c. If there are two bonds with equal maturity and credit risk, the bond which is callable will have a higher yield to maturity than the bond which is noncallable.
d. Answers a and c are correct.
e. Answers b and c are correct.

ANSWER: E

12.   Which of the following statements is most correct?

a.   All else equal, a 1-year bond will have a higher (i.e., better) bond rating than a 20-year bond.
b.   A 20-year bond with semiannual interest payments has higher price risk (i.e., interest rate risk) than a 5-year bond with semiannual interest payments.
c.   10-year zero coupon bonds have higher reinvestment rate risk than 10-year, 10 percent coupon bonds.
d.   If a callable bond is trading at a premium, then you would expect to earn the yield-to-maturity.
e.   Statements a and b are correct.

ANSWER: E

13.   You intend to purchase a 10-year, $1,000 face value bond that pays interest of $60 every 6 months. If your nominal annual required rate of return is 10 percent with semiannual compounding, how much should you be willing to pay for this bond?

a. $ 826.31
b. $1,086.15
c. $ 957.50
d. $1,431.49
e. $1,124.62

ANSWER: E

14.   Assume that you wish to purchase a 20-year bond that has a maturity value of $1,000 and makes semiannual interest payments of $40. If you require a 10 percent nominal yield to maturity on this investment, what is the maximum price you should be willing to pay for the bond?

a. $619
b. $674
c. $761
d. $828
e. $902

ANSWER: D

15.   You are the owner of 100 bonds issued by Euler, Ltd. These bonds have 8 years remaining to maturity, an annual coupon payment of $80, and a par value of $1,000. Unfortunately, Euler is on the brink of bankruptcy. The creditors, including yourself, have agreed to a postponement of the next 4 interest payments (otherwise, the next interest payment would have been due in 1 year). The remaining interest payments, for Years 5 through 8, will be made as scheduled. The postponed payments will accrue interest at an annual rate of 6 percent, and they will then be paid as a lump sum at maturity 8 years hence. The required rate of return on these bonds, considering their substantial risk, is now 28 percent. What is the present value of each bond?

a. $538.21
b. $426.73
c. $384.84
d. $266.88
e. $249.98

ANSWER: D

16. Marie Snell recently inherited some bonds (face value $100,000) from her father, and soon thereafter she became engaged to Sam Spade, a University of Florida marketing graduate. Sam wants Marie to cash in the bonds so the two of them can use the money to "live like royalty" for two years in Monte Carlo. The 2 percent annual coupon bonds mature on January 1, 2022, and it is now January 1, 2002. Interest on these bonds is paid annually on December 31 of each year, and new annual coupon bonds with similar risk and maturity are currently yielding 12 percent. If Marie sells her bonds now and puts the proceeds into an account which pays 10 percent compounded annually, what would be the largest equal annual amounts she could withdraw for two years, beginning today (i.e., two payments, the first payment today and the second payment one year from today)?

a. $13,255
b. $29,708
c. $12,654
d. $25,305
e. $14,580

ANSWER: A

Stocks and Their Valuation

CMBA Objective Correlations

- Describe the process of valuing corporate securities.

- Describe the major characteristics of preferred and common stock.

Sample Questions

1. Which of the following statements is most correct?

   a. Preferred stockholders have priority over common stockholders.
   b. A big advantage of preferred stock is that preferred stock dividends are tax deductible for the issuing corporation.
   c. Most preferred stock is owned by corporations.
   d. Statements a and b are correct.
   e. Statements a and c are correct.

   ANSWER: E

2. Which of the following statements is most correct?

   a. One of the advantages to the firm associated with financing using preferred stock rather than common stock is that control of the firm is not diluted.
   b. Preferred stock provides steadier and more reliable income to investors than common stock.
   c. One of the advantages to the firm of financing with preferred stock is that 70 percent of the dividends paid out are tax deductible.
   d. Statements a and c are correct.
   e. Statements a and b are correct.

   ANSWER: E

3. Which of the following statements is most correct?

   a. One of the advantages of financing with stock is that a greater proportion of stock in the capital structure can reduce the risk of a takeover bid.
   b. A firm with classified stock can pay different dividends to each class of shares.
   c. One of the advantages of financing with stock is that a firm's debt ratio will decrease.
   d. Both statements b and c are correct.
   e. All of the statements above are correct.

   ANSWER: D

4. A stock expects to pay a year-end dividend of $2.00 a share (i.e., D_1 = $2.00; assume that last year's dividend has already been paid). The dividend is expected to fall 5 percent a year, forever (i.e., g = -5%). The company's expected and required rate of return is 15 percent. Which of the following statements is most correct?

   a. The company's stock price is $10.
   b. The company's expected dividend yield 5 years from now will be 20 percent.
   c. The company's stock price 5 years from now is expected to be $7.74.
   d. Both answers b and c are correct.
   e. All of the above answers are correct.

   ANSWER: E

5. The expected rate of return on the common stock of Northwest Corporation is 14 percent. The stock's dividend is expected to grow at a constant rate of 8 percent a year. The stock currently sells for $50 a share. Which of the following statements is most correct?

   a. The stock's dividend yield is 8 percent.
   b. The stock's dividend yield is 7 percent.
   c. The current dividend per share is $4.00.
   d. The stock price is expected to be $54 a share in one year.
   e. The stock price is expected to be $57 a share in one year.

   ANSWER: D

6. The Jones Company has decided to undertake a large project. Consequently, there is a need for additional funds. The financial manager plans to issue preferred stock with a perpetual annual dividend of $5 per share and a par value of $30. If the required return on this stock is currently 20 percent, what should be the stock's market value?

   a. $150
   b. $100
   c. $ 50
   d. $ 25
   e. $ 10

   ANSWER: D

7. Johnston Corporation is growing at a constant rate of 6 percent per year. It has both common stock and non-participating preferred stock outstanding. The cost of preferred stock (k_{ps}) is 8 percent. The par value of the preferred stock is $120, and the stock has a stated dividend of 10 percent of par. What is the market value of the preferred stock?

   a. $125
   b. $120
   c. $175
   d. $150
   e. $200

   ANSWER: D

8.   A share of preferred stock pays a quarterly dividend of $2.50. If the price of this preferred stock is currently $50, what is the nominal annual rate of return?

a.   12%
b.   18%
c.   20%
d.   23%
e.   28%

ANSWER: D

9.   A share of preferred stock pays a dividend of $0.50 each quarter. If you are willing to pay $20.00 for this preferred stock, what is your nominal (not effective) annual rate of return?

a.   10%
b.   8%
c.   6%
d.   12%
e.   14%

ANSWER: A

10.   Assume that you plan to buy a share of XYZ stock today and to hold it for 2 years. Your expectations are that you will not receive a dividend at the end of Year 1, but you will receive a dividend of $9.25 at the end of Year 2. In addition, you expect to sell the stock for $150 at the end of Year 2. If your expected rate of return is 16 percent, how much should you be willing to pay for this stock today?

a. $164.19
b. $ 75.29
c. $107.53
d. $118.35
e. $131.74

ANSWER: D

11.   Waters Corporation has a stock price of $20 a share. The stock's year-end dividend is expected to be $2 a share ($D_1 = \$2.00$). The stock's required rate of return is 15 percent and the stock's dividend is expected to grow at the same constant rate forever. What is the expected price of the stock seven years from now?

a. $28
b. $53
c. $27
d. $23
e. $39

ANSWER: A

12. Berg Inc. has just paid a dividend of $2.00. Its stock is now selling for $48 per share. The firm is half as risky as the market. The expected return on the market is 14 percent, and the yield on U.S. Treasury bonds is 11 percent. If the market is in equilibrium, what rate of growth is expected?

   a. 13%
   b. 10%
   c. 4%
   d. 8%
   e. -2%

   ANSWER: D

13. Grant Corporation's stock is selling for $40 in the market. The company's beta is 0.8, the market risk premium is 6 percent, and the risk-free rate is 9 percent. The previous dividend was $2 (i.e., $D_0 = \$2$) and dividends are expected to grow at a constant rate. What is the growth rate for this stock?

   a. 5.52%
   b. 5.00%
   c. 13.80%
   d. 8.80%
   e. 8.38%

   ANSWER: E

14. Carlson Products, a constant growth company, has a current market (and equilibrium) stock price of $20.00. Carlson's next dividend, D_1, is forecasted to be $2.00, and Carlson is growing at an annual rate of 6 percent. Carlson has a beta coefficient of 1.2, and the required rate of return on the market is 15 percent. As Carlson's financial manager, you have access to insider information concerning a switch in product lines which would not change the growth rate, but would cut Carlson's beta coefficient in half. If you buy the stock at the current market price, what is your expected percentage capital gain?

   a. 23%
   b. 33%
   c. 43%
   d. 53%
   e. There would be a capital loss.

   ANSWER: C

Evaluating Cash Flows

CMBA Objective Correlations

- Distinguish between the various techniques used to make capital budgeting decisions.

Sample Questions

1.   A major *disadvantage* of the payback period method is that it

   a.   Is useless as a risk indicator.
   b.   Ignores cash flows beyond the payback period.
   c.   Does not directly account for the time value of money.
   d.   All of the answers above are correct.
   e.   Only answers b and c are correct.

   ANSWER: E

2.   Which of the following statements is most correct?

   a.   If a project's internal rate of return (IRR) exceeds the cost of capital, then the project's net present value (NPV) must be positive.
   b.   If Project A has a higher IRR than Project B, then Project A must also have a higher NPV.
   c.   The IRR calculation implicitly assumes that all cash flows are reinvested at a rate of return equal to the cost of capital.
   d.   Answers a and c are correct.
   e.   None of the answers above is correct.

   ANSWER: A

3.   Project A has an internal rate of return (IRR) of 15 percent. Project B has an IRR of 14 percent. Both projects have a cost of capital of 12 percent. Which of the following statements is most correct?

   a.   Both projects have a positive net present value (NPV).
   b.   Project A must have a higher NPV than Project B.
   c.   If the cost of capital were less than 12 percent, Project B would have a higher IRR than Project A.
   d.   Statements a and c are correct.
   e.   Statements a, b, and c are correct.

   ANSWER: A

4.   A project has an up-front cost of $100,000. The project's WACC is 12 percent and its net present value is $10,000. Which of the following statements is most correct?

    a.   The project should be rejected since its return is less than the WACC.
    b.   The project's internal rate of return is greater than 12 percent.
    c.   The project's modified internal rate of return is less than 12 percent.
    d.   All of the above answers are correct.
    e.   None of the above answers is correct.

ANSWER: B

5.   Projects L and S each have an initial cost of $10,000, followed by a series of positive cash inflows. Project L has total, undiscounted cash inflows of $16,000, while S has total undiscounted inflows of $15,000. Further, at a discount rate of 10 percent, the two projects have identical NPVs. Which project's NPV will be *more sensitive* to changes in the discount rate? (Hint: Projects with steeper NPV profiles are more sensitive to discount rate changes.)

    a.   Project S.
    b.   Project L.
    c.   Both projects are equally sensitive to changes in the discount rate since their NPVs are equal at all costs of capital.
    d.   Neither project is sensitive to changes in the discount rate, since both have NPV profiles which are horizontal.
    e.   The solution cannot be determined unless the timing of the cash flows is known.

ANSWER: B

6.   Two mutually exclusive projects each have a cost of $10,000. The total, undiscounted cash flows from Project L are $15,000, while the undiscounted cash flows from Project S total $13,000. Their NPV profiles cross at a discount rate of 10 percent. Which of the following statements best describes this situation?

    a.   The NPV and IRR methods will select the same project if the cost of capital is *greater than* 10 percent; for example, 18 percent.
    b.   The NPV and IRR methods will select the same project if the cost of capital is *less than* 10 percent; for example, 8 percent.
    c.   To determine if a ranking conflict will occur between the two projects the cost of capital is needed as well as an additional piece of information.
    d.   Project L should be selected at any cost of capital, because it has a higher IRR.
    e.   Project S should be selected at any cost of capital, because it has a higher IRR.

ANSWER: A

7.   Assume a project has normal cash flows (that is, the initial cash flow is negative, and all other cash flows are positive). Which of the following statements is most correct?

a.   All else equal, a project's IRR increases as the cost of capital declines.
b.   All else equal, a project's NPV increases as the cost of capital declines.
c.   All else equal, a project's MIRR is unaffected by changes in the cost of capital.
d.   Answers a and b are correct.
e.   Answers b and c are correct.

ANSWER: B

8.   Which of the following statements is most correct? The modified IRR (MIRR) method:

a.   Always leads to the same ranking decision as NPV for independent projects.
b.   Overcomes the problem of multiple rates of return.
c.   Compounds cash flows at the cost of capital.
d.   Overcomes the problems of cash flow timing and project size that lead to criticism of the regular IRR method.
e.   Answers b and c are correct.

ANSWER: E

9.   Which of the following statements is correct?

a.   Because discounted payback takes account of the cost of capital, a project's discounted payback is normally shorter than its regular payback.
b.   The NPV and IRR methods use the same basic equation, but in the NPV method the discount rate is specified and the equation is solved for NPV, while in the IRR method the NPV is set equal to zero and the discount rate is found.
c.   If the cost of capital is _less than_ the crossover rate for two mutually exclusive projects' NPV profiles, a NPV/IRR conflict will not occur.
d.   If you are choosing between two projects which have the same life, and if their NPV profiles cross, then the smaller project will probably be the one with the steeper NPV profile.
e.   If the cost of capital is relatively high, this will favor larger, longer-term projects over smaller, shorter-term alternatives because it is good to earn high rates on larger amounts over longer periods.

ANSWER: B

10.   In comparing two mutually exclusive projects of equal size and equal life, which of the following statements is most correct?

a.   The project with the higher NPV may not always be the project with the higher IRR.
b.   The project with the higher NPV may not always be the project with the higher MIRR.
c.   The project with the higher IRR may not always be the project with the higher MIRR.
d.   All of the answers above are correct.
e.   Answers a and c are correct.

ANSWER: E

Cash Flow Estimation and Risk Analysis

CMBA Objective Correlations

- Describe the process of forecasting cash flows in capital budgeting problems.

- Describe the implementation of risk analysis in capital budgeting problems.

Sample Questions

1. When evaluating a _new_ project, the firm should consider all of the following factors _except_:

    a. Changes in working capital attributable to the project.
    b. Previous expenditures associated with a market test to determine the feasibility of the project, if the expenditures have been expensed for tax purposes.
    c. The current market value of any equipment to be replaced.
    d. The resulting difference in depreciation expense if the project involves replacement.
    e. All of the statements above should be considered.

    ANSWER: B

2. Which of the following statements is most correct?

    a. The rate of depreciation will often affect operating cash flows, even though depreciation is not a cash expense.
    b. Corporations should fully account for sunk costs when making investment decisions.
    c. Corporations should fully account for opportunity costs when making investment decisions.
    d. All of the answers above are correct.
    e. Answers a and c are correct.

    ANSWER: E

3. Which of the following statements is most correct?

    a. Sunk costs should be incorporated into capital budgeting decisions.
    b. Opportunity costs should be incorporated into capital budgeting decisions.
    c. Relevant externalities should be incorporated into capital budgeting decisions.
    d. Answers b and c are correct.
    e. Answers a, b, and c are correct.

    ANSWER: D

4.   A company is considering an expansion project. The company's CFO plans to calculate the project's NPV by discounting the relevant cash flows (which include the initial up-front costs, the operating cash flows, and the terminal cash flows) at the company's cost of capital (WACC). Which of the following factors should the CFO include when estimating the relevant cash flows?

    a.   Any sunk costs associated with the project.
    b.   Any interest expenses associated with the project.
    c.   Any opportunity costs associated with the project.
    d.   Answers b and c are correct.
    e.   All of the answers above are correct.

ANSWER: C

5.   Adams Audio is considering whether to make an investment in a new type of technology. Which of the following factors should the company consider when it decides whether to undertake the investment?

    a.   The company has already spent $3 million researching the technology.
    b.   The new technology will affect the cash flows produced by its other operations.
    c.   If the investment is not made, then the company will be able to sell one of its laboratories for $2 million.
    d.   All of the factors above should be considered.
    e.   Factors b and c should be considered.

ANSWER: E

6.   A firm is considering the purchase of an asset whose risk is greater than the current risk of the firm, based on any method for assessing risk. In evaluating this asset, the decision maker should

    a.   Increase the IRR of the asset to reflect the greater risk.
    b.   Increase the NPV of the asset to reflect the greater risk.
    c.   Reject the asset, since its acceptance would increase the risk of the firm.
    d.   Ignore the risk differential if the asset to be accepted would comprise only a small fraction of the total assets of the firm.
    e.   Increase the cost of capital used to evaluate the project to reflect the higher risk of the project.

ANSWER: E

7.   Risk in a revenue-producing project can best be adjusted for by

    a.   Ignoring it.
    b.   Adjusting the discount rate upward for increasing risk.
    c.   Adjusting the discount rate downward for increasing risk.
    d.   Picking a risk factor equal to the average discount rate.
    e.   Reducing the NPV by 10 percent for risky projects.

ANSWER: B

8. A company estimates that an average-risk project has a WACC of 10 percent, a below-average-risk project has a WACC of 8 percent, and an above-average-risk project has a WACC of 12 percent. Which of the following independent projects should the company accept?

   a. Project A has average risk and an IRR = 9 percent.
   b. Project B has below-average risk and an IRR = 8.5 percent.
   c. Project C has above-average risk and an IRR = 11 percent.
   d. All of the projects above should be accepted.
   e. None of the projects above should be accepted.

   ANSWER: B

9. Sanford & Son Inc. is thinking about expanding their business by opening another shop on property they purchased 10 years ago. Which of the following items should be included in the analysis of this endeavor?

   a. The property was cleared of trees and brush 5 years ago at a cost of $5,000.
   b. The new shop is expected to affect the profitability of the existing shop since some current customers will transfer their business to the new shop. Sanford and Son estimate that profits at the existing shop will decrease by 10 percent.
   c. Sanford & Son can lease the entire property to another company (that wants to grow flowers on the lot) for $5,000 per year.
   d. Both statements b and c should be included in the analysis.
   e. All of the statements above should be included in the analysis.

   ANSWER: D

10. Pickles Corp. is a company which sells bottled iced tea. The company is thinking about expanding its operations into the bottled lemonade business. Which of the following factors should the company incorporate into its capital budgeting decision as it decides whether or not to enter the lemonade business?

   a. If the company enters the lemonade business, its iced tea sales are expected to fall 5 percent as some consumers switch from iced tea to lemonade.
   b. Two years ago the company spent $3 million to renovate a building for a proposed project which was never undertaken. If the project is adopted, the plan is to have the lemonade produced in this building.
   c. If the company doesn't produce lemonade, it can lease the building to another company and receive after-tax cash flows of $500,000 a year.
   d. All of the statements above are correct.
   e. Answers a and c are correct.

   ANSWER: E

11. Which of the following statements is most correct?

   a. Capital budgeting analysis for expansion and replacement projects is essentially the same because the types of cash flows involved are the same.
   b. In estimating net cash flows for the purpose of capital budgeting, interest and dividend payments should not be included since the effects of these items are already included in the weighted average cost of capital.
   c. When equipment is sold, companies receive a tax credit as long as the salvage value is less than the initial cost of the equipment.
   d. All of the answers above are correct.
   e. None of the answers above is correct.

   ANSWER: B

12. In theory, the decision maker should view market risk as being of primary importance. However, within-firm, or corporate, risk is relevant to a firm's

   a. Well-diversified stockholders, because it may affect debt capacity and operating income.
   b. Management, because it affects job stability.
   c. Creditors, because it affects the firm's credit worthiness.
   d. All of the answers above are correct.
   e. Only answers a and c are correct.

   ANSWER: D

13. Cochran Corporation has a weighted average cost of capital of 11 percent for projects of average risk. Projects of below-average risk have a cost of capital of 9 percent, while projects of above-average risk have a cost of capital equal to 13 percent. Projects A and B are mutually exclusive, whereas all other projects are independent. None of the projects will be repeated. The following table summarizes the cash flows, internal rate of return (IRR), and risk of each of the projects.

Year (t)	Project A	Project B	Project C	Project D	Project E
0	-$200,000	-$100,000	-$100,000	-$100,000	-$100,000
1	66,000	30,000	30,000	30,000	40,000
2	66,000	30,000	30,000	30,000	25,000
3	66,000	40,000	30,000	40,000	30,000
4	66,000	40,000	40,000	50,000	35,000
IRR	12.110%	14.038%	10.848%	16.636%	11.630%
Project Risk	Below Average	Below Average	Average	Above Average	Above Average

Which projects will the firm select for investment?

   a. Projects: A, B, C, D, E
   b. Projects: B, C, D, E
   c. Projects: B, D
   d. Projects: A, D
   e. Projects: B, C, D

   ANSWER: D

Capital Structure Decisions

CMBA Objective Correlations

- Explain how to create value through financing decisions.

- Show how to relate a firm's financing mix to its investment decisions.

Sample Questions

1. Which of the following statements is most correct?

   a. Since debt financing raises the firm's financial risk, raising a company's debt ratio will always increase the company's WACC.
   b. Since debt financing is cheaper than equity financing, raising a company's debt ratio will always reduce the company's WACC.
   c. Increasing a company's debt ratio will typically reduce the marginal cost of both debt and equity financing; however, it still may raise the company's WACC.
   d. Statements a and c are correct.
   e. None of the statements above is correct.

   ANSWER: E

2. Ridgefield Enterprises has total assets of $300 million. The company currently has no debt in its capital structure. The company's basic earning power is 15 percent. The company is contemplating a recapitalization where it will issue debt at 10 percent and use the proceeds to buy back shares of the company's common stock. If the company proceeds with the recapitalization, its operating income, total assets, and tax rate will remain the same. Which of the following will occur as a result of the recapitalization?

   a. The company's ROA will decline.
   b. The company's ROE will increase.
   c. The company's basic earning power will decline.
   d. Answers a and b are correct.
   e. All of the above answers are correct.

   ANSWER: D

3. Which of the following events is likely to encourage a company to raise its target debt ratio?

   a. An increase in the corporate tax rate.
   b. An increase in the personal tax rate.
   c. An increase in the company's operating leverage.
   d. Statements a and c are correct.
   e. All of the statements above are correct.

   ANSWER: A

4. Which of the following would increase the likelihood that a company would increase its debt ratio in its capital structure?

a. An increase in costs incurred when filing for bankruptcy.
b. An increase in the corporate tax rate.
c. An increase in the personal tax rate.
d. A decrease in the firm's business risk.
e. Statements b and d are correct.

ANSWER: E

5. Which of the following statements is *false*? As a firm increases its operating leverage for a given quantity of output, this

a. changes its operating cost structure.
b. increases its business risk.
c. increases the standard deviation of its EBIT.
d. increases the variability in earnings per share.
e. decreases its financial leverage.

ANSWER: E

6. If debt financing is used, which of the following is *true*?

a. The percentage change in net operating income is greater than a given percentage change in net income.
b. The percentage change in net operating income is equal to a given percentage change in net income.
c. The percentage change in net income relative to the percentage change in net operating income depends on the interest rate charged on debt.
d. The percentage change in net operating income is less than the percentage change in net income.
e. The degree of operating leverage is greater than 1.

ANSWER: D

7. Company A and Company B have the same total assets, operating income (EBIT), tax rate, and business risk. Company A, however, has a much higher debt ratio than Company B. Company A's basic earning power (BEP) exceeds its cost of debt financing (k_d). Which of the following statements is most correct?

a. Company A has a higher return on assets (ROA) than Company B.
b. Company A has a higher times interest earned (TIE) ratio than Company B.
c. Company A has a higher return on equity (ROE) than Company B, and its risk, as measured by the standard deviation of ROE, is also higher than Company B's.
d. Statements b and c are correct.
e. All of the statements above are correct.

ANSWER: C

8.   Which of the following statements is most correct?

a.   A firm can use retained earnings without paying a flotation cost. Therefore, while the cost of retained earnings is not zero, the cost of retained earnings is generally lower than the after-tax cost of debt financing.
b.   The capital structure that minimizes the firm's cost of capital is also the capital structure that maximizes the firm's stock price.
c.   The capital structure that minimizes the firm's cost of capital is also the capital structure that maximizes the firm's earnings per share.
d.   If a firm finds that the cost of debt financing is currently less than the cost of equity financing, an increase in its debt ratio will always reduce its cost of capital.
e.   Statements a and b are correct.

ANSWER: B

9.   A consultant has collected the following information regarding Young Publishing:

Total assets	$3,000 million	Tax rate	40%
Operating income (EBIT)	$800 million	Debt ratio	0%
Interest expense	$0 million	WACC	10%
Net income	$480 million	M/B ratio	1.00×
Share price	$32.00	EPS = DPS	$3.20

The company has no growth opportunities (g = 0), so the company pays out all of its earnings as dividends (EPS = DPS). Young's stock price can be calculated by simply dividing earnings per share by the required return on equity capital, which currently equals the WACC because the company has no debt.

The consultant believes that the company would be much better off if it were to change its capital structure. After meeting with investment bankers, the consultant concludes that the company could issue $1,200 million of debt at a before-tax cost of 7 percent, leaving the company with interest expense of $84 million. The $1,200 million raised from the debt issue would be used to repurchase stock at $32 per share. The repurchase will have no effect on the firm's EBIT; however, after the repurchase, the cost of equity will increase to 11 percent. If the firm follows the consultant's advice, what will be its estimated stock price after the capital structure change?

a. $32.00
b. $33.48
c. $31.29
d. $32.59
e. $34.72

ANSWER: E

10. Etchabarren Electronics has made the following forecast for the upcoming year based on the company's current capitalization:

Interest expense	$2,000,000
Operating income (EBIT)	$20,000,000
Earnings per share	$3.60

The company has $20 million worth of debt outstanding and all of its debt yields 10 percent. The company's tax rate is 40 percent. The company's price earnings ratio has traditionally equaled 12, so the company forecasts that under the current capitalization its stock price will be $43.20 at year end.

The company's investment bankers have suggested that the company do a recapitalization. Their suggestion is to issue enough new bonds at a yield of 10 percent to repurchase 1 million shares of common stock. Assume that the stock can be repurchased at today's $40 stock price.

Assume that the repurchase will have no effect on the company's operating income; however, the repurchase will increase the company's dollar interest expense. Also, assume that as a result of the increased financial risk the company's price earnings ratio will be 11.5 after the repurchase. Given these assumptions, what would be the expected year-end stock price if the company proceeded with the recapitalization?

a. $48.30
b. $42.56
c. $44.76
d. $40.34
e. $46.90

ANSWER: A

Initial Public Offerings and Investment Banking

CMBA Objective Correlations

- Describe an initial public offering (IPO).
- Recognize the major characteristics of investment banking.

Sample Questions

1. Which of the following is *not* an advantage of going public?

    a. It allows a firm's founders to diversify their holdings.
    b. It increases the liquidity of the stock.
    c. It establishes a value for the firm.
    d. It makes it easier to raise new equity capital in the future.
    e. All of the above are advantages of going public.

    ANSWER: E

2. When new common stock is offered for sale to the public through investment bankers, the investment bankers may provide potential investors with information contained in a statement called the

    a. Indenture.
    b. Trust agreement.
    c. "Red herring" prospectus.
    d. Proxy.
    e. Security agreement.

    ANSWER: C

3. Which of the following statements is most correct?

    a. One danger a family-owned business faces when it goes public is the loss of absolute voting control of the company, because there is no way to keep new stockholders from voting.
    b. The market is less active for small companies' shares, so these stocks must be included on the SEC's list in order to inform investors of their existence. Therefore, "listed shares" as the term is generally used refers to shares of smaller as opposed to larger companies.
    c. Before a company can offer a new issue of common stock to the public, it must get approval from the SEC for the price at which the stock can be sold. If the SEC thinks the proposed price is too high, then the company's prospectus is deemed to be a "red herring," and the stock cannot be sold.
    d. The *preemptive right* refers to stockholders' right to elect a company's board of directors.
    e. Each of the above statements is false.

    ANSWER: E

4. Which of the following *advantages* of going public simultaneously implies a potential *disadvantage* of going public?

    a. Facilitates in stockholder diversification.
    b. Changes liquidity of the firm's stock.
    c. Alters the difficulty associated with obtaining capital.
    d. Establishes a market value for the firm.
    e. Changes name recognition of the company.

    ANSWER: A

5. Which of the following statements concerning common stock and the investment banking process is *false*?

    a. The preemptive right gives each existing common stockholder the right to purchase his or her proportionate share of a new stock issue.
    b. If a firm sells 1,000,000 new shares of Class B stock, the transaction occurs in the *primary* market.
    c. Listing a large firm's stock is often considered to be beneficial to stockholders because the increases in liquidity and status probably outweigh the additional costs to the firm.
    d. Stockholders have the right to elect the firm's directors, who in turn select the officers who manage the business. If stockholders are dissatisfied with management's performance, an outside group may ask the stockholders to vote for it in an effort to take control of the business. This action is called a *tender offer*.
    e. A large issue of new stock could cause the stock price to fall. This loss is called "market pressure," and it is treated as a flotation cost because it is a cost associated with the new issue.

    ANSWER: D

6. Mesmer Analytic, a biotechnology firm, floated an initial public offering of 2,000,000 shares at a price of $5.00 per share. The firm's owner/managers held 60 percent of the company's $1.00 par value authorized and issued stock following the public offering. One month after the IPO, the firm's board of directors declared a one-time dividend of $0.50 per share payable to all stockholders, meaning that the owner/managers would receive an immediate dividend, in part out of the pockets of the new public stockholders. What was the book value per share of the firm before and after the special dividend was paid?

    a. $2.60; $2.10
    b. $2.60; $2.60
    c. $2.60; $2.30
    d. $1.60; $1.10
    e. $1.60; $1.00

    ANSWER: A

7.   Basic Buildings Inc. decided to go public with a $5,000,000 new equity issue at the beginning of January, 1999. Its investment bankers agreed to take a smaller fee now (6 percent of par value versus 10 percent) in exchange for a 1-year option to purchase an additional 200,000 shares of the company at $5.00 per share. The investment banking firm expects to exercise its option and purchase the 200,000 shares in exactly one year's time when the stock price is expected to be $6.50 per share. However, if the stock price is actually $12.00 per share one year from now, what is the present value of the entire underwriting agreement to the investment banker? Assume that the investment banker's required return on such arrangements is 15 percent and ignore any tax considerations.

    a. $ 300,000
    b. $ 642,782
    c. $1,400,000
    d. $1,700,000
    e. $1,517,391

ANSWER: E

Current Asset Management

CMBA Objective Correlations

- Define working capital management.

- Describe the process of managing working capital assets and liabilities.

Sample Questions

1. Other things held constant, which of the following will cause an increase in working capital?

    a. Cash is used to buy marketable securities.
    b. A cash dividend is declared and paid.
    c. Merchandise is sold at a profit, but the sale is on credit.
    d. Long-term bonds are retired with the proceeds of a preferred stock issue.
    e. Missing inventory is written off against retained earnings.

    ANSWER: C

2. Which of the following statements concerning the cash budget is true?

    a. Depreciation expense is not explicitly included, but depreciation effects are implicitly included in estimated tax payments.
    b. Cash budgets do not include financial expenses such as interest and dividend payments.
    c. Cash budgets do not include cash inflows from long-term sources such as bond issues.
    d. Answers a and b above.
    e. Answers a and c above.

    ANSWER: A

3. Which of the following statements is most correct?

    a. A cash management system which *minimizes collections float* and *maximizes disbursement float* is better than one with higher collections float and lower disbursement float.
    b. A cash management system which *maximizes collections float* and *minimizes disbursement float* is better than one with lower collections float and higher disbursement float.
    c. The use of a *lockbox* is designed to minimize cash theft losses. If the cost of the lockbox is less than theft losses saved, then the lockbox should be installed.
    d. Other things held constant, a firm will need an identical line of credit if it can arrange to pay its bills by the 5th of each month than if its bills come due uniformly during the month.
    e. The statements above are all false.

    ANSWER: A

4.   Which of the following statements is most correct?

a.   A good cash management system would minimize disbursement float and maximize collections float.
b.   If a firm begins to use a well-designed lockbox system, this will reduce its customers' net float.
c.   In the early 1980's, the prime interest rate hit a high of 21 percent. In 1995 the prime rate was considerably lower. That sharp interest rate decline has increased firms' concerns about the efficiency of their cash management programs.
d.   If a firm can get its customers to permit it to pay by wire transfers rather than having to write checks, this will increase its net float and thus reduce its required cash balances.
e.   A firm which has such an efficient cash management system that it has positive net float can have a negative checkbook balance at most times and still not have its checks bounce.

ANSWER: E

5.   Which of the following statements about current asset management is most correct?

a.   A positive net float means that a company has more cash available for its use than the amount shown in the company's books.
b.   Use of a lockbox reduces the possibility that petty cash will be lost.
c.   Depreciation has an impact on the cash budget.
d.   Both a and c are correct.
e.   All of the statements above are correct.

ANSWER: D

6.   Which of the following might be attributed to efficient inventory management?

a.   High inventory turnover ratio.
b.   Low incidence of production schedule disruptions.
c.   High total assets turnover.
d.   All of the answers above.
e.   Only answers a and c above.

ANSWER: D

7.   Which of the following actions are likely to reduce the length of a company's cash conversion cycle?

a.   Adopting a just-in-time inventory system which reduces the inventory conversion period.
b.   Reducing the average days sales outstanding (DSO) on its accounts receivable.
c.   Reducing the amount of time the company takes to pay its suppliers.
d.   All of the answers above are correct.
e.   Answers a and b are correct.

ANSWER: E

8. Which of the following statements is most correct?

   a. The cash balances of most firms consist of transactions, compensating, precautionary, and speculative balances. The total desired cash balance can be determined by calculating the amount needed for each purpose and then summing them together.
   b. The easier a firm's access to borrowed funds the higher its precautionary balances will be, in order to protect against sudden increases in interest rates.
   c. For some firms, holding highly liquid marketable securities is a substitute for holding cash because the marketable securities accomplish the same objective as cash.
   d. Firms today are more likely to rely on cash than on reserve borrowing power or marketable securities for speculative purposes because of the need to move quickly.
   e. Each of the statements above is false.

   ANSWER: C

9. Which of the following statements is most correct?

   a. Shorter-term cash budgets, in general, are used primarily for planning purposes while longer-term budgets are used for actual cash control.
   b. The cash budget and the capital budget are planned separately and although they are both important to the firm, they are independent of each other.
   c. Since depreciation is a non-cash charge, it does not appear on nor have an effect on the cash budget.
   d. The target cash balance is set optimally such that it need not be adjusted for seasonal patterns and unanticipated fluctuations in receipts, although it is changed to reflect long-term changes in the firm's operations.
   e. The typical actual cash budget will reflect interest on loans and income from investment of surplus cash. These numbers are expected values and actual results might turn out different.

   ANSWER: E

10. Which of the following statements is most correct?

   a. A firm which makes 90 percent of its sales on credit and 10 percent for cash is growing at a rate of 10 percent annually. If the firm maintains stable growth it will also be able to maintain its accounts receivable at its current level, since the 10 percent cash sales can be used to manage the 10 percent growth rate.
   b. In managing a firm's accounts receivable it is possible to increase credit sales per day yet still keep accounts receivable fairly steady if the firm can shorten the length of its collection period.
   c. If a firm has a large percentage of accounts over 30 days old, it is a sign that the firm's receivables management needs to be reviewed and improved.
   d. Since receivables and payables both result from sales transactions, a firm with a high receivables-to-sales ratio should also have a high payables-to-sales ratio.
   e. All of the statements above are false.

   ANSWER: B

11.   Which of the following statements is *incorrect* about working capital policy?

a. A company may hold a relatively large amount of cash if it anticipates uncertain sales levels in the coming year.
b. Credit policy has an impact on working capital since it has the potential to influence sales levels and the speed with which cash is collected.
c. The cash budget is useful in determining future financing needs.
d. Holding minimal levels of inventory can reduce inventory carrying costs and cannot lead to any adverse effects on profitability.
e. Managing working capital levels is important to the financial staff since it influences financing decisions and overall profitability of the firm.

ANSWER: D

12.   Chadmark Corporation's budgeted monthly sales are $3,000. Forty percent of its customers pay in the first month and take the 2 percent discount. The remaining 60 percent pay in the month following the sale and don't receive a discount. Chadmark's bad debts are very small and are excluded from this analysis. Purchases for next month's sales are constant each month at $1,500. Other payments for wages, rent, and taxes are constant at $700 per month. Construct a single month's cash budget with the information given. What is the average cash gain or (loss) during a typical month for Chadmark Corporation?

a. $2,600
b. $ 800
c. $ 776
d. $ 740
e. $ 728

ANSWER: C

13.   Gaston Piston Corp. has annual sales of $50,000,000 and maintains an average inventory level of $15,000,000. The average accounts receivable balance outstanding is $10,000,000. The company makes all purchases on credit and has always paid on the 30th day. The company is now going to take full advantage of trade credit and pay its suppliers on the 40th day. If sales can be maintained at existing levels but inventory can be lowered by $2,000,000 and accounts receivable lowered by $2,000,000, what will be the net change in the cash conversion cycle? (Assume there are 360 days in the year.)

a. -14.4 days
b. -18.8 days
c. -28.8 days
d. -25.6 days
e. -38.8 days

ANSWER: E

Mergers and Acquisitions

CMBA Objective Correlations

- Describe the corporate motives for mergers and acquisitions.

- Describe the process of evaluating mergers and acquisitions.

Sample Questions

1. Firms use defensive tactics to fight off undesired mergers. These tactics include

    a. Raising antitrust issues.
    b. Taking poison pills.
    c. Getting a white knight to bid for the firm.
    d. Repurchasing their own stock.
    e. All of the above.

    ANSWER: E

2. Which of the following are given as reasons for the high level of merger activity in the U.S. during the 1980s?

    a. Synergistic benefits arising from mergers.
    b. Reduction in competition resulting from mergers.
    c. Attempts to stabilize earnings by diversifying.
    d. All of the above.
    e. Both a and c above.

    ANSWER: E

3. Which of the following statements is most correct?

    a. Tax considerations often play a part in mergers. If one firm has excess cash, purchasing another firm exposes the purchasing firm to additional taxes. Thus, firms with excess cash rarely undertake mergers.
    b. The smaller the synergistic benefits of a particular merger, the greater the incentive to bargain in negotiations, and the higher the probability that the merger will be completed.
    c. Since mergers are frequently financed by debt more than equity, financial economies which imply a lower cost of debt or greater debt capacity are rarely a relevant rationale for mergers.
    d. Managers who purchase other firms often assert that the new combined firm will enjoy benefits from diversification such as more stable earnings. However, since shareholders are free to diversify their own holdings at lower cost, such a rationale is generally not a valid motive for publicly held firms.

    ANSWER: D

4. Which of the following statements is most correct?

    a. The high value of the U.S. dollar relative to Japanese and European currencies in the 1980s, made U.S. companies comparatively inexpensive to foreign buyers, spurring many mergers.
    b. During the 1980s, the Reagan and Bush administrations tried to foster greater competition and they were adamant about preventing the loss of competition; thus, most large mergers were disallowed.
    c. The expansion of the junk bond market made debt more freely available for large acquisitions and LBOs in the 1980s, and thus, it resulted in an increased level of merger activity.
    d. Increased nationalization of business and a desire to scale down and focus on producing in one's home country virtually halted international mergers in the 1980s.
    e. Answers a and b are correct.

    ANSWER: C

5. Which of the following statements is most correct?

    a. A firm acquiring another firm in a horizontal merger will not have its required rate of return affected because the two firms will have similar betas.
    b. Financial theory says that the choice of how to pay for a merger is really irrelevant because, although it may affect the firm's capital structure, it will not affect the firm's overall required rate of return.
    c. The basic rationale for any financial merger is synergy and thus, development of pro-forma cash flows is the single most important part of the analysis.
    d. In most mergers, the benefits of synergy and the price premium the acquirer pays over market price are summed and then divided equally between the shareholders of the acquiring and target firms.
    e. The primary rationale for any operating merger is synergy, but it is also possible that mergers can include aspects of both operating and financial mergers.

    ANSWER: E

6. Which of the following statements is most correct?

    a. Firms that get acquired usually have a market price below book value before the merger offer is made. However, once the initial offer is made, the price can rise above book value, but the purchase price, especially in large acquisitions, will remain within 20 percent of book value.
    b. When Texaco purchased Getty Oil, many financial analysts felt that the deal made sense because it increased Texaco's market share and expanded its shrinking oil reserves. This merger exemplified the belief among the natural resource companies that buying reserves through acquisitions was less costly than exploring and finding them in the field.
    c. When Mobil Oil Company tried to acquire Conoco, another oil company, stockholders were concerned that the U.S. Justice Department would try to block this merger because it would lessen competition. Thus, antitrust considerations affected this proposed horizontal merger.
    d. Answers b and c are correct.
    e. All of the statements above are false.

    ANSWER: D

7.	American Hardware, a national hardware chain, is considering purchasing a smaller chain, Eastern Hardware. American's analysts project that the merger will result in incremental net cash flows with a present value of $72.52 million, and they have determined that the appropriate discount rate for valuing Eastern is 16 percent. Eastern has 4 million shares outstanding. Eastern's current price is $16.25. What is the maximum price per share that American should offer?

	a. $16.25
	b. $16.97
	c. $17.42
	d. $18.13
	e. $19.00

	ANSWER:	D

8.	American Pizza, a national pizza chain, is considering purchasing a smaller chain, Eastern Pizza. American's analysts project that the merger will result in incremental net cash flows of $2 million in Year 1, $4 million in Year 2, $5 million in Year 3, and $117 million in Year 4. (The Year 4 cash flow includes a terminal value of $107 million.) The acquisition would be made immediately, if it is undertaken. Eastern's post-merger beta is estimated to be 2.0, and its post-merger tax rate would be 34 percent. The risk-free rate is 8 percent, and the market risk premium is 4 percent. What is the appropriate discount rate for valuing the acquisition?

	a. 17%
	b. 16%
	c. 15%
	d. 14%
	e. 12%

	ANSWER:	B

9.	Firm A, which is considering a vertical merger with another firm, Firm T, currently has a required return of 13 percent. The required return of the target firm, Firm T, is 18 percent. The expected return on the market is 12 percent and the risk-free rate is 6 percent. Assume the market is in equilibrium. If the combined firm will be one and one-half times as large as the acquiring firm using book values what will be the beta of the new merged firm?

	a. 1.20
	b. 1.45
	c. 1.59
	d. 1.72
	e. 2.00

	ANSWER:	B

Magiclean Corporation (Questions 10-13)

Magiclean Corporation is considering an acquisition of Dustvac Company. Dustvac has a capital structure of 50 percent debt, 50 percent equity, with a current book value of $10 million in assets. Dustvac's pre-merger beta is 1.36 and is not likely to be altered as a result of the proposed merger. Magiclean's pre-merger beta is 1.02 and both it and Dustvac face a 40 percent tax rate. Magiclean's capital structure is 40 percent debt and 60 percent equity, and it has

$24 million in total assets. The net cash flows from Dustvac available to Magiclean's stockholders are estimated at $4.0 million for each of the next three years and terminal value of $19.0 million in Year 4. Additionally, new debt issued by the combined firm would yield 10 percent before-tax, and the cost of equity is estimated at 12.59 percent. Currently, the risk-free rate is 6.0 percent and the market risk premium is 5.88 percent.

10.   What is the merged firm's WACC?

a. 9.30%
b. 9.76%
c. 10.19%
d. 12.59%
e. 13.06%

ANSWER: B

11.   What is the merged firm's new beta?

a. 1.02
b. 1.06
c. 1.12
d. 1.19
e. 1.22

ANSWER: C

12.   What is the appropriate discount rate Magiclean should use to discount the equity cash flows from Dustvac?

a. 15.52%
b. 14.00%
c. 13.84%
d. 13.14%
e. 10.47%

ANSWER: B

13.   What is the present value of the Dustvac cash inflows to Magiclean? (Round your answer to the closest thousand dollars.)

a. $31,000,000
b. $25,620,000
c. $22,847,000
d. $20,536,000
e. $14,695,000

ANSWER: D

14. Pit Row Auto, a national autoparts chain, is considering purchasing a smaller chain, Southern Auto. Pit Row's analysts project that the merger will result in incremental net cash flows of $2 million in Year 1, $4 million in Year 2, $5 million in Year 3, and $117 million in Year 4. The Year 4 cash flow *includes* a terminal value of $107 million. Assume all cash flows occur at the end of the year. The acquisition would be made immediately, if it is undertaken. Southern's post-merger beta is estimated to be 2.0, and its post-merger tax rate would be 34 percent. The risk-free rate is 8 percent, and the market risk premium is 4 percent. What is the value of Southern Auto to Pit Row Auto's shareholders?

a. $60.35 million
b. $67.00 million
c. $72.52 million
d. $81.93 million
e. $88.23 million

ANSWER: C

15. Modal Systems currently has total assets of $10 million and a debt to total assets (D/TA) ratio of 30 percent. Modal is considering purchasing Quickswitch Company which has total assets of $6 million and a D/TA ratio of 70 percent. If the component costs of capital for the combined firm will be 12 percent before-tax on debt and 15 percent on equity, and the firm's tax rate is 40 percent, what is the WACC for the merged firm?

a. 15.00%
b. 13.65%
c. 12.66%
d. 11.49%
e. 9.75%

ANSWER: D

Macroeconomics

Measuring Economic Variables

CMBA Objective Correlations

- Describe the calculation and limits in use of published statistics (e.g., GDP, unemployment rate, inflation rate).

- Evaluate a macroeconomic forecast.

- Explain how the inequality of withdrawals and injections affect GDP changes.

Sample Questions

1. Which of the following is the correct definition of gross domestic product (GDP)?

    a. total of all final goods and services produced by domestic residents in a given period valued at market prices
    b. total of all exchanges that occur within a nation's borders in a given period valued at market prices
    c. total of all final goods and services produced within a nation's borders in a given period valued at market prices
    d. total of all final and intermediate goods and services produced within a nation's borders in a given period valued at market prices

ANSWER: c

2. Which of the following would be excluded from GDP?

    a. value of a purchase of stocks
    b. value of a purchase of bonds
    c. value of auto parts purchased by an automobile company
    d. all of the above
    e. none of the above

ANSWER: d

3. Based on the definition of GDP, we know that depreciation expense:

    a. is excluded from GDP
    b. is included in GDP
    c. is excluded from GDP and included in gross national product (GNP)
    d. is included in GDP and excluded from GNP

ANSWER: b

4. The product approach to GDP indicates that GDP equals the sum of:

    a.   consumption spending, net investment, government spending and net export spending
    b.   consumption spending, gross investment, government spending and net export spending
    c.   consumption spending, inventory investment, government spending and net export spending
    d.   consumption spending, gross investment and government spending

ANSWER: b

5. Suppose a country legalizes all forms of gambling. Based on our understanding of the definition of GDP, we would expect:

    a.   GDP will increase
    b.   the size of the underground economy will increase
    c.   the size of the underground economy will decrease
    d.   both a and c

ANSWER: d

6. Based on our understanding of the definition of GDP, we would expect that a <u>reduction</u> in the tax rate will tend to cause:

    a.   GDP to increase and the size of the underground economy to increase
    b.   GDP to increase and the size of the underground economy to decrease
    c.   GDP to decrease and the size of the underground economy to increase
    d.   GDP to decrease and the size of the underground economy to decrease

ANSWER: b

7. Suppose nominal GDP decreased during a given year. Based on this information, it is always true that:

    a.   real GDP fell during the year
    b.   the GDP deflator fell during the year
    c.   real GDP and/or the GDP deflator fell during the year
    d.   both real GDP and the GDP deflator fell during the year

ANSWER: c

8. Suppose <u>nominal</u> GDP increased by 7% in 1997 (over its previous level in 1996). Given this information, we know with certainty that:

    a. the aggregate price level (i.e., the GDP deflator) increased in 1997
    b. real GDP increased in 1997
    c. real GDP did not change in 1997
    d. more information is needed to ANSWER this question

ANSWER: d

9. Suppose nominal GDP in 1982 was <u>less</u> than real GDP in 1982. Given this information, we know with certainty that:

    a.   the price level in 1982 was greater than the price level in the base year
    b.   the price level in 1982 was less than the price level in the base year
    c.   real GDP in 1982 was less than real GDP in the base year
    d.   real GDP in 1982 was greater than real GDP in the base year

ANSWER: b

10. Which of the following expressions represents real GDP?

    a.   Y/P
    b.   PxY
    c.   P/Y
    d.   Pxy

ANSWER: a

11. Which of the following expressions represents nominal GDP?

    a.   Y/P
    b.   PxY
    c.   P/Y
    d.   Pxy

ANSWER: d

12. In the base year, we know that:

    a.   real GDP always exceeds nominal GDP
    b.   real GDP is always less than nominal GDP
    c.   real GDP equals nominal GDP
    d.   the GDP deflator (P) is greater than 1

ANSWER: c

13. In the base year, we know that:

    a.   the GDP deflator (P) is greater than 1
    b. $P = 1$
    c. $P < 1$
    d. $P = y/Y$

ANSWER: b

14. Suppose the GDP deflator in 1998 equals 1.27. This indicates that:

    a.   real GDP in 1998 is 27% higher than in the base year
    b.   nominal GDP in 1998 is 27% higher than in the base year
    c.   the overall price level in 1998 is 27% higher than in the base year
    d.   both b and c

ANSWER: c

15. Which of the following is (are) a fixed-weight price index?

    a.   GDP deflator
    b.   CPI
    c.   PPI
    d.   both b and c

ANSWER: d

16. Suppose that: (1) the GDP deflator increased by 4% in 1995; and (2) nominal GDP increased by 6% in 1995. Given this information, we know with certainty that:

    a.   real GDP (y) increased in 1995
    b.   y decreased in 1995
    c.   y fell during 1995 <u>and</u> the aggregate price level increased in 1995
    d.   more information is needed to ANSWER this question

ANSWER: a

17. Which of the following explains why the CPI might overstate the true rate of inflation?

    a.   the failure of the CPI to take into account changes in products' quality
    b.   the failure of the CPI to take into account consumer's changes in spending as relative prices change
    c.   the failure of the CPI to take into account the growth of discount retail stores
    d.   all of the above

ANSWER: d

18. The CPI tends to overstate the true rate of inflation because:

    a.   it places too much weight on goods whose relative prices have fallen
    b.   it places too much weight on goods whose relative prices have increased
    c.   it places too little weight on goods whose relative prices have fallen
    d.   it places too little weight on goods whose relative prices have increased
    e.   both b and c

ANSWER: e

19. Suppose nominal GDP increased during a given year. Based on this information, it is always true that:

    a. real GDP increased during the year
    b. the GDP deflator increased during the year
    c. real GDP and/or the GDP deflator increased during the year
    d. both real GDP and the GDP deflator increased during the year

ANSWER: c

20. Suppose <u>nominal</u> GDP decreased by 4% in 2000 (over its previous level in 1999). Given this information, we know with certainty that:

    a. the aggregate price level (i.e., the GDP deflator) decreased in 2000
    b. real GDP decreased in 2000
    c. real GDP did not change in 2000
    d. more information is needed to ANSWER this question

ANSWER: d

21. Which of the following expressions represents the GDP deflator?

    a. Y/y
    b. y/Y
    c. $y \times Y$
    d. Pxy

ANSWER: a

22. If $Y > y$, we know with certainty that:

    a. $P > 1$
    b. $P = 1$
    c. $P < 1$
    d. $P = 0$

ANSWER: a

23. If $Y < y$, we know with certainty that:

    a. $P > 1$
    b. $P = 1$
    c. $P < 1$
    d. $P = 0$

ANSWER: c

Classical Macroeconomic Theory

CMBA Objective Correlations

- Recognize how components of the economic environment (unemployment, inflation, growth, fiscal and monetary policy) affect firm actions.

- Understand how changes in various components of aggregate demand (consumer demand, investment demand, government demand, net foreign demand) affect the macro economy.

- Evaluate the effectiveness of policies designed to stimulate aggregate demand and those designed to stimulate aggregate supply.

- Order the components of the federal budget by size, and analyze the impact of budget items on firm decisions.

Sample Questions

1. Which of the following expressions represents the marginal product of labor?

    a. y/N
    b. $y = F(N)$
    c. $\Delta y/\Delta N$
    d. $y - N$

ANSWER: c

2. The law of diminishing marginal returns indicates that the marginal product of labor:

    a. is greater, the higher the level of employment
    b. is lower, the higher the level of employment
    c. does not change as the level of employment changes
    d. is an upward sloping curve

ANSWER: b

3. Profit-maximizing firms will increase production when:

    a. marginal cost > marginal revenue
    b. marginal cost = marginal revenue
    c. marginal cost < marginal revenue
    d. the marginal product of labor is greater than zero

ANSWER: c

4. Suppose the current market wage is $20 and that the marginal product of labor at the firm's current output level is 5 (i.e., $MP_N = 5$). Given this information, we know that the:

    a.   marginal cost of producing output is $100
    b.   marginal cost of producing output is $20
    c.   marginal cost of producing output is $4
    d.   marginal cost of producing output is $5

ANSWER: c

5. In a graph with the current market wage on the vertical axis, labor demand is represented by:

    a.   the aggregate production function ($y = F(N)$)
    b.   the marginal product of labor
    c.   the value of the marginal product of labor
    d.   both b and c

ANSWER: c

6. In a graph with the current market wage on the vertical axis, we know that a 5% increase in the price level will cause:

    a.   no shift in the labor demand curve
    b.   a rightward shift in the labor demand curve
    c.   a leftward shift in the labor demand curve
    d.   firms to reduce their demand for labor
    e.   both c and d

ANSWER: b

7. Which of the following represents the Cambridge equation? Circle all that apply.

    a. $M^d = kxPxY$
    b. $M^d = Pxy$
    c. $M^d = kxY$
    d. $M^d = VxPxY$

ANSWER: a and c

8. In the Cambridge equation, which of the following events will cause an increase in nominal money demand? Circle all that apply.

    a.   increase in P
    b.   reduction in P
    c.   increase in Y
    d.   increase in k
    e.   reduction in k

ANSWER: a, c and d

9. In the Cambridge equation, which of the following events will cause a reduction in nominal money demand? Circle all that apply.

    a.   increase in P
    b.   reduction in P
    c.   increase in Y
    d.   increase in k
    e.   reduction in k

ANSWER: b and e

10. The aggregate demand schedule has its particular shape because of the effects of:

    a.   changes in P on the real wage
    b.   changes in k on the demand for money balances
    c.   changes in the quantity supplied of money on nominal purchasing power
    d.   changes in P on nominal income earnings and the desire to hold nominal money balances

ANSWER: d

11. An increase in the price level (P) will cause:

    a.   a leftward shift in y^s
    b.   a rightward shift in y^s
    c.   a rightward shift in y^d
    d.   a leftward shift in y^d
    e.   none of the above

ANSWER: e

12. Which of the following events will cause a rightward shift in the aggregate demand schedule?

    a.   increase in P
    b.   reduction in P
    c.   increase in k
    d.   increase in M

ANSWER: d

13. Suppose we assume that oil is an additional factor of production. Based on your understanding of the classical model, a reduction in the quantity of oil will cause:

    a.   an increase in P and an increase in y
    b.   an increase in P and a reduction in y
    c.   a reduction in P and a reduction in y
    d.   a reduction in P and an increase in y

ANSWER: b

14. Suppose we assume that oil is an additional factor of production. Based on your understanding of the classical model, an increase in the quantity of oil will cause:

    a. an increase in P and an increase in y
    b. an increase in P and a reduction in y
    c. a reduction in P and a reduction in y
    d. a reduction in P and an increase in y

ANSWER: d

15. Based on your understanding of the classical model, an increase in labor force participation that causes an increase in the supply of labor will cause:

    a. an increase in P and an increase in y
    b. an increase in P and a reduction in y
    c. a reduction in P and a reduction in y
    d. a reduction in P and an increase in y

ANSWER: d

16. Based on your understanding of the classical model, a reduction in labor force participation that causes a reduction in the supply of labor will cause:

    a. an increase in P and an increase in y
    b. an increase in P and a reduction in y
    c. a reduction in P and a reduction in y
    d. a reduction in P and an increase in y

ANSWER: b

17. Based on your understanding of the classical model, an increase in government spending will cause:

    a. an increase in P and an increase in y
    b. an increase in P and no change in y
    c. no change in P and no change in y
    d. a reduction in P and an increase in y

ANSWER: c

18. Based on your understanding of the classical model, a reduction in government spending will cause:

    a. an increase in P and an increase in y
    b. an increase in P and no change in y
    c. no change in P and no change in y
    d. a reduction in P and an increase in y

ANSWER: c

19. Based on your understanding of the classical model and of the determination of the exchange rate (E), an increase in the money supply will cause:

    a.   an increase in P and an increase in E
    b.   an increase in P and a reduction in E
    c.   a reduction in P and a reduction in E
    d.   a reduction in P and an increase in E

ANSWER: a

20. A reduction in the size of the budget deficit will cause which of the following? Circle all that apply.

    a.   an increase in the real interest rate
    b.   a reduction in the real interest rate
    c.   an increase in investment
    d.   an increase in private consumption

ANSWER: b, c and d

21. Economic growth is important because:

    a.   increases in per-capita real GDP represent equal increases in the average living standard of a nation's residents
    b.   increases in per-capita real GDP reflect equal and proportionate increases in the income of all residents in an economy
    c.   growth has a cumulative effect on per-capita real GDP over the years
    d.   all of the above

ANSWER: c

22. Over long periods of time, we observe that small differences in economic growth rates:

    a.   tend to have a small effect on future per-capita real GDP levels
    b.   tend to have a large effect on future per-capita real GDP levels
    c.   tend to cancel each other out
    d.   do not seem to affect future per-capita real GDP levels

ANSWER: b

The Theory of Economic Growth

CMBA Objective Correlations

- Understand the causes of economic growth (more capital, more labor, more productivity), and predict the consequences of firms for each of these causes.

- Evaluate changes in national protectionist policies.

Sample Questions

1. Which of following is used to measure economic growth?

    a. the rate of change in real output ($\Delta y/y$)
    b. the rate of change in per-capita nominal GDP
    c. the rate of change in the capital stock
    d. none of the above

ANSWER: d

2. Compounded growth refers to:

    a. the rate of growth in per-capita real GDP
    b. the change in the level of per-capita real GDP over time
    c. the rate of change in the level of real GDP ($\Delta y/y$)
    d. the change in the rate of growth in per-capita real GDP

ANSWER: b

3. Macroeconomists believe that increases in economic growth generally cause:

    a. increases in the standard of living
    b. intergenerational externalities
    c. increases in the level of per-capita real GDP
    d. all of the above

ANSWER: d

4. Which of the following expressions represents a nation's overall output growth rate? For this question, assume that all ß's are less than one.

    a. $\text{ß}_N(\Delta N/N) + \text{ß}_K(\Delta K/K)$
    b. $\Delta A/A$
    c. $\text{ß}_N(\Delta N/N) + \text{ß}_K(\Delta K/K) + \Delta A/A$
    d. $\text{ß}_N(\Delta N/N) + \text{ß}_K(\Delta K/K) + \text{ß}_A(\Delta A/A)$

ANSWER: c

5. Suppose $\beta_N = .6$. Given this information, we know that:

    a. $\Delta y/y = 6\%$
    b. the overall output growth is 6%
    c. a 5% increase in employment will cause, all else fixed, a 3% increase in overall output growth
    d. a 1% increase in employment will cause, all else fixed, a 6% increase in overall output growth

ANSWER: c

6. An increase in labor productivity will cause:

    a. an increase in the real wage
    b. the aggregate production function to shift
    c. an increase in equilibrium output
    d. all of the above

ANSWER: d

7. Suppose the U.S. economy experiences a simultaneous increase in labor force participation and reduction in labor productivity. Given this information, we know with certainty that:

    a. per-capita real GDP falls
    b. the real wage falls
    c. employment falls
    d. per-capita real GDP increases
    e. economic growth decreases

ANSWER: b

8. An increase in capital accumulation, all else fixed, will tend to cause:

    a. an increase in economic growth
    b. a reduction in economic growth
    c. no effect on economic growth
    d. an ambiguous effect on economic growth

ANSWER: a

9. An increase in the marginal product of capital will tend to cause:

    a. an increase in the demand for loanable funds
    b. an increase in investment
    c. an increase in the real interest rate
    d. all of the above

ANSWER: d

10. An increase in household saving will tend to cause:

    a.   a reduction in the level of real GDP
    b.   an increase in economic growth
    c.   an increase in the real interest rate
    d.   an increase in the demand for loanable funds

ANSWER: b

11. An increase in government spending which results in an increase in the size of the budget deficit will tend to cause:

    a.   an increase in economic growth
    b.   a reduction in the real interest rate
    c.   a reduction in capital and reduction in economic growth
    d.   an increase in investment

ANSWER: c

12. An increase in the marginal product of capital will cause a reduction in employment (i.e., the use of labor) when:

    a.   capital and labor are substitutes
    b.   capital and labor are complements
    c.   per-capita real GDP increases
    d.   economic growth increases

ANSWER: a

13. According to new growth theory, which of the following is crucial to economic growth?

    a.   labor force participation
    b.   international trade
    c.   capital accumulation
    d.   technological growth

ANSWER: d

14. New growth theorists believe that economic growth:

    a.   can be self-perpetuating
    b.   is caused solely by capital accumulation
    c.   is determined primarily by labor force participation
    d.   none of the above

ANSWER: a

15. Economists who favor protectionism believe that:

    a. free trade will yield the highest level of economic growth
    b. increased competition will raise the standard of living
    c. pure competition may not be the best market structure to promote economic growth
    d. quotas and tariffs should not be used

ANSWER: c

16. Opponents of protectionism believe that:

    a. free trade will allow new ideas and technology to be more easily diffused around the world in the absence of trade restrictions
    b. quotas and tariffs will increase economic growth
    c. free trade will reduce economic growth
    d. all of the above

ANSWER: a

17. An increase in labor supply will tend to cause:

    a. an increase in the real wage and an increase in per capita output
    b. a reduction in the real wage an increase in per capita output
    c. a reduction in the real wage and a reduction in per capita output
    d. an increase in the real wage and a reduction in per capita output

ANSWER: b

18. A reduction in labor supply will tend to cause:

    a. an increase in the real wage and an increase in per capita output
    b. a reduction in the real wage an increase in per capita output
    c. a reduction in the real wage and a reduction in per capita output
    d. an increase in the real wage and a reduction in per capita output

ANSWER: d

19. An increase in labor productivity will tend to cause:

    a. an increase in the real wage and an increase in per capita output
    b. a reduction in the real wage an increase in per capita output
    c. a reduction in the real wage and a reduction in per capita output
    d. an increase in the real wage and a reduction in per capita output

ANSWER: a

Money in the Traditional Keynesian System

CMBA Objective Correlations

- Explain how the money supply is expanded and contracted, and interpret the language of the Federal Reserve.

- Define the yield curve and understand shifts in the curve.

Sample Questions

1. Which of the following events will cause an increase in the supply of real money balances?

    a. a reduction in M
    b. an increase in P
    c. a reduction in P
    d. a reduction in the interest rate
    e. an increase in the interest rate

ANSWER: c

2. Based on your understanding of the market for real money balances, a reduction in the nominal money supply will tend to cause:

    a. a reduction in the interest rate and a leftward shift in the money demand schedule
    b. a reduction in the interest rate and no change in the money demand schedule
    c. an increase in the interest rate and a leftward shift in the money demand schedule
    d. an increase in the interest rate and no change in the money demand schedule

ANSWER: d

3. Based on your understanding of the market for real money balances, a reduction in the price level will tend to cause:

    a. a reduction in the interest rate and a leftward shift in the money demand schedule
    b. a reduction in the interest rate and no shift in the money demand schedule
    c. an increase in the in the interest rate and a leftward shift in the money demand schedule
    d. an increase in the interest rate and no shift in the money demand schedule

ANSWER: b

4. Based on your understanding of the market for real money balances, the increased use of credit cards will tend to cause:

    a. a reduction in the interest rate and a leftward shift in the money demand schedule
    b. a reduction in the interest rate and no shift in the money demand schedule
    c. an increase in the in the interest rate and a leftward shift in the money demand schedule
    d. an increase in the interest rate and no shift in the money demand schedule

ANSWER: a

5. As money demand becomes less interest rate elastic, we know that:

   a. the IS schedule becomes more interest rate elastic
   b. the IS schedule becomes less interest rate elastic
   c. the LM schedule becomes more interest rate elastic
   d. the LM schedule becomes less interest rate elastic

ANSWER: d

6. An increase in the nominal money supply will tend to cause:

   a. the LM schedule to shift up
   b. the LM schedule to shift down
   c. the LM schedule to become more interest rate elastic
   d. the LM schedule to become less interest rate elastic

ANSWER: b

7. An increase in the price level will tend to cause:

   a. the LM schedule to shift up
   b. the LM schedule to shift down
   c. the LM schedule to become more interest rate elastic
   d. the LM schedule to become less interest rate elastic

ANSWER: a

8. As investment becomes less interest rate elastic, we know that:

   a. the IS schedule becomes more interest rate elastic
   b. the IS schedule becomes less interest rate elastic
   c. the LM schedule becomes more interest rate elastic
   d. the LM schedule becomes less interest rate elastic

ANSWER: b

9. A reduction in taxes will tend to cause:

   a. a leftward shift in the IS schedule
   b. a rightward shift in the IS schedule
   c. the LM schedule to shift down
   d. the LM schedule to shift up

ANSWER: b

10. Suppose the Fed increases the money supply. In which of the following cases will this increase in the money supply likely have the greatest effect on output?

    a. inelastic money demand and inelastic investment
    b. inelastic money demand and elastic investment
    c. elastic money demand and inelastic investment
    d. elastic money demand and elastic investment

ANSWER: b

11. Suppose the Fed reduces the money supply. In which of the following cases will this reduction in the money supply likely have the smallest effect on output?

    a. inelastic money demand and inelastic investment
    b. inelastic money demand and elastic investment
    c. elastic money demand and inelastic investment
    d. elastic money demand and elastic investment

ANSWER: c

12. As the interest elasticity of money demand decreases, we know that a reduction in government spending will cause:

    a. a relatively larger reduction in output
    b. a relatively smaller reduction in the interest rate
    c. a relatively larger increase in investment
    d. all of the above

ANSWER: c

13. For this question, assume that banks do not hold excess reserves and that individuals do not hold currency. Suppose the required reserve ratio is 20% (q = .20). Given this information, a Fed purchase of $20 million of government securities will eventually cause the money supply to:

    a. increase by $100 million
    b. increase by $40 million
    c. decrease by $100 million
    d. decrease by $50 million

ANSWER: a

14. For this question, assume that banks do not hold excess reserves and that individuals do not hold currency. Suppose the required reserve ratio is 25% (q = .25). Given this information, a Fed purchase of $10 million of government securities will eventually cause the money supply to:

    a. increase by $25 million
    b. increase by $40 million
    c. decrease by $25 million
    d. decrease by $50 million

ANSWER: b

15. For this question, assume that banks do not hold excess reserves and that individuals do not hold currency. Suppose the required reserve ratio is 20% (q = .20). Given this information, a Fed sale of $20 million of government securities will eventually cause the money supply to:

    a. increase by $100 million
    b. increase by $40 million
    c. decrease by $100 million
    d. decrease by $50 million

ANSWER: c

16. For this question, assume that banks do not hold excess reserves and that individuals do not hold currency. Suppose the required reserve ratio is 25% (q = .25). Given this information, a Fed sale of $10 million of government securities will eventually cause the money supply to:

    a. increase by $25 million
    b. increase by $40 million
    c. decrease by $25 million
    d. decrease by $50 million
    e. none of the above

ANSWER: e

17. Suppose the economy is affected by variations in money demand. To limit the variations in output caused by these shocks, the Fed should implement which of the following in response to a reduction in money demand?

    a. increase the money supply
    b. leave the money supply constant
    c. reduce the money supply to return the interest rate to its original level
    d. pursue a monetary aggregate target

ANSWER: c

18. Suppose the economy is affected by variations in autonomous expenditures. To limit the variations in output caused by these shocks, the Fed should implement which of the following in response to a reduction in autonomous expenditures?

    a. pursue a policy which effectively makes the LM schedule horizontal
    b. leave the money supply constant
    c. reduce the money supply to return the interest rate to its original level
    d. pursue an interest rate target

ANSWER: b

19. Suppose the economy is affected by variations in autonomous expenditures. To limit the variations in output caused by these shocks, the Fed should implement which of the following in response to an increase in autonomous expenditures?

    a.   pursue a policy which effectively makes the LM schedule horizontal
    b.   leave the money supply constant
    c.   increase the money supply to return the interest rate to its original level
    d.   pursue an interest rate target

ANSWER: b

Inflation

CMBA Objective Correlations

- Understand the causes of inflation, and predict how an inflationary period will affect the firm.

- Understand the causes and cures for hyperinflation.

- Distinguish among the types of unemployment and the policies for dealing with them.

Sample Questions

1. The unemployment rate equals:

   a. the percentage of the total population 16 to 65 years of age who are unemployed
   b. the percentage of the total population 16 to 65 years of age who are not actively searching for employment
   c. the percentage of the civilian labor force that is unemployed
   d. the percentage of the civilian labor force who are not actively searching for employment

ANSWER: c

2. Which of the following is NOT included in the civilian labor force? Circle all that apply.

   a. people not employed who have stopped searching for work
   b. people not employed who are actively searching for work
   c. people confined to an institution
   d. people in the military

ANSWER: a, c and d

3. The natural rate of unemployment is defined as the ratio of:

   a. those who are frictionally and structurally unemployed to the civilian labor force
   b. those who are frictionally and cyclically unemployed to the civilian labor force
   c. those who are cyclically and structurally unemployed to the civilian labor force
   d. those who are cyclically and frictionally unemployed to the civilian labor force

ANSWER: a

4. As the number of discouraged workers increases, all else fixed, we would expect:

   a. an increase in the unemployment rate
   b. a reduction in the unemployment rate
   c. no change in the unemployment rate
   d. an ambiguous effect on the unemployment rate

ANSWER: b

5. As the number of discouraged workers decreases, all else fixed, we would expect:

   a. an increase in the unemployment rate
   b. a reduction in the unemployment rate
   c. no change in the unemployment rate
   d. an ambiguous effect on the unemployment rate

ANSWER: a

6. Frictional unemployment refers to:

   a. that portion of the labor force consisting of individuals who qualify for employment but who are temporarily out of work
   b. that portion of the labor force consisting of individuals who are unemployed because of business-cycle fluctuations
   c. that portion of the labor force consisting of individuals who would like to work but who lack skills and other attributes needed to obtain work
   d. the natural unemployment rate

ANSWER: a

7. Cyclical unemployment refers to:

   a. that portion of the labor force consisting of individuals who qualify for employment but who are temporarily out of work
   b. that portion of the labor force consisting of individuals who are unemployed because of business-cycle fluctuations
   c. that portion of the labor force consisting of individuals who would like to work but who lack skills and other attributes needed to obtain work
   d. the natural unemployment rate

ANSWER: b

8. Structural unemployment refers to:

   a. that portion of the labor force consisting of individuals who qualify for employment but who are temporarily out of work
   b. that portion of the labor force consisting of individuals who are unemployed because of business-cycle fluctuations
   c. that portion of the labor force consisting of individuals who would like to work but who lack skills and other attributes needed to obtain work
   d. the natural unemployment rate

ANSWER: c

9. Which of the following reports do stock traders ignore?

   a. aggregate nonfarm payrolls
   b. unemployment rate
   c. hours worked
   d. hourly pay

ANSWER: b

10. The natural rate of unemployment consists of which of the following?

    a.   frictional unemployment and cyclical unemployment
    b.   frictional unemployment and structural unemployment
    c.   structural unemployment and cyclical unemployment
    d.   structural unemployment, cyclical unemployment, and frictional unemployment

ANSWER: b

11. Which of the following is NOT included in the natural rate of unemployment?

    a.   frictional unemployment
    b.   structural unemployment
    c.   cyclical unemployment
    d.   none of the above

ANSWER: c

12. Which of the following will tend to rise the most when the economy enters a recession?

    a.   frictional unemployment
    b.   structural unemployment
    c.   cyclical unemployment
    d.   none of the above

ANSWER: c

13. The Phillips curve illustrates the relationship between:

    a.   the interest rate and investment
    b.   the price level and IS-LM equilibrium
    c.   inflation and unemployment
    d.   changes in the nominal money stock and the interest rate

ANSWER: c

14. The Phillips curve indicates that increases in aggregate demand will have the greatest effect on the price level when:

    a.   output is relatively low
    b.   the unemployment rate is relatively high
    c.   the unemployment rate is relatively low
    d.   none of the above

ANSWER: c

15. The Phillips curve indicates that increases in aggregate demand will have the smallest effect on the price level when:

    a.   output is relatively low
    b.   output is relatively high
    c.   the unemployment rate is relatively low
    d.   none of the above

ANSWER: a

16. The Phillips curve indicates that reductions in aggregate demand will have the greatest effect on the price level when:

    a.   output is relatively low
    b.   the unemployment rate is relatively high
    c.   the unemployment rate is relatively low
    d.   none of the above

ANSWER: c

17. The Phillips curve indicates that reductions in aggregate demand will have the smallest effect on the price level when:

    a.   output is relatively low
    b.   output is relatively high
    c.   the unemployment rate is relatively low
    d.   none of the above

ANSWER: a

18. Which of the following represents a cost of inflation and inflation variability?

    a.   resources expended to economize on money holdings
    b.   redistribution of resources from creditors to debtors
    c.   redistribution of real incomes from individuals to the government
    d.   all of the above
    e.   none of the above.

ANSWER: d

19. Monetarists argue that in the long run, we know that:

    a.   workers are fully informed about prices
    b.   expected inflation rates equal the actual inflation rate
    c.   the actual unemployment rate will equal the natural unemployment rate
    d.   all of the above
    e.   none of the above
ANSWER: d

20. The natural rate of unemployment:

    a. stems from structural and frictional unemployment
    b. is that unemployment rate consistent with the unemployment rate which occurs when the economy is on its long-run growth path
    c. is that unemployment rate which occurs when full information is available
    d. all of the above
    e. none of the above

ANSWER: d

21. An increase in expected inflation will tend to cause:

    a. no change in the unemployment rate in the long run
    b. a reduction in the unemployment in the long run
    c. no change in actual inflation in the long run
    d. none of the above

ANSWER: a

22. The monetarist view of the Phillips curve indicates that a reduction in the actual inflation rate will tend to cause:

    a. a reduction in the unemployment rate in the short run
    b. an increase in the unemployment rate in the short run
    c. a reduction in the unemployment rate in the long run
    d. an increase in the natural rate of unemployment in the long run

ANSWER: b

23. A prediction of the political business cycle theory is that:

    a. the short run Phillips curve is vertical
    b. economies in democratic societies will experience short run reductions in the unemployment rate at the expense of higher inflation
    c. the long run Phillips curve is downward sloping
    d. economies will experience simultaneous reductions in inflation and reductions in unemployment

ANSWER: b

24. Stagflation refers to:

    a. the effects of changes in inflation on the unemployment rate in the short run
    b. the effects of changes in inflation on the unemployment rate in the long run
    c. a period of simultaneous increases in the inflation rate and increases in the unemployment rate
    d. the effects of reductions in aggregate demand on unemployment and inflation in the short run

ANSWER: c

Macroeconomic Policy

CMBA Objective Correlations

- Explain how changes in monetary policy are transmitted to changes in inflation and unemployment, and why the transmissions mechanisms may not work as predicted.

Sample Questions

1. Which of the following represents the recognition lag?

    a. the amount of time between the need for a macroeconomic policy action and the realization of that need
    b. the amount of time between the realization of the need for a macroeconomic policy action and the actual implementation of that policy
    c. the amount of time between the implementation of a policy action and its macroeconomic effects
    d. none of the above

ANSWER: a

2. Which of the following represents the response lag?

    a. the amount of time between the need for a macroeconomic policy action and the realization of that need
    b. the amount of time between the realization of the need for a macroeconomic policy action and the actual implementation of that policy
    c. the amount of time between the implementation of a policy action and its macroeconomic effects
    d. none of the above

ANSWER: b

3. Which of the following represents the transmission lag?

    a. the amount of time between the need for a macroeconomic policy action and the realization of that need
    b. the amount of time between the realization of the need for a macroeconomic policy action and the actual implementation of that policy
    c. the amount of time between the implementation of a policy action and its macroeconomic effects
    d. none of the above

ANSWER: c

4. Which of the following statements about monetary policy is most likely true?

    a. the recognition lag is the longest of the lags
    b. the response lag is the longest of the lags
    c. the transmission lag is the shortest of the lags
    d. the response lag is the shortest of the lags

ANSWER: d

5. Which of the following statements about monetary and fiscal policy is most likely true?

    a. the recognition lag for monetary policy is longer than it is for fiscal policy
    b. the recognition lag for monetary policy is shorter than it is for fiscal policy
    c. the response lag for monetary policy is longer than it is for fiscal policy
    d. the response lag for monetary policy is shorter than it is for fiscal policy

ANSWER: d

6. For countercyclical policy to be successful, we know that:

    a. the policy maker's contribution to real income should increase when real income increases
    b. the policy maker's contribution to real income should increase when real income decreases
    c. the policy maker's contribution to real income should decrease when real income decreases
    d. the policy maker's contribution to real income should not change as real income changes

ANSWER: b

7. For countercyclical policy to be successful, we know that:

    a. the policy maker's contribution to real income should increase when real income increases
    b. the policy maker's contribution to real income should decrease when real income decreases
    c. the policy maker's contribution to real income should decrease when real income increases
    d. the policy maker's contribution to real income should not change as real income changes

ANSWER: c

8. The existence of time lags can cause:

    a. the policy maker's contribution to real income to increase when real income increases
    b. the policy maker's contribution to real income to increase when real income decreases
    c. the policy maker's contribution to real income to decrease when real income increases
    d. the policy maker's contribution to real income should not change as real income changes

ANSWER: a

9. Procyclical policy would occur when:

    a. the policy maker's contribution to real income increases as real income decreases
    b. the policy maker's contribution to real income decreases as real income decreases
    c. the policy maker's contribution to real income decrease as real income increases
    d. the policy maker's contribution to real income does not change as real income changes

ANSWER: b

10. Since time lags can cause macroeconomic policy to be procyclical, some economists have argued that policy makers should:

    a.   use discretionary policy making
    b.   adopt policy rules
    c.   undertake macroeconomic policy responses on an ad hoc basis
    d.   all of the above

ANSWER: b

Use the following graph to answer the next nine questions (#11 - #19).

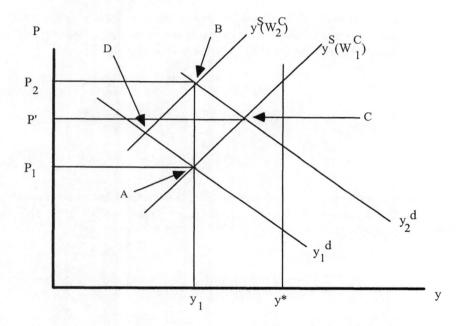

11. In the above graph, assume that y_1 represents the full-information level of output and that y^* is the capacity level of output. Which of the following points represents a commitment policy equilibrium?

    a.   A
    b.   B
    c.   C
    d.   D

ANSWER: a

12. In the above graph, assume that y_1 represents the full-information level of output and that y^* is the capacity level of output. Which of the following points represents a discretionary policy equilibrium?

    a.   A
    b.   B
    c.   C
    d.   D

ANSWER: b

13. In the above graph, assume that y_1 represents the full-information level of output and that y^* is the capacity level of output. Which of the following represents the inflation bias arising from discretionary policy?

    a. $P_2 - P_1$
    b. $P_2 - P'$
    c. $P' - P_1$
    d. $y^* - y_1$

ANSWER: a

14. In the above graph, assume that y_1 represents the full-information level of output and that y^* is the capacity level of output. Which of the following points will occur if: (1) workers and firms expect the policy maker to attempt to increase output; <u>and</u> (2) the policy maker does NOT attempt to increase output?

    a.   A
    b.   B
    c.   C
    d.   D

ANSWER: d

15. In the above graph, assume that y_1 represents the full-information level of output and that y^* is the capacity level of output. Which of the following points will occur if: (1) workers and firms do NOT expect the policy maker to attempt to increase output; <u>and</u> (2) the policy maker DOES attempt to increase output?

    a.   A
    b.   B
    c.   C
    d.   D

ANSWER: c

16. In the above graph, assume that y_1 represents the full-information level of output and that y^* is the capacity level of output. Which of the following points will occur if: (1) workers and firms expect the policy maker to attempt to increase output; <u>and</u> (2) the policy maker DOES attempt to increase output?

    a.   A
    b.   B
    c.   C
    d.   D

ANSWER: b

17. In the above graph, assume that y_1 represents the full-information level of output and that y^* is the capacity level of output. Which of the following points will occur if: (1) workers and firms do NOT expect the policy maker to attempt to increase output; <u>and</u> (2) the policy maker does NOT attempt to increase output?

    a. A
    b. B
    c. C
    d. D

ANSWER: a

18. The time inconsistency problem indicates that which of the following points will occur?

    a. A
    b. B
    c. C
    d. D

ANSWER: b

19. Assuming that policy credibility exists, which of the following points will occur?

    a. A
    b. B
    c. C
    d. D

ANSWER: a

International Dimensions of Macroeconomic Policy

CMBA Objective Correlations

- Explain how international translation and transaction risk may affect firm balance sheet and income statement.

- Justify a decision to hedge international risk.

- Explain the various tools for hedging international risk (e.g., currency options, futures, and forward contracts).

- Recognize the special risks firms may face in operating in countries that use flexible exchange rates, pegged exchange rates, exchange controls, or currency boards to determine exchange rates.

- Show the connection between inflation rate and exchange rate.

Sample Questions

1. Which of the following represents 'accounting risk'?

    a. the effects of changes in the exchange rate on the market value of an individual's foreign asset holdings
    b. the effects of changes in the exchange rate on the value of a financial asset relating to the funding of a foreign-currency-denominated transaction
    c. the effects of changes in the exchange rate on the underlying rates of return on financial assets denominated in other currencies
    d. the effects of changes in the exchange rate on net exports

ANSWER: a

2. Which of the following represents 'transaction risk'?

    a. the effects of changes in the exchange rate on the market value of an individual's foreign asset holdings
    b. the effects of changes in the exchange rate on the value of a financial asset relating to the funding of a foreign-currency-denominated transaction
    c. the effects of changes in the exchange rate on the underlying rates of return on financial assets denominated in other currencies
    d. the effects of changes in the exchange rate on net exports

ANSWER: b

3. Which of the following represents 'currency risk'?

    a. the effects of changes in the exchange rate on the market value of an individual's foreign asset holdings
    b. the effects of changes in the exchange rate on the value of a financial asset relating to the funding of a foreign-currency-denominated transaction
    c. the effects of changes in the exchange rate on the underlying rates of return on financial assets denominated in other currencies
    d. the effects of changes in the exchange rate on net exports

ANSWER: c

4. Which of the following can be used to hedge against foreign exchange risk?

    a. forward currency contracts
    b. interest rate forward contracts
    c. interest rate swaps
    d. all of the above

ANSWER: d

5. Which of the following is a rationale for fixed exchange rates?

    a. monetary policy has a relatively greater effect on output with fixed exchange rates and perfect capital mobility
    b. hedging is not a costless activity
    c. fiscal policy has a relatively greater effect on output with flexible exchange rates and perfect capital mobility
    d. all of the above

ANSWER: b

6. Which of the following represents a rationale for flexible exchange rates?

    a. the use of a single currency increases foreign exchange risks
    b. adjustments in the exchange rate permit more rapid price and output adjustments to changes in supply and demand conditions
    c. hedging costs are relatively small
    d. all of the above

ANSWER: b

7. Suppose the economy's private payments balance is initially equal to zero. Also assume that exchange rates are fixed and that financial capital is imperfectly mobile. A monetary expansion will have which of the following effects in the short run?

    a. the interest rate will fall
    b. output will increase
    c. a private payments deficit will occur
    d. all of the above

ANSWER: d

8. Suppose the economy's private payments balance is initially equal to zero. Also assume that exchange rates are fixed and that financial capital is imperfectly mobile. A monetary contraction will have which of the following effects in the short run?

    a. the IS schedule will shift to the left
    b. the BP schedule will shift to the left
    c. output will fall
    d. all of the above

ANSWER: c

9. Suppose the economy's private payments balance is initially equal to zero. Also assume that exchange rates are fixed and that financial capital is imperfectly mobile. A monetary expansion will have which of the following effects in the short run?

    a. a private payments surplus caused primarily by a reduction in imports when capital mobility is low
    b. a private payments surplus caused primarily by a capital inflow when capital mobility is low
    c. a private payments deficit caused primarily by an increase in imports when capital mobility is high
    d. a private payments deficit caused primarily by a capital outflow when capital mobility is high

ANSWER: d

10. Suppose the economy's private payments balance is initially equal to zero. Also assume that exchange rates are fixed and that financial capital is imperfectly mobile. Suppose the central bank increases the money supply. Which of the following actions will be part of the sterilization process associated with this initial increase in the money supply?

    a. sale of U.S. government securities
    b. reduction in its holdings of foreign exchange reserves
    c. purchase of U.S. government securities
    d. all of the above

ANSWER: c

11. Suppose the economy's private payments balance is initially equal to zero. Also assume that exchange rates are fixed and that financial capital is imperfectly mobile. Suppose the central bank reduces the money supply. Which of the following actions will be part of the sterilization process associated with this initial reduction in the money supply?

    a. sale of U.S. government securities
    b. increase in its holdings of foreign exchange reserves
    c. purchase of U.S. government securities
    d. all of the above

ANSWER: a

12. Suppose the economy's private payments balance is initially equal to zero. Also assume that exchange rates are fixed and that the economy is initially operating at point A. Also assume that the central bank does NOT pursue sterilization procedures. Given this information, we know that a reduction in government spending will cause in the long run:

    a. a private payments deficit
    b. a private payments surplus
    c. an increase in the money supply
    d. a reduction in the money supply

ANSWER: d

13. Suppose the economy's private payments balance is initially equal to zero. Also assume that exchange rates are flexible and that financial capital is imperfectly mobile. We know that a depreciation will cause:

    a. both the IS schedule and BP schedule to shift to the left
    b. both the IS schedule and BP schedule to shift to the right
    c. the IS schedule to shift to the right and the BP schedule to shift to the left
    d. the IS schedule to shift to the left and the BP schedule to shift to the right

ANSWER: b

14. Suppose the economy's private payments balance is initially equal to zero. Also assume that exchange rates are flexible and that financial capital is imperfectly mobile. We know that an increase in the money supply will cause in the long run:

    a. the BP schedule to shift to the left
    b. the BP schedule to shift to the right
    c. no shift in the BP schedule
    d. uncertain effects on the BP schedule

ANSWER: b

15. Suppose the economy's private payments balance is initially equal to zero. Also assume that exchange rates are flexible and that financial capital is imperfectly mobile. We know that an increase in the money supply will cause in the long run:

    a. a depreciation of the currency
    b. the BP schedule to shift to the right
    c. the IS schedule to shift to the right
    d. all of the above

ANSWER: d

16. Suppose the economy's private payments balance is initially equal to zero. Also assume that exchange rates are flexible and that financial capital is imperfectly mobile. We know that a reduction in the money supply will cause in the short run:

    a. a private payments deficit
    b. a private payments surplus
    c. no effect on the private payments balance
    d. uncertain effects on the private payments balance

ANSWER: b

17. Suppose the economy's private payments balance is initially equal to zero. Also assume that exchange rates are flexible and that financial capital is imperfectly mobile. Suppose government spending increases. We know that as capital becomes more mobile that this increase in government spending will likely cause in the short run:

    a. a private payments deficit
    b. a private payments surplus
    c. a depreciation of the currency
    d. a rightward shift in the BP schedule

ANSWER: b

18. Suppose the economy's private payments balance is initially equal to zero. Also assume that exchange rates are flexible and that financial capital is imperfectly mobile. Suppose government spending increases. We know that as capital becomes less mobile that this increase in government spending will likely cause in the short run:

    a.   a private payments deficit
    b.   a private payments surplus
    c.   an appreciation of the currency
    d.   a leftward shift in the IS schedule

ANSWER: a

Use the following graph to answer the next three questions (#19 - #21).

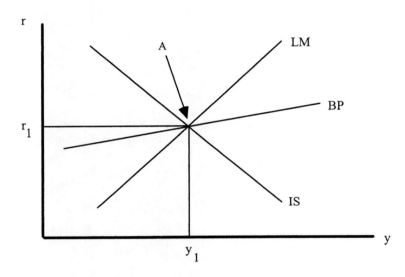

19. Suppose the economy's private payments balance is initially equal to zero. Also assume that exchange rates are flexible and that the economy is initially operating at point A. Given this information, we know that a reduction in government spending will cause in the short run:

    a.   a private payments deficit
    b.   a private payments surplus
    c.   the BP schedule to shift to the left
    d.   an appreciation of the currency

ANSWER: a

20. Suppose the economy's private payments balance is initially equal to zero. Also assume that exchange rates are flexible and that the economy is initially operating at point A. Given this information, we know that an increase in government spending will cause in the short run:

    a.   a private payments deficit
    b.   a private payments surplus
    c.   the BP schedule to shift to the right
    d.   a depreciation of the currency

ANSWER: b

21. Suppose the economy's private payments balance is initially equal to zero. Also assume that exchange rates are flexible and that the economy is initially operating at point A. Given this information, we know that an increase in government spending will cause in the long run:

    a.   a private payments deficit
    b.   a private payments surplus
    c.   the BP schedule to shift to the right
    d.   an appreciation of the currency

ANSWER: d

Microeconomics

Demand and Supply

CMBA Objective Correlations

- Apply the supply and demand model to changes in price and quantity. Analyze the forces that shift supply and demand curves.

Sample Questions

1. If demand increases while supply decreases for a particular good:
   a. its equilibrium price will increase while the quantity of the good produced and sold could increase, decrease, or remain constant.
   b. the quantity of the good produced and sold will decrease while its equilibrium price could increase, decrease, or remain constant.
   c. the quantity of the good produced and sold will increase while its equilibrium price could increase, decrease or remain constant.
   d. its equilibrium price will decrease while the quantity of the good produced and sold could increase, decrease, or remain constant.

ANSWER: A

2. Shortage is a condition of:
   a. excess supply.
   b. a deficiency in demand.
   c. market equilibrium.
   d. excess demand.

ANSWER: D

3. Derived demand is directly determined by:
   a. utility.
   b. the profitability of using inputs to produce output.
   c. the ability to satisfy consumer desires.
   d. personal consumption.

ANSWER: B

4. A demand curve expresses the relation between the quantity demanded and:
   a. income.
   b. advertising.
   c. price.
   d. all of the above.

ANSWER: C

5. Change in the quantity demanded is:
    a. a movement along a single demand curve.
    b. an upward shift from one demand curve to another.
    c. a reflection of change in one or more of the nonprice variables in the product demand function.
    d. a downward shift from one demand curve to another.

ANSWER: A

6. A supply curve expresses the relation between the quantity supplied and:
    a. technology.
    b. wage rates.
    c. price.
    d. all of the above.

ANSWER: C

7. Change in the quantity supplied reflects a:
    a. change in price.
    b. switch from one supply curve to another.
    c. change in one or more nonprice variables.
    d. shift in supply.

ANSWER: A

8. Holding all else equal, an unnecessary increase in federally-mandated auto safety requirements leads to a decrease in:
    a. auto demand.
    b. the quantity of autos supplied.
    c. auto supply.
    d. the quantity of autos demanded.

ANSWER: C

9. Holding all else equal, an increase in mandatory payments by employers for universal health care coverage for workers would lead to a decrease in the:
    a. supply of workers.
    b. the quantity supplied of workers.
    c. the quantity demanded of workers.
    d. demand for workers.

ANSWER: D

10. The demand for inputs is derived from the:
    a. profit motive.
    b. utility of supply.
    c. utility of consumption.
    d. market demand function.

ANSWER: A

11. The effect on sales of an increase in price is a decrease in:
    a. the quantity demanded.
    b. demand.
    c. supply.
    d. the quantity supplied.

ANSWER: A

12. Demand is the total quantity of a good or service that customers:
    a. are willing to purchase.
    b. are able to purchase.
    c. are willing and able to purchase.
    d. need.

ANSWER: C

13. Demand for consumption goods and services is:
    a. derived demand.
    b. direct demand.
    c. product demand.
    d. utility.

ANSWER: B

14. Derived demand is the:
    a. demand for inputs used in production.
    b. demand for products other than raw materials.
    c. first derivative of the demand function.
    d. demand for consumption products.

ANSWER: A

15. The demand function for a product states the relation between the aggregate quantity demanded and:
    a. all factors that influence demand.
    b. the aggregate quantity supplied.
    c. consumer utility.
    d. the market price, holding all the other factors that influence demand constant.

ANSWER: A

16. Change in the quantity demanded is caused by a change in:
    a. advertising.
    b. wage rates.
    c. raw material costs.
    d. price.

ANSWER: D

17. The demand curve for automobiles will shift to the right if:
    a. interest rates increase.
    b. advertising expenditures increase.
    c. the price of steel decreases.
    d. the price of automobiles decreases.

ANSWER: B

18. Change in the quantity supplied is caused by a change in:
    a. income.
    b. weather.
    c. energy costs.
    d. price.

ANSWER: D

19. The supply of a product does not depend on:
    a. raw material costs.
    b. wage rates.
    c. consumer incomes.
    d. technology.

ANSWER: C

20. If the production of two goods is complementary a decrease in the price of one will:
    a. increase supply of the other.
    b. increase the quantity supplied of the other.
    c. decrease the price of the other.
    d. decrease supply of the other.

ANSWER: D

21. Farmers in certain areas of the U.S. can grow either wheat or corn. If the price of corn increases the:
    a. supply of wheat will shift to the right.
    b. supply of wheat will shift to the left.
    c. supply of both corn and wheat will shift, but in opposite directions.
    d. supply of corn will shift to the right.

ANSWER: B

22. The supply curve expresses the relation between the aggregate quantity supplied and:
    a. price, holding constant the effects of all other variables.
    b. aggregate quantity demanded, holding constant the effects of all other variables.
    c. profit, holding constant the effects of all other variables.
    d. each factor that affects supply.

ANSWER: A

Demand Analysis

CMBA Objective Correlations

- Predict how rational and irrational decisions by consumers affect firms.

- Distinguish between cost and price.

- Calculate price and income elasticity coefficients

- Recognize the importance of cross elasticity.

- Apply elasticity concept to production and pricing decisions in firms.

- Explain how advertising should change the slope and position of the demand curve.

Sample Questions

1. All combinations of goods and services that provide the same utility are identified by the:
   a. law of diminishing marginal utility.
   b. law of constant marginal utility.
   c. law of increasing marginal utility.
   d. indifference curve.

ANSWER: D

2. The increase in overall consumption made possible by a price cut is the:
   a. income effect.
   b. substitution effect.
   c. income and substitution effect.
   d. consumption effect.

ANSWER: A

3. The point advertising elasticity reveals the:
   a. percentage change in demand following a change in advertising.
   b. percentage change in the quantity demanded following a change in advertising.
   c. percentage change in advertising following a change in the quantity demanded.
   d. percentage change in advertising following a change in demand.

ANSWER: A

4. If $P_1 = \$5$, $Q_1 = 10,000$, $P_2 = \$6$ and $Q_2 = 5,000$, then at point P_2 the point price elasticity ε_P equals:
    a. -6.
    b. -2.5.
    c. -4.25.
    d. -0.12.

ANSWER: A

5. If $MC = \$25$ and $\varepsilon_P = -2.5$, the profit-maximizing price equals:
    a. $25.
    b. $17.86.
    c. $41.67.
    d. $35.

ANSWER: C

6. The concept of cross-price elasticity is used to examine the responsiveness of demand:
    a. to changes in income.
    b. for one product to changes in the price of another.
    c. to changes in "own" price.
    d. to changes in income.

ANSWER: B

7. When the cross-price elasticity $\varepsilon_{PX} = 3$:
    a. demand rises by 3% with a 1% increase in the price of X.
    b. the quantity demanded rises by 3% with a 1% increase in the price of X.
    c. the quantity demanded rises by 1% with a 3% increase in the price of X.
    d. demand rises by 1% with a 3% increase in the price of X.

ANSWER: A

8. Goods for which $\varepsilon_1 > 1$ are often referred to as:
    a. cyclical normal goods.
    b. noncyclical normal goods.
    c. being relatively unaffected by changing income.
    d. inferior goods.

ANSWER: A

9. If $\varepsilon_P = -3$ and $MC = \$1.32$, the profit-maximizing price is:
    a. $3.00.
    b. $1.98.
    c. $1.32.
    d. $1.76.

ANSWER: B

10. If MR = $25,000 - $300Q and MC = $5,000 + $100Q, the profit-maximizing price is:
    a. $50.
    b. $25,000.
    c. $17,500.
    d. $10,000.

ANSWER: C

11. Elasticity is the:
    a. percentage change in a dependent variable, Y, resulting from a one-percent change in the value of an independent variable, X.
    b. change in a dependent variable, Y, resulting from a change in the value of an independent variable, X.
    c. change in an independent variable, X, resulting from a change in the value of a dependent variable, Y.
    d. percentage change in an independent variable, X, resulting from a one-percent change in the value of a dependent variable, Y.

ANSWER: A

12. Point elasticity measures elasticity:
    a. over a given range of a function.
    b. at a spot on a function.
    c. along an arc.
    d. before non-price effects.

ANSWER: B

13. With elastic demand, a price increase will:
    a. lower marginal revenue.
    b. lower total revenue.
    c. increase total revenue.
    d. lower marginal and total revenue.

ANSWER: B

14. With inelastic demand, a price increase produces:
    a. a less than proportionate decline in quantity demanded.
    b. lower total revenue.
    c. lower marginal revenue.
    d. lower marginal and total revenue.

ANSWER: A

15. A direct relation between the price of one product and the demand for another holds for all:
    a. complements.
    b. substitutes.
    c. normal goods.
    d. inferior goods.

ANSWER: B

16. A utility function is a descriptive statement that relates total utility to:
    a. income.
    b. the production of goods and services.
    c. the consumption of goods and services.
    d. prices.

ANSWER: C

17. According to the law of diminishing marginal utility:
    a. as the consumption of a given product rises, the added benefit eventually diminishes.
    b. as the production cost for a given product rises, the added benefit eventually diminishes.
    c. the demand curve for some products is upward-sloping.
    d. as the price of a given product rises, the added benefit eventually diminishes.

ANSWER: A

18. Given limited budgets, consumers obtain the most satisfaction if they purchase goods and services that:
    a. provide the highest level of marginal utility.
    b. provide the highest level of total utility.
    c. provide the highest level of marginal utility per dollar spent.
    d. cost the least.

ANSWER: C

19. An indifference curve is a set of market baskets that:
    a. contain the same goods.
    b. provide the same utility.
    c. have identical marginal rates of substitution.
    d. can be obtained for the same cost.

ANSWER: B

20. An increase in the quantity purchased following a price cut is:
    a. unrelated to the law of diminishing marginal utility.
    b. inconsistent with the law of diminishing marginal utility.
    c. inconsistent with utility-maximizing behavior.
    d. consistent with the law of diminishing marginal utility.

ANSWER: D

21. The marginal rate of substitution is always equal to:
    a. the marginal utility of either product.
    b. the total utility of either product.
    c. minus one times the ratio of marginal utilities for each product.
    d. the slope of the budget constraint.

ANSWER: C

22. If the quantity of Good X is measured on the horizontal axis and the quantity of Good Y is measured on the vertical axis, the slope of the budget constraint will decrease if the:
    a. price of X decreases.
    b. price of Y decreases.
    c. marginal utility of X decreases.
    d. budget decreases.

ANSWER: A

23. Income and substitution effects explain change in the quantity of a good consumed that result from a change in:
    a. consumer preferences.
    b. price.
    c. price of other goods.
    d. income.

ANSWER: B

24. The change to a new indifference curve following a rise in aggregate consumption caused by a price cut is:
    a. a price effect.
    b. an income effect.
    c. a substitution effect.
    d. a consumption effect.

ANSWER: B

25. The demand for a product tends to be inelastic if:
    a. it is expensive.
    b. a small proportion of consumer's income is spent on the good.
    c. consumers are quick to respond to price changes.
    d. it has many substitutes.

ANSWER: B

26. Two products are complements if the:
    a. cross-price elasticity of demand is less than zero.
    b. cross-price elasticity of demand equals zero.
    c. cross-price elasticity of demand is greater than zero.
    d. price elasticity of demand for each good is greater than zero.

ANSWER: A

27. If the income elasticity of demand for a good is greater than one, the good is:
    a. a noncyclical normal good.
    b. a cyclical normal good.
    c. neither a normal nor an inferior good.
    d. an inferior good.

ANSWER: B

Cost Analysis and Estimation

CMBA Objective Correlations

- Describe how fixed cost, marginal cost and average cost differ.

- Evaluate changes in the minimum wage.

- Calculate the minimum point on an average cost function.

Sample Questions

1. The breakeven level of output occurs where:
   a. marginal cost equals average cost.
   b. marginal profit equals zero.
   c. total profit equals zero.
   d. marginal cost equals marginal revenue.

ANSWER: C

2. Total revenue is maximized at the point where:
   a. marginal revenue equals zero.
   b. marginal cost equals zero.
   c. marginal revenue equals marginal cost.
   d. marginal profit equals zero.

ANSWER: A

3. Total cost minimization occurs at the point where:
   a. MC = 0.
   b. MC = AC.
   c. AC = 0.
   d. Q = 0.

ANSWER: D

4. Marginal profit equals:
   a. the change in total profit following a one-unit change in output.
   b. the change in total profit following a managerial decision.
   c. average revenue minus average cost.
   d. total revenue minus total cost.

ANSWER: A

5. Marginal cost is:
   a. the change in output following a one-dollar change in cost.
   b. the change in cost following a one-unit change in output.
   c. the change in average cost following a one-unit change in output.
   d. the change in cost following a managerial decision.

ANSWER: B

6. At the profit-maximizing level of output:
   a. marginal revenue equals marginal cost.
   b. marginal cost equals zero.
   c. average profit equals zero.
   d. marginal profit equals average profit.

ANSWER: A

7. The percentage change in profit that results from a 1% change in units sold equals:
   a. the cost elasticity.
   b. the returns to scope economies.
   c. marginal profit.
   d. the degree of operating leverage.

ANSWER: D

8. The amount that must be paid for an item under prevailing market conditions is:
   a. historical cost.
   b. replacement cost.
   c. incremental cost.
   d. current cost.

ANSWER: D

9. The foregone value associated with the current rather than next-best use of a given asset is:
   a. replacement cost.
   b. implicit cost.
   c. explicit cost.
   d. opportunity cost.

ANSWER: D

10. Incremental cost is the change in:
    a. total cost caused by a given managerial decision.
    b. noncash expenses caused by a given managerial decision.
    c. out-of-pocket costs caused by a given managerial decision.
    d. variable cost caused by a given managerial decision.

ANSWER: A

11. Noncash expenses are:
    a. explicit costs.
    b. sunk costs.
    c. incremental costs.
    d. implicit costs.

ANSWER: D

12. In the decision process, management should ignore:
    a. implicit costs.
    b. historical costs.
    c. sunk costs.
    d. incremental costs.

ANSWER: C

13. Fixed costs include:
    a. variable labor expenses.
    b. output-related energy costs.
    c. output-related raw material costs.
    d. variable interest costs for borrowed capital.

ANSWER: D

14. Marginal cost equals:
    a. average variable cost at its maximum point.
    b. the change in total fixed cost divided by the change in quantity.
    c. the change in total variable cost divided by the change in quantity.
    d. total cost divided by quantity.

ANSWER: C

15. If the productivity of variable factors is decreasing in the short-run:
    a. marginal cost must increase as output increases.
    b. average cost must decrease as output increases.
    c. average cost must increase as output increases.
    d. marginal cost must decrease as output increases.

ANSWER: A

16. A firm's capacity is the output:
    a. maximum that can be produced in the long-run.
    b. level where short-run average costs are minimized.
    c. level where long-run average costs are minimized.
    d. maximum that can be produced in the short-run.

ANSWER: B

17. Minimum efficient scale is the output level where:
    a. long-run average cost is first minimized.
    b. long-run marginal cost is first minimized.
    c. long-run total cost is first minimized.
    d. short-run average cost is first minimized.

ANSWER: A

18. The change in cost caused by a given managerial decision is:
    a. implicit cost.
    b. incremental cost.
    c. explicit cost.
    d. opportunity cost.

ANSWER: B

The following information applies to Questions 19 and 20.

U-Do-It Furniture, Inc., sells hardwood chairs, in both kits and fully assembled forms. Customers who assemble their own chairs benefit from the lower kit price of $35 per chair. "Full-service" customers enjoy the luxury of an assembled chair, but pay a higher price of $60 per chair. Both kit and fully assembled chair prices are stable. The company has observed the following relation between the number of assembly workers employed per day and assembled chair output:

Number of Chairs Finished	Workers per day
0	0
1	5
2	9
3	12
4	14
5	15

19. How many assemblers would U-Do-It Furniture employ at a daily wage rate of $75?

    a. 1 assembler
    b. 2 assemblers
    c. 3 assemblers
    d. 4 assemblers

ANSWER: C

20. What is the highest daily wage rate U-Do-It Furniture would pay to hire four assemblers per day?

    a. $40
    b. $45
    c. $50
    d. $55

ANSWER: C

Perfect Competition and Monopoly

CMBA Objective Correlations

- Distinguish between commodity and monopoly pricing.

- Describe a disequilibrium price, and predict market changes that result.

- Evaluate the use of antitrust laws and deregulation as methods of dealing with monopoly power.

Sample Questions

1. For a firm in perfectly competitive market equilibrium:
   a. MR < AR.
   b. P > AC.
   c. P > MR.
   d. P = MC.

ANSWER: D

2. For a firm in perfectly competitive market equilibrium:
   a. MC < AC.
   b. MR > AR.
   c. P < AC.
   d. MR = MC.

ANSWER: D

3. Government-mandated wage arbitration for employers can enhance efficiency when the labor market involves:
   a. monopoly.
   b. excess seller power.
   c. perfect competition.
   d. monopsony.

ANSWER: D

4. Above-normal profits in a perfectly competitive industry are caused by:
   a. increases in demand that are successfully anticipated.
   b. decreases in cost that are successfully anticipated.
   c. increases in productivity that are successfully anticipated.
   d. luck.

ANSWER: D

5. In long-run equilibrium, monopoly prices are set a level where:
   a. price exceeds marginal revenue.
   b. industry demand equals industry supply.
   c. industry demand is less than industry supply.
   d. price exceeds average revenue.

ANSWER: A

6. For a monopoly in equilibrium:
   a. MR = MC.
   b. MC ≤ AC.
   c. MR ≤ AR.
   d. P ≥ AC.

ANSWER: A

7. The level of competition in a given market tends to increase if:
   a. minimum efficient scale of firms increases.
   b. the number of substitutes increase.
   c. significant barriers to exit are imposed.
   d. the number of potential entrants decreases.

ANSWER: B

8. In a perfectly competitive market:
   a. sellers and buyers have perfect information.
   b. entry and exit are difficult.
   c. sellers produce similar, but not identical products.
   d. each seller can affect the market price by changing output.

ANSWER: A

9. The demand curve for a unique product without substitutes is:
   a. upward sloping.
   b. downward sloping.
   c. horizontal.
   d. vertical.

ANSWER: D

10. In the short run, a perfectly competitive firm will shut down and produce nothing if:
   a. excess profits equal zero.
   b. total cost exceeds total revenue.
   c. total variable cost exceeds total revenue.
   d. the market price falls below the minimum average total cost.

ANSWER: C

11. In the long run, firms will exit a perfectly competitive industry if:
   a. excess profits exceed zero.
   b. excess profits are less than zero.
   c. total profit equals zero.
   d. excess profits equal zero.

ANSWER: B

12. A monopolist maximizes profits by producing a level of output where:
    a.   P = AC.
    b.   P > MC.
    c.   P < MC.
    d.   P = MC.

ANSWER: B

13. In the short run, a monopolist will:
    a.   shut down if price equals average total cost.
    b.   shut down if price is less than average total cost.
    c.   shut down if price is less than average variable cost.
    d.   never shut down.

ANSWER: C

14. In general, a perfectly competitive industry will sell:
    a.   less output at lower prices than monopoly.
    b.   more output at higher prices than monopoly.
    c.   less output at higher prices than monopoly.
    d.   more output at lower prices than monopoly.

ANSWER: D

15. At the profit maximizing level of output for a monopolist:
    a.   P = AR and AR = AC.
    b.   P = MC and MR > MC.
    c.   P > MC and MR = MC.
    d.   P = MR and AC = MC.

ANSWER: C

16. A monopsony employer facing a perfectly competitive supply of labor would pay a wage:
    a.   greater than the perfectly competitive wage.
    b.   equal to marginal revenue product.
    c.   greater than marginal revenue product.
    d.   less than the perfectly competitive wage.

ANSWER: D

17. Wages for labor will be highest in labor markets consisting of:
    a.   perfectly competitive buyers and a monopolist.
    b.   a monopsonist and perfectly competitive sellers.
    c.   a monopsonist and monopolist.
    d.   perfectly competitive buyers and sellers.

ANSWER: A

18. In monopoly and perfectly competitive markets, profits are maximized when:
    a.   MC = AC.
    b.   P > AC.
    c.   MR = MC.
    d.   MR = P.

ANSWER: C

19. Perfect competition is inconsistent with:
    a.   economic profits.
    b.   economic losses.
    c.   barriers to exit.
    d.   hard-to-measure product quality.

ANSWER: D

20. The labor market confrontation between Major League Baseball and the Players Association is an example of:
    a.   natural monopoly.
    b.   countervailing power.
    c.   price takers.
    d.   market structure.

ANSWER: B

21. A body of law that provides a means for victims of accidents and injury to receive just compensation is called:
    a.   the tort system.
    b.   antitrust law.
    c.   regulatory policy.
    d.   the criminal justice system.

ANSWER: A

22. A natural monopoly exists if:
    a.   marginal revenue is falling as output expands.
    b.   price equals average cost.
    c.   average cost falls as output expands.
    d.   marginal revenue equals marginal cost.

ANSWER: C

23. Government seeks to aid economic efficiency in the case of natural monopoly through:
    a.   creating government-financed corporations to compete with the natural monopolist.
    b.   subsidizing competitors.
    c.   price regulation.
    d.   breaking the natural monopolist up into smaller competitors.

ANSWER: C

24. The F.T.C. enforces antitrust laws by:
    a.   sentencing individuals up to three years imprisonment.
    b.   awarding triple damages.
    c.   issuing cease and desist orders.
    d.   imposing fines on corporations up to $1 million.

ANSWER: C

Monopolistic Competition and Oligopoly

CMBA Objective Correlations

- Differentiate among various forms of industrial organization (pure competition, monopolistic competition, oligopoly, monopoly).

- Recognize how the competitive environment affects firm decisions.

Sample Questions

1. For a firm in monopolistically competitive market equilibrium:
   a. $MC \geq AC$.
   b. $MR \leq AR$.
   c. $MR = MC$.
   d. $P \geq AC$.

ANSWER: C

2. In oligopoly equilibrium:
   a. $MC = AC$.
   b. $MC > AC$.
   c. $MR = MC$.
   d. $MC > AC$.

ANSWER: C

3. A perfectly functioning cartel results in a:
   a. monopoly equilibrium.
   b. oligopoly equilibrium.
   c. perfectly competitive equilibrium.
   d. monopolistically competitive equilibrium.

ANSWER: A

4. A successfully exploited niche market involves elements of:
   a. perfect competition.
   b. monopolistic competition.
   c. monopoly.
   d. monopsony.

ANSWER: C

5. A union with an exclusive contract to supply labor enjoys:
   a. monopsony in the labor market.
   b. monopoly in the labor market.
   c. oligopoly in the labor market.
   d. oligopsony in the labor market.

ANSWER: B

6. In both monopolistic competition and oligopoly market structures;
    a. there is easy entry and exit.
    b. consumers perceive differences among the products of various competitors.
    c. economic profits may be earned in the long run.
    d. there are many sellers.

ANSWER: B

7. When prices in monopolistically competitive markets exceed those in a perfectly competitive equilibrium, this difference is the cost of:
    a. information.
    b. market power.
    c. inefficiency.
    d. product differentiation.

ANSWER: D

8. Monopolistic competition always entails:
    a. declining LRAC.
    b. vigorous price competition.
    c. increasing LRAC.
    d. constant LRAC.

ANSWER: B

9. In a monopolistically competitive industry, firms:
    a. offer products that are not perfect substitutes.
    b. make decisions in light of expected reactions from other firms.
    c. set price equal to marginal cost.
    d. are price takers.

ANSWER: A

10. The demand curve faced by a firm in a monopolistically competitive industry is:
    a. the downward sloping industry demand curve.
    b. downward sloping.
    c. more elastic than the perfectly competitive firm's demand curve.
    d. horizontal.

ANSWER: B

11. A monopolistically competitive firm will earn short run positive economic profits if it can set a price:
    a. equal to minimum average cost.
    b. higher than average cost.
    c. equal to marginal revenue.
    d. higher than minimum average cost.

ANSWER: B

12. A perfectly functioning cartel leads to a price/output combination identical to an industry that is:
    a. monopolistic.
    b. monopolistically competitive.
    c. oligopolistic.
    d. perfectly competitive.

ANSWER: A

13. Oligopolistic firms:
    a. seldom earn economic profits.
    b. always produce differentiated products.
    c. always produce homogenous products.
    d. make decisions expecting reactions from competitors.

ANSWER: D

14. The demand faced by an industry price leader is:
    a. market demand.
    b. market demand plus the demand for output by follower firms.
    c. market demand less the supply of output by follower firms.
    d. kinked.

ANSWER: C

15. The industry supply curve is derived through the horizontal summation of firm:
    a. average cost curves.
    b. marginal revenue curves.
    c. marginal cost curves.
    d. demand curves.

ANSWER: C

16. The kinked demand curve theory of oligopoly assumes that rival firms:
    a. react to price increases.
    b. react to price increases and decreases.
    c. do not react to price changes.
    d. react to price decreases.

ANSWER: D

17. In equilibrium monopolistic competition results in:
    a. $P > AC$ and $MR = MC$.
    b. $P = MR$ and $AC = MC$.
    c. $P < MR$ and $AC < MC$.
    d. $P = AC$ and $MR = MC$.

ANSWER: D

18. Equilibrium in oligopoly markets is characterized by:
    a. $P > AC$ and $MR = MC$.
    b. $P = MR$ and $AC = MC$.
    c. $P < MR$ and $AC < MC$.
    d. $P = AC$ and $MR = MC$.

ANSWER: D

19. A firm should increase advertising if the net marginal revenue derived is:
   a. equal to the marginal cost of advertising.
   b. greater than the marginal cost of advertising.
   c. greater than zero.
   d. less than the marginal cost of advertising.

ANSWER: B

20. Concentration ratios:
   a. overstate the relative importance of firms in local markets.
   b. ignore potential entrants.
   c. measure the degree of buyer concentration.
   d. understate the relative importance of domestic firms when import competition is important.

ANSWER: B

21. The vigor of competition always decreases with a fall in:
   a. product differentiation.
   b. barriers to entry.
   c. the level of available information.
   d. the number of competitors.

ANSWER: C

22. Within a single market the cross-price elasticity of demand is:
   a. positive.
   b. negative.
   c. zero.
   d. irrelevant.

ANSWER: A

23. The four-firm concentration ratio will rise following:
   a. a rise in imports.
   b. a fall in imports.
   c. a merger between the two largest firms in the industry.
   d. small firm entry.

ANSWER: C

24. A kinked demand curve results from:
   a. different competitor reactions .
   b. competitor price reactions.
   c. an absence of competitor price reactions.
   d. supply imbalance.

ANSWER: A

Pricing Practices

CMBA Objective Correlations

- Justify a marginal-cost pricing decision. Explain how fixed costs enter pricing decisions.

- Apply the wage-pricing model to trade union behavior.

- Explain how a firm can achieve a profit-maximizing price.

Sample Questions

1. A 50% markup on cost is equivalent to a markup on price of:
   a. 25%.
   b. 33%.
   c. 50%.
   d. 100%.

ANSWER: B

2. A 50% markup on price is equivalent to a markup on cost of:
   a. 25%.
   b. 33%.
   c. 50%.
   d. 100%.

ANSWER: D

3. When $\varepsilon_P = -2$, the optimal markup on cost is:
   a. 100%.
   b. 67%
   c. 50%.
   d. 33%.

ANSWER: A

4. When $\varepsilon_P = -1$, the optimal markup on price is:
   a. 100%.
   b. 67%
   c. 50%.
   d. 33%.

ANSWER: A

5. When transferred products can be sold in perfectly competitive external markets, the optimal transfer price is the:
   a. external market price.
   b. marginal revenue of the transferred-to (buying) division.
   c. marginal revenue in the output market.
   d. marginal cost of the transferring (selling) division.

ANSWER: A

6. The most prevalent pricing practice employed by business firms is setting price equal to:
   a. average revenue.
   b. average cost.
   c. average variable cost plus a charge for overhead and profit margin.
   d. marginal revenue.

ANSWER: C

7. If a firm charges a price of $6 for a product with a cost of $4, the markup on cost equals:
   a. 67%.
   b. 33%.
   c. 150%.
   d. 50%.

·ANSWER: D

8. If a firm charges a price of $5 for a product with a cost of $2, the markup on price equals:
   a. 60%.
   b. 150%.
   c. 250%.
   d. 40%.

ANSWER: A

9. If markup on price equals 20%, markup on cost equals:
   a. 25%.
   b. 67%.
   c. 400%.
   d. 20%.

ANSWER: A

10. Profit margin equals:
    a. marginal cost minus marginal revenue.
    b. average cost minus average revenue.
    c. average cost minus average variable cost.
    d. price minus cost.

ANSWER: D

11. During off-peak periods, firms should base their markup pricing on:
    a. fully allocated costs.
    b. incremental costs.
    c. sunk costs.
    d. historical costs.

ANSWER: B

12. The optimal markup on price will fall following an increase in:
    a. cost.
    b. revenue.
    c. the price elasticity of demand.
    d. price.

ANSWER: C

13. If marginal cost is $20 and the price elasticity of demand is -5, the optimal price is:
    a. $25.
    b. $30.
    c. $100.
    d. $24.

ANSWER: A

14. If the price elasticity of demand is -2, the optimal markup on price is:
    a. 50%.
    b. 67%.
    c. 100%.
    d. 20%.

ANSWER: A

15. When engaging in short-run incremental analysis, managers should ignore:
    a. fixed costs.
    b. implicit costs.
    c. explicit costs.
    d. effects on the costs of already existing products.

ANSWER: A

16. Successful price discrimination requires:
    a. the ability to prevent transfers among customers in different submarkets.
    b. inelastic demand in each submarket.
    c. constant marginal costs.
    d. identical price elasticities among submarkets.

ANSWER: A

17. A firm supplying a single product to two distinct submarkets will maximizes profits by equating:
    a. average revenue in each market to average cost.
    b. average revenue in each market to marginal cost.
    c. marginal revenue in each market to marginal cost.
    d. price in each market to marginal cost.

ANSWER: C

18. When products A and B are produced in fixed proportions, profits will be maximized when marginal cost:
    a. equals marginal revenue of B.
    b. of B equals zero.
    c. equals marginal revenue of A plus B.
    d. equals marginal revenue of A.

ANSWER: C

19. If $\varepsilon_P = -3$, the optimal markup on price is:
    a. 33%.
    b. 50%.
    c. 300%.
    d. 25%.

ANSWER: A

20. If $\varepsilon_P = -3$, the optimal markup on cost is:
    a. 33%.
    b. 50%.
    c. 300%.
    d. 25%.

ANSWER: B

21. If the optimal markup on price is 50%, the optimal markup on cost is:
    a. 100%.
    b. 75%.
    c. 50%.
    d. 25%.

ANSWER: A

22. If the optimal markup on cost is 25%, the optimal markup on price is:
    a. 20%.
    b. 25%.
    c. 50%.
    d. 100%.

ANSWER: A

23. If MC = \$4 and ε_P = -2, the optimal markup on price is:
   a. \$8.
   b. \$4.
   c. \$2.
   d. 33%.

ANSWER: B

24. Price discrimination exists when:
   a. prices are set according to the price elasticity of demand.
   b. markups differ.
   c. prices differ.
   d. costs differ.

ANSWER: B

25. With price discrimination, lower prices are charged when:
   a. the price elasticity of demand is high.
   b. the price elasticity of demand is low.
   c. the cross-price elasticity of demand is high.
   d. the cross-price elasticity of demand is low.

ANSWER: A

Marketing

Marketing Strategy and Tactics

CMBA Objective Correlations

- Given a firm's particular marketing strategy (product/service, price, place, or promotion), select the appropriate corresponding marketing strategy (product/service, price, place, or promotion) for the firm.

- Given a particular market scenario, select the appropriate marketing strategy (product/service, price, place, or promotion) for a firm.

- Describe the relationship between type of decision-making (routinized, limited, extended) and marketing strategy (product/service, price, place, or promotion).

Sample Questions

1. The marketing mix _____.
    a. consists of product, pricing, distribution, and promotion decisions
    b. deals with delegating authority
    c. is how products are perceived by consumers in the marketplace
    d. consists of homogeneous groups of consumers who have similar wants and needs
    e. all of the above

ANSWER: A

2. _____ identifies important trends in the environment and then considers the potential impact of these changes on the firm's existing marketing strategy.
    a. Integrated marketing communications
    b. marketing channels
    c. marketing mix
    d. promotion mix
    e. environmental scanning

ANSWER: E

3. Marketing plan strategies in the area of product may include
    a. determining the variable costs of a product and establishing profit margin.
    b. changing packaging graphics and repositioning the product.
    c. selecting marketing channels and the level of customer service.
    d. determining the advertising message and the media vehicles.

ANSWER: B

4. Marketing plan strategies in the area of pricing may include
    a. determining the variable costs of a product and establishing profit margin.
    b. changing packaging graphics and repositioning the product.
    c. selecting marketing channels and the level of customer service.
    d. determining the advertising message and the media vehicles.

ANSWER: B

5. Marketing plan strategies in the area of promotion may include
    a. determining the variable costs of a product and establishing profit margin.
    b. changing packaging graphics and repositioning the product.
    c. selecting marketing channels and the level of customer service.
    d. determining the advertising message and the media vehicles.

ANSWER: D

6. Marketing plan strategies in the area of place, or distribution, may include
    a. determining the variable costs of a product and establishing profit margin.
    b. changing packaging graphics and repositioning the product.
    c. selecting marketing channels and the level of customer service.
    d. determining the advertising message and the media vehicles.

ANSWER: C

7. Which of the following is the best example of a marketing objective with an accompanying marketing strategy to achieve the objective?
    a. Objective: to achieve high brand awareness; strategy: to expand the product line.
    b. Objective: to achieve industry leadership; strategy: to improve the packaging.
    c. Objective: to increase profit margins; strategy: to decrease the product's price
    d. Objective: to achieve 20% market share; strategy: to expand the product line.

ANSWER: D

8. Which of the following is the best example of a cost leadership strategy?
    a. Compaq Computer sells many different types of computers.
    b. Maxwell House sells Colombian Supreme coffee under the Maxwell House brand.
    c. American Express sells its Gold Card to upper middle income users.
    d. Honda sells high volume and low priced Honda Civic cars.

ANSWER: D

9. As a generic competitive strategy, differentiation
    a. is practiced by firms with the highest quality brands.
    b. is practiced by firms with a niche market segment.
    c. is practiced by firms with large economies of scale.
    d. is practiced by firms with many employees.

ANSWER: A

10. Which of the following is the best example of a differentiation strategy?
   a. Compaq Computer sells many different types of computers.
   b. Maxwell House sells Colombian Supreme coffee under the Maxwell House brand.
   c. American Express sells its Gold Card to upper middle income users.
   d. Honda sells high volume and low priced Honda Civic cars.

ANSWER: B

11. As a generic competitive strategy, focus
   a. is practiced by firms with the highest quality brands.
   b. is practiced by firms with a niche market segment.
   c. is practiced by firms with large economies of scale.
   d. is practiced by firms with many employees.

ANSWER: B

12. Which of the following is the best example of a focus strategy?
   a. Compaq Computer sells many different types of computers.
   b. Maxwell House sells Colombian Supreme coffee under the Maxwell House brand.
   c. American Express sells its Gold Card to upper middle income users.
   d. Honda sells high volume and low priced Honda Civic cars.

ANSWER: C

13. The two main strategies practiced by market leaders in an industry are
   a. market expansion and defense of market share.
   b. market expansion and market flanking attacks.
   c. defense of market share and frontal attacks.
   d. defense of market share and guerrilla warfare.

ANSWER: A

14. A major baking soda marketer discovered that consumers were using its product in a variety of ways: for baking, for deodorizing refrigerators, for cleaning teeth, and for deodorizing garbage disposals. As a result, the company began to market these new uses more aggressively to the same group of people. Which of the following strategies best describes the above?
   a. Market development.
   b. Diversification.
   c. Market penetration.
   d. Product development.

ANSWER: C

15. A large pharmaceutical firm discovered that taking one aspirin a day was useful for preventing heart attacks. As a result, it began to market its aspirin brand as preventive medicine for consumers interested in maintaining good cardiovascular health, rather than just a reactive medicine for consumers with headaches. Which of the following strategies best describes the above?
    a. Market development.
    b. Diversification.
    c. Market penetration.
    d. Product development.

ANSWER: A

16. A car manufacturer attempts to trade its current customer base to an improved and more expensive version of the car model which the customers own. Which of the following strategies best describes the above?
    a. Market development.
    b. Diversification.
    c. Market penetration.
    d. Product development.

ANSWER: D

17. A large tobacco company acquires a major packaged foods product company to enter new markets. Which of the following strategies best describes the above?
    a. Market development.
    b. Diversification.
    c. Market penetration.
    d. Product development.

ANSWER: B

18. Daimler-Benz, the maker of Mercedes-Benz automobiles, decided to get into the aerospace and transport equipment business. Which of the following strategies best describes the above?
    a. Complementary diversification.
    b. Additive diversification.
    c. Conglomerate diversification.
    d. Collaboration.

ANSWER: C

19. IBM acquired Lotus, the maker of Lotus 1-2-3 and other software. Which of the following strategies best describes the above?
    a. Complementary diversification.
    b. Additive diversification.
    c. Conglomerate diversification.
    d. Collaboration.

ANSWER: A

Marketing Research and Information Systems

CMBA Objective Correlations

- Describe the benefits and drawbacks of research contact methods (personal, mail, telephone, online).

- Given a firm's particular research objective, select the appropriate research approach (focus group, survey, etc).

Sample Questions

1. The first step of the market research process is _____.
   a. search secondary data sources databases
   b. to meet the problem and determine how to solve it
   c. problem recognition
   d. undertake thorough primary research
   e. analyze information

   ANSWER: C

2. Which of the following is NOT one of the stages on the market research process?
   a. meet and define problem and determine how to solve it
   b. problem recognition
   c. undertake quick and dirty primary research
   d. hire a market research specialist
   e. undertake thorough primary research

   ANSWER: D

3. In the _____ stage of the market research process, the marketer is considering the value of highly accurate information.
   a. problem recognition
   b. meet and define problem and determine how to solve it
   c. undertake thorough primary research
   d. search secondary data sources and databases
   e. undertake quick and dirty primary research

   ANSWER: B

4. Which of the following stages of the market research process would the marketer select the sampling frame of a study.
   a. meet and define problem and determine how to solve it
   b. undertake quick-and-dirty primary research
   c. problem recognition
   d. undertake thorough primary research
   e. search secondary data sources and own databases

   ANSWER: D

5. A marketer who is choosing the survey technique, is in the _____ stage of the market research process.
   a. undertake quick-and-dirty primary research
   b. search secondary data sources and databases
   c. problem recognition
   d. undertake thorough primary research
   e. present findings

   ANSWER: D

6. Which of the following is a carefully recruited group of six to twelve people who participate in a freewheeling one- to two-hour discussion that focuses on a particular subject?
   a. moderating session
   b. team building session
   c. focus group
   d. discussion group
   e. conversational team

   ANSWER: C

7. The leader of a focus group is called the _____.
   a. team leader
   b. team builder
   c. team organizer
   d. group leader
   e. moderator

   ANSWER: E

8. A basis for selecting focus group members would include _____.
   a. age
   b. gender
   c. income
   d. occupation
   e. all of the above

   ANSWER: E

9. A _____ sample is that part of a sample that is left unchanged and serves as a basis of comparison to allow analysis or the results of the experiment.
   a. marginal
   b. experimental
   c. convenience
   d. control
   e. planned

   ANSWER: D

10. Which of the following types of information allow identification of customer segments based on geographical location and demographic information?
    a. psychographic
    b. behavioral
    c. geodemographic
    d. attitudinal
    e. motivational

    ANSWER: C

11. Which of the following is NOT a survey method in marketing research?
    a. direct/cold mailing
    b. mail panels
    c. telephone
    d. observation
    e. mall intercept

    ANSWER: D

12. Which of the following is the most flexible survey method?
    a. focus groups
    b. telephone
    c. personal in-home
    d. mall intercept
    e. mail panels

    ANSWER: D

13. The survey method where a researcher can get the greatest quantity of information is _____.
    a. observation
    b. personal in-home
    c. telephone
    d. mall intercept
    e. direct/cold mailing

    ANSWER: B

14. Which of the following survey methods provides the greatest degree of control?
    a. personal in-home
    b. mall intercept
    c. observation
    d. telephone
    e. mail panel

    ANSWER: A

15. The _____ survey method is best for asking sensitive questions of respondents.
    a. focus groups
    b. mall intercept
    c. personal in-home
    d. telephone
    e. direct/cold mailing

    ANSWER: E

16. The direct/cold mailing survey method is best when _____.
    a. it is a complex survey
    b. a huge quantity of data is required from the respondents
    c. there are sensitive or embarrassing questions
    d. a high response rate is needed
    e. a high level of sample control is needed

    ANSWER: C

17. Response rates tend to be highest with the _____ survey method.
    a. focus group
    b. telephone
    c. personal in-home
    d. mall intercept
    e. mail panel

    ANSWER: C

18. Which of the following survey methods is most appropriate in measuring opinions of people in low incidence categories?
    a. mailing of direct/cold
    b. telephone
    c. mail panels
    d. mall intercept
    e. calling

    ANSWER: C

Business-to-Business Marketing

CMBA Objective Correlations

- Given a particular marketing objective for a company, select the appropriate person(s) (initiator, influencer, decider, buyer, user) at whom to direct a marketing campaign.

- Describe the differences between consumer and organizational markets.

- Given a particular problem encountered by a firm attempting to sell to an organizational buyer, infer the most likely cause.

Sample Questions

1. The business market consists of the following three components:
   a. commercial enterprises, resellers, and government.
   b. manufacturers, institutions and defense.
   c. manufacturers, service organizations and defense.
   d. commercial enterprises, service organizations and government.
   e. commercial enterprises, institutions, and government.

   ANSWER: E

2. The factors that distinguish business marketing from consumer marketing are:
   a. the level of effort spent on developing marketing strategy.
   b. the nature of the customer and how the customer uses the product.
   c. the goals and objectives established for marketing activities.
   d. whether the products will be consumed or used for other purposes.
   e. all of the above.

   ANSWER: B

3. Products like calculators are purchased in both consumer and business markets. What distinguishes business marketing from consumer marketing is:
   a. the intended use of the product and the intended consumer.
   b. the importance of price.
   c. the importance of quality.
   d. the number of new customers that may exist in the consumer market.
   e. the fact that buyers in the consumer market may not ever work in a business.

   ANSWER: A

4. Institutional customers are:
   a. Made up of government buying organizations as well as schools and hospitals.
   b. More similar to governments than corporations in the way they buy.
   c. Frequently staffed by professionals who often play key roles in the purchasing process.
   d. Similar to business in that they always use purchasing agents to make key buying decisions.
   e. Usually more difficult to satisfy because of the diversity of their needs.

   ANSWER: C

5. Although business and consumer markets differ, they are similar in that:
   a. Consumer markets are dependent on derived demand to stimulate growth.
   b. Understanding customer needs and satisfying them effectively is the key to marketing success.
   c. Both markets experience extreme fluctuations in demand.
   d. Both focus equal attention on the emphasis placed on personal selling.
   e. All of the above.

   ANSWER: B

6. The demand for business products and services tend to fluctuate more than the demand for household consumer goods because:
   a. Business products and services usually require marketing managers to have knowledge about a wider array of market situations.
   b. It is more difficult to forecast demand for business products.
   c. There are more final consumers, which makes demand for consumer goods more stable.
   d. Consumer products marketers smooth out demand by heavy use of advertising.
   e. Major swings in demand for consumer goods caused by changes in economic conditions will result in large changes in the demand for products to make the consumer goods.

   ANSWER: E

7. DuPont, a very large business marketer, will advertise to final consumers primarily to:
   a. stimulate demand for products using their materials.
   b. decrease the derived demand for nylon products.
   c. expand demand for DuPont materials sold to institutions.
   d. create a favorable image of consumer products.
   e. all the above.

   ANSWER: A

8. The same product may elicit markedly different purchasing patterns in different organizations. As a result:
   a. Business marketers need to focus their strategies on all buying influences.
   b. Attention needs to be focused on buying situations rather than on products.
   c. The modified rebuy tends to predominate the types of situations encountered.
   d. Products need to be classified on the basis of their buying characteristics.
   e. Purchasing patterns tend to vary considerably between different business customers.

   ANSWER: B

9. Organizational buyers do not have well-defined criteria that can be applied to the procurement problem in:
   a. Selective response behavior.
   b. Modified rebuy situations.
   c. New task buying situations.
   d. Straight rebuy situations.
   e. Purchasing expensive accessory equipment.

   ANSWER: C

10. The decision used by organizational buyers in the straight rebuy situation is:
    a. Limited problem solving.
    b. Routine problem solving.
    c. Extended problem solving.
    d. Modified problem solving.
    e. Any of the above.

    ANSWER: B

11. The marketers task in the straight rebuy situation:
    a. depends on whether the seller is an "in" supplier or an "out" supplier.
    b. is focused on understanding the information requirements of the buyer.
    c. is straight forward in that all the seller has to do is convince the buyer to shop around.
    d. depends on how long the seller has been unable to effectively solve their need.
    e. is based upon creating a positive image in the minds of all decision influencers.

    ANSWER: A

12. In the modified rebuy situation, organizational decision makers:
    a. Are not receptive to alternative solutions to their purchasing need.
    b. Usually have limited understanding of their requirements.
    c. Believe it is worthwhile to seek additional information and consider alternative solutions.
    d. Operate in a stage of extended problem solving.
    e. Lack strong predispositions toward a particular solution.

    ANSWER: C

13. In the modified rebuy situation, the marketing effort:
    a. Should be focused on the strengths of competitive offers.
    b. Depends on how much information is needed by the buyer.
    c. Is difficult to develop because the seller lacks knowledge of the buyer's feelings of risk associated with the purchase decision.
    d. Depends on whether the marketer is an "in" supplier or an "out" supplier.
    e. All the above.

    ANSWER: D

14. The buying decisions of organizations are influenced by:
    a. Environmental factors.
    b. Organizational factors.
    c. Group factors.
    d. Individual factors.
    e. All the above affect buying decisions.

    ANSWER: E

15. The key environmental factor that shapes organizational buying behavior is:
    a. Weather.
    b. Trends and fads.
    c. Politics.
    d. Corporate culture.
    e. All the above.

    ANSWER: C

16. The buying center is:
    a. Composed of individuals who are formally assigned to it.
    b. An office assigned to make purchase decisions.
    c. Generally found only in commercial enterprises.
    d. Given only an advisory role in the purchase decision.
    e. Made up of personnel who participate in the purchase decision or who share goals associated with the decision.

    ANSWER: E

17. The composition of the buying center:
    a. Evolves during the purchasing process.
    b. Varies from one purchasing situation to another.
    c. Varies from firm to firm.
    d. Cannot be identified by the organization chart.
    e. All the above.

    ANSWER: E

18. Because organizational buying is a process rather than an isolated act,
    a. The individuals involved remain constant during the process.
    b. The buying center is often given detailed responsibilities based on strategic priorities.
    c. Different individuals are important to the process at different times.
    d. The process can be halted and easily restarted.
    e. The buying group will be established prior to assessing alternative purchasing solutions.

    ANSWER: C

19. It is important for the business marketer to identify the members of the buying center and understand:
    a. Who is the most senior level person in the buying center.
    b. Each participant's relative influence and evaluative criteria.
    c. Each participant's function and relative influence.
    d. Each participant's influence, function, title and evaluative criteria.
    e. The role each member will play and how long they have held membership in the buying center.

    ANSWER: B

20. In the buying center, the individual who actually makes the buying decision, whether or not they have the formal authority to do so, is performing the role of:
    a. User.
    b. Decider.
    c. Gatekeeper.
    d. Buyer.
    e. Influencer.

    ANSWER: B

21. Individuals who control the flow of information into the buying center are performing the role of:
    a. User.
    b. Gatekeeper.
    c. Implementer.
    d. Decider.
    e. Buyer.

    ANSWER: B

22. Within the buying center, an individual who has formal authority for selecting a supplier and all procedures connected with securing the product is performing the role of:
    a. Decider.
    b. User.
    c. Influencer.
    d. Buyer.
    e. Gatekeeper.

    ANSWER: D

Segmenting, Targeting, and Positioning Products and Services

CMBA Objective Correlations

- Given certain market characteristics (size; demographic, geographic, psychographic, and/or behavioral descriptors), select the appropriate segmentation scheme for a firm.

- Given a particular product/service, identify the appropriate target market for a firm.

- Given characteristics (competitors' sizes and positions) of a particular market, select the appropriate positioning strategy for a firm.

- Describe the criteria for segmenting markets.

Sample Questions

1. Which of the following is NOT a good example of matching the marketing mix to the target market?
   a. Advertising luxury automobiles in a Teen magazine
   b. Playing soft romantic music at an expensive restaurant
   c. Offering music discounts to students
   d. Advertising mascara a fashion magazine
   e. Giving pizza coupons to college students

   ANSWER: A

2. Obler Company has developed a shoe that comfortable fits people whose second toe is far longer than the first. This firm is practicing:
   a. Mass marketing.
   b. Specialization.
   c. Market retention.
   d. Niche marketing.
   e. Market penetration.

   ANSWER: D

3. Blake's is a highly renowned clothes retailer. The price for a men's dress shirt in the store is in the $100-200 range. Which of the following would be the least viable target marketing strategy?
   a. Advertising in the arts section of a local newspaper.
   b. Using zip codes for affluent neighborhoods to target direct mail.
   c. Directly contacting local upscale businesses.
   d. Posting flyers at the local discount store.
   e. Advertising in a local business magazine.

   ANSWER: D

4. RV Village, a company that sells recreational vehicles (RVs), has determined that most purchasers of RVs are between the ages of 35 and 54 with an annual income over $75,000. This information about the market will help RV Village to:
   a. Increase brand loyalty.
   b. Offer fewer products.
   c. Create a customized marketing mix.
   d. Reduce opportunities available for product sales.
   e. Increase the price on most models of RVs.

   ANSWER: C

5. A firm advertising golf equipment in a teenage fashion magazine would most likely see:
   a. An increase in product sales and a decrease in costs.
   b. A decrease in product sales and an increase in costs.
   c. More teenagers playing golf.
   d. An increase in marketing cost effectiveness.
   e. An increase in sales of most golf equipment.

   ANSWER: B

6. 2000 census data revealed that the number of teens will increase from 23.2 million to 26 million in the next five years. Considering that the numbers of teens in the marketplace is large and growing and that teens' favorite food is pizza, a new pizza franchise known as The Popular Pizza Place with locations next to high schools in many cities is being developed. This is an example of which of the following advantages of target marketing?
   a. Defining the market for analysis
   b. Assessing demand potential
   c. Identifying competitors
   d. Product positioning
   e. Identifying market opportunities

   ANSWER: E

7. An advertisement for cookware shows a woman working over a stove preparing a meal for her husband. The slogan reads "Helping you serve the king of your castle!" This advertisement is an example of which of the following target market disadvantages?
   a. Increased costs
   b. Stereotyping
   c. Unethical advertising
   d. Faux segmentation
   e. Decreased brand loyalty

   ANSWER: B

8. Slide and Sleigh, a company that manufacturers snow sleds, conducted research to determine which geographic areas of the country had annual snow fall rates in excess of 25 inches each year. This is an example of which of the following steps in the target marketing selection process?
    a. Identification of the total market
    b. Profile each selected segment
    c. Select positioning strategy
    d. Develop and implement appropriate marketing mix
    e. Monitor, evaluate, and control

    ANSWER: A

9. A manufacturer determines that there are a large number of boat owners that earn more than $100,000 in his area. A yacht is developed aimed at this group of customers. This is an example of:
    a. positioning segmenting.
    b. post hoc segmenting.
    c. a priori segmenting.
    d. unethical segmenting.
    e. cluster segmenting.

    ANSWER: C

10. Tasty Tea Company has existing data about their customers that regularly buy their products. The company sends their best customers coupons knowing they will be more likely to purchase even more of the product. This is an example of:
    a. Positioning segmentation.
    b. Post hoc segmentation.
    c. Priori segmentation.
    d. Unethical segmentation.
    e. Clustering.

    ANSWER: B

11. Elvira Electronics has decided to use a picture of a space ship on all its advertisements, packaging, etc., to better inform potential consumers that its products are "out of this world." This determination most likely occurred during which of the following steps in the target marketing selection process?
    a. Identify the total market
    b. Determine bases for segmentation
    c. Profile each selected segment
    d. Assess potential profitability of each segment
    e. Select positioning strategy

    ANSWER: E

12. Salt is an example of a product that likely does not meet which of the following criteria for successful segmentation?
    a. Measurable
    b. Accessible
    c. Heterogeneous
    d. Accessible
    e. Substantial

    ANSWER: C

13. To justify segmenting a target market, the segment must be:
    a. The right age.
    b. In the geographical region.
    c. The right gender.
    d. Accessible and reachable.
    e. Heterogeneous.

    ANSWER: D

14. Betty Crocker has developed one marketing mix strategy that is appropriate for all members of the total market. This is known as a(n):
    a. Concentrated targeting strategy.
    b. Differentiated targeting strategy.
    c. External factor strategy.
    d. Undifferentiated targeting strategy.
    e. Target market strategy.

    ANSWER: D

15. Which of the following would be the best targeting strategy for Morton's Salt?
    a. Concentrated strategy.
    b. Undifferentiated strategy.
    c. Differentiated strategy.
    d. External factor strategies.
    e. Target market strategy.

    ANSWER: B

16. Coca-Cola has one marketing mix aimed at ten different segments. This is an example of a(n):
    a. Cluster strategy.
    b. Undifferentiated strategy.
    c. Differentiated strategy.
    d. Concentrated strategy.
    e. Unconcentrated strategy.

    ANSWER: D

17. When a firm develops different marketing mixes specially tailored for each of two market segments, it is using a(n):
    a. Unconcentrated strategy.
    b. Concentrated strategy.
    c. Undifferentiated strategy.
    d. Differentiated strategy.
    e. Target market strategy.

    ANSWER: D

18. When considering strategic targeting factors, two major categories must be considered. These are:
    a. Why and when to implement.
    b. How and where to implement the strategies.
    c. Strategic and external factors.
    d. Homogeneous demand vs. heterogeneous demand.
    e. Competitive vs. economic factors.

    ANSWER: C

19. Golden Years Vitamin Group is targeting a product to consumers over age 60 and living in Florida. This is an example of _____ segmentation.
    a. Psychographic.
    b. Demographic.
    c. Benefit sought.
    d. Usage.
    e. Geodemographic.

    ANSWER: E

20. When segmenting market of teenagers that snowboard in Colorado, which of the following segmentation bases are being used?
    a. Benefit sought and demographics
    b. Psychographics and geographics
    c. Psychographics, demographics, and geographics
    d. Demographics, benefit sought, and psychographics
    e. Usage rate, demographics, geographics

    ANSWER: C

21. If Ford Motor Company decided to develop a new car model aimed at consumers who are slightly rebellious, like jazz music, are democrats, and volunteer for charity work regularly, they would be using which of the following bases for segmentation?
    a. Demographics
    b. Psychographics
    c. Benefits sought
    d. Behavior or usage
    e. Geographics

    ANSWER: B

22. The famous Miller Lite beer advertising campaign that told heavy beer drinkers that Miller Lite was "less filling, tastes great" is an example of market segmentation based on:
    a. demographics.
    b. geographics.
    c. situation.
    d. behavior.
    e. psychographics.

    ANSWER: D

23. There are some consumers who want toothpaste to whiten their teeth while other consumers want toothpaste to fight cavities. These differences provide an opportunity for using which of the following segmentation variables?
    a. Demographic
    b. Benefit sought
    c. Behavior
    d. Geographic
    e. Psychographic

    ANSWER: B

24. The golden arches of McDonald's is an example of using a(n) _____ to position their product in consumers' minds:
    a. symbol
    b. attribute
    c. product class
    d. market
    e. competitor

    ANSWER: A

25. The Marlboro man is an example of positioning a product by:
    a. Product attributes.
    b. Price/quality.
    c. Product class.
    d. Competition.
    e. Product user.

    ANSWER: E

26. If Dell Computer segmented its business customers into different segments based on size and speed of order, Dell would be using which of the following segmentation descriptors?
    a. Purchasing approaches
    b. Product use
    c. Demographics
    d. Geographics
    e. Situation

    ANSWER: A

27. A large restaurant chain has the same brand of icemaker as a smaller chain. Ice machines at the large chain do not need servicing by the seller because they have their own repairperson. Knowing this, the seller may revise its marketing mix and segment markets based on:
    a. Product usage.
    b. Resource allocations.
    c. Expenditure.
    d. Purchasing approaches.
    e. Situational factors.

    ANSWER: A

Product Decisions and New Product Development

CMBA Objective Correlations

- Given a particular product life cycle stage (introduction, growth, maturity, or decline), identify the role played by a specific marketing mix variable (product/service, price, place, or promotion).

- Given a particular product life cycle stage (introduction, growth, maturity, or decline), select the appropriate marketing strategy (product/service, price, place, or promotion).

- Describe the marketing objective of a firm whose product/service is in a particular stage of the product life cycle (introduction, growth, maturity, or decline).

- Describe the primary risk associated with filling a product line.

- Describe the primary rationale for brand extensions.

- Describe the differences between products and services.

- Given a firm's growth objective, select the appropriate product/service strategy.

- Given acquisition costs, revenue, contribution margin, discount rate, and loyalty period, calculate lifetime customer value.

- Describe customer perceived value.

Sample Questions

1. A product is classified as a consumer product if it is:
   a. to be used in assembling a finished product
   b. a major capital good
   c. purchased by a consumer for household use
   d. used in support of business operations
   e. not a service offering

   ANSWER: C

2. The depth of a firm's product mix is defined by the:
   a. number of brands a company markets across its product lines
   b. number of different product lines a company offers
   c. full set of products a company markets
   d. group of related items in a company's product portfolio
   e. number of brands within a particular product line

   ANSWER: E

3. Which of the following is not an advantage to a firm that offers multiple product lines?
   a. Allows more products to manage and account for
   b. Avoids product obsolescence
   c. Offsets cyclical product sales fluctuations
   d. Protection against competitive action
   e. Achieves greater market impact

   ANSWER: A

4. At one time, Phillip Morris, Inc. paid four times the book value for both Kraft and General Foods companies. Which of the following reasons justifies why that decision was warranted?
    a. Other firms were also bidding for these companies, driving the purchase price up.
    b. Management of the acquired companies was able to negotiate a good price.
    c. They expected the new products to be commercialized by these firms in the future to increase the value of the firms by this much.
    d. The reputation and good will of their brand names (their brand equity) were worth the price in the long-run.
    e. They made a poor management decision.

    ANSWER: D

5. When using a market development growth strategy, a firm:
    a. seeks to sell more of its existing products to new markets.
    b. seeks to sell more of its existing products to existing markets.
    c. seeks to grow in existing markets by developing new products for those markets.
    d. develops growth in new markets through developing new products that appeal to these markets.
    e. grows its current market by cutting prices.

    ANSWER: A

6. In a product diversification growth strategy, a firm will:
    a. seek to sell more of its existing products to new markets.
    b. seek to sell more of its existing products to existing markets.
    c. seek to grow in existing markets by developing new products for those markets.
    d. develop growth in new markets through developing new products that appeal to these markets.
    e. grow its current market by cutting prices.

    ANSWER: D

7. Most of the new products commercialized by firms are considered:
    a. New-to-the-world
    b. New product lines
    c. Improvements to existing products
    d. Repositionings of current products
    e. Cost reductions

    ANSWER: C

8. During the growth stage of the product life cycle:
    a. sales start a long-term decline, as substitute products offer superior sets of benefits.
    b. the market is saturated because the vast majority have become regular product purchasers.
    c. there is rapidly increasing market demand and new competitors entering the market.
    d. a few early adopters try the product, generating sales that are slowly growing.
    e. demand is stagnant.

    ANSWER: C

9. The mature stage of the product life cycle is characterized by:
   a. sales that start a long-term decline, as substitute products offer superior sets of benefits.
   b. a saturated market, because the vast majority have become regular product purchasers.
   c. rapidly increasing market demand and new competitors entering the market.
   d. no market, because no one is now purchasing the product.
   e. a few early adopters trying the product, generating sales that are slowly growing.

   ANSWER: B

10. During the decline stage of the product life cycle:
    a. sales start a long-term decline, as substitute products offer superior sets of benefits.
    b. the market is saturated because the vast majority have become regular product purchasers.
    c. there is rapidly increasing market demand and new competitors entering the market.
    d. a few early adopters try the product, generating sales that are slowly growing.
    e. there is constant demand as replacement sales take place.

    ANSWER: A

11. Which of the following must be adapted to meet the special opportunities and challenges of each stage of the product life cycle?
    a. The organizational structure of the firm
    b. The management structure of the firm
    c. The marketing strategy and tactics for the product
    d. The manufacturing strategy for the product
    e. The project leader

    ANSWER: C

12 Which of the following groups of terms best describes a service?
   a. objects, devices, and performances
   b. effort, objects, and deeds
   c. things, devices, and performances
   d. objects, devices, and things
   e. deeds, effort, and performances

   ANSWER: E

13. Services can be characterized by all of the following characteristics except for:
    a. Intangibility.
    b. Homogeneity.
    c. Perishability.
    d. Inseparability.
    e. Heterogeneity.

    ANSWER: B

14. Which of the following statements is false?
    a. Services cannot be touched or seen in the same manner as goods.
    b. Consumer judgements about services tend to be more subjective than objective.
    c. The consumption of services is often separated by time and space.
    d. Services tend to vary from one transaction to the next.
    e. Services cannot be inventoried.

    ANSWER: C

15. There are four unique service characteristics that distinguish goods from services. The one that is the primary source of the other three characteristics is:
    a. intangibility.
    b. inseparability.
    c. homogeneity.
    d. perishability.
    e. heterogeneity.

    ANSWER: A

16. In comparison to goods, services are more subjectively evaluated due to _____.
    a. intangibility
    b. inseparability
    c. homogeneity
    d. perishability
    e. heterogeneity

    ANSWER: A

17. Product attributes that can be determined prior to purchase such as price, fit, feel, and color are called:
    a. search attributes.
    b. cognitive attributes.
    c. experience attributes.
    d. involvement attributes.
    e. credence attributes.

    ANSWER: A

18. Product attributes that can be evaluated only during and after the production process, such as a meal at a restaurant or the quality of a haircut, are called:
    a. search attributes.
    b. cognitive attributes.
    c. experience attributes.
    d. involvement attributes.
    e. credence attributes.

    ANSWER: C

19. Services are primarily characterized by which of the following types of attributes?
    a. search and cognitive
    b. experience and credence
    c. cognitive and involvement
    d. search and experience
    e. search and credence

    ANSWER: B

20. _____ focuses the firm's marketing efforts toward the existing customer base.
    a. Customer retention
    b. Conquest marketing
    c. Services marketing
    d. Market expansion
    e. Product development

    ANSWER: A

21. _____ seeks new customers by offering discounts and developing promotions that encourage new business.
    a. Customer retention
    b. Frequency marketing
    c. Conquest marketing
    d. Relationship marketing
    e. Aftermarketing

    ANSWER: C

Marketing Channels and Distribution

CMBA Objective Correlations

- Describe yield management.

- Given a particular product/service type, select the appropriate distribution strategy (direct, intensive, selective, exclusive).

- Explain the role of the channel.

- Describe the difference between a channel and a supply chain.

Sample Questions

1. The _____ channel is that part of the channel involved in buying, selling, and transferring title.
   a. Facilitating
   b. Physical
   c. Advertising
   d. Sales
   e. Form

   ANSWER: D

2. _____ are part of the sales channel.
   a. Public storage firms
   b. Insurance companies
   c. Market research firms
   d. Transportation companies
   e. Consumers

   ANSWER: E

3. _____ are part of the sales channel.
   a. Retailers
   b. Finance companies
   c. Insurance companies
   d. Public storage firms
   e. Transportation companies

   ANSWER: A

4. _____ are part of the facilitating channels.
   a. Manufacturers
   b. Retailers
   c. Consumers
   d. Transportation companies
   e. None of the above

   ANSWER: D

5. The form or shape that a marketing channel takes to perform the tasks necessary to make products available to consumers is usually referred to as _____.
   a. distribution channels
   b. channel length
   c. channel structure
   d. channel intensity
   e. channel flow

   ANSWER: C

6. Channel structure is _____.
   a. the form or shape that a marketing channel takes to perform the tasks necessary to make products available to consumers
   b. the network of organizations that creates time, place, and possession utilities for consumers and business users
   c. the number of levels in a marketing channel
   d. the number of intermediaries at each level of the marketing channel
   e. the effort to reduce the number of transactions between producers and consumers

   ANSWER: A

7. Channel length _____.
   a. consists of all the businesses and institutions who are involved in performing the functions of buying, selling, and transferring title
   b. is the number of levels in a marketing channel
   c. refers to the number of intermediaries at each level of the marketing channel
   d. refers to the actual movement of the product from the manufacturer to the final consumers
   e. refers to the broad set of principles by which a firm seeks to achieve its distribution objectives to satisfy its customers

   ANSWER: B

8. The number of channels in a marketing channel is known as _____.
   a. channel structure
   b. channel intensity
   c. channel length
   d. channel flows
   e. channel systems

   ANSWER: C

9. A factor that would influence the length of the channel structure would include _____.
   a. geographical dispersion of customer base
   b. perishability of the product
   c. weight of the product
   d. behavior patterns of the customer base
   e. all of the above

   ANSWER: E

10. A firm is using _____ distribution when all possible intermediaries at a particular level of the channel are used.
    a. Priority
    b. Intensive
    c. Selective
    d. Intentional
    e. Exclusive

    ANSWER: B

11. Intensive distribution would most likely be used for _____.
    a. soda pop
    b. fur coats
    c. Trucks
    d. Computers
    e. football helmets

    ANSWER: A

12. Selective distribution would most likely be used for _____.
    a. Diet Pepsi
    b. Rolex watches
    c. Levi's jeans
    d. Gillette razor blades
    e. Hallmark greeting cards

    ANSWER: C

13. Selective distribution is associated with the distribution of _____.
    a. convenience goods
    b. impulse goods
    c. unsought goods
    d. shopping goods
    e. specialty goods

    ANSWER: D

14. A firm is using _____ distribution when only one intermediary is used at a particular level of the channel to cover a defined territory.
    a. Intensive
    b. Selective
    c. Inclusive
    d. Exclusive
    e. Planned

    ANSWER: D

15. The number of intermediaries at each level of the marketing channel is known as _____.
    a. channel length
    b. channel design
    c. channel flow
    d. channel intensity
    e. channel structure

    ANSWER: D

16. An example of _____ would be a grocery store selling items such as greeting cards and flowers.
    a. mixing strategies
    b. scrambled merchandising
    c. reversal strategies
    d. upside down planning
    e. product differentiation

    ANSWER: B

17. The analysis, planning, organizing, and controlling of a firm's marketing channels is known as _____.
    a. channel structure
    b. marketing channel power
    c. marketing channel management
    d. interorganizational context
    e. channel strategy

    ANSWER: C

18. Marketing channel management deals with the _____ of a firm's marketing channels.
    a. Analysis
    b. Planning
    c. Organizing
    d. Controlling
    e. all of the above

    ANSWER: E

19. Channel management that extends beyond a firm's own organization into other independent businesses is _____.
    a. marketing channel management
    b. interorganizational context
    c. marketing channel power
    d. channel length
    e. channel dispersion

    ANSWER: B

20. The broad set of principles by which a firm seeks to achieve its distribution objectives is known as _____.
    a. channel design
    b. channel strategy
    c. channel flow
    d. channel structure
    e. channel management

    ANSWER: B

21. The process of developing new channels where none had existed before, or making significant modifications to existing channels is known as _____.
    a. channel strategy
    b. channel design
    c. channel flow
    d. channel diagramming
    e. channel intensity

    ANSWER: B

22. The first phase of channel design is _____.
    a. developing the hypothesis
    b. specifying distribution tasks that need to be performed by the channel
    c. setting distribution objectives
    d. Considering alternative channel structures
    e. choosing an optimal channel structure

    ANSWER: C

23. Which of the following is NOT one of the phases of channel design?
    a. choosing an optimal channel structure
    b. Considering alternative channel structures
    c. setting distribution objectives
    d. developing the hypothesis
    e. specifying the distribution tasks that need to be performed by the channel

    ANSWER: D

24. The _____ would be what the firm would like its channel strategy to accomplish in terms of meeting the needs of its customers.
    a. Distribution objectives
    b. channel design
    c. channel structure
    d. channel flow
    e. channel plan

    ANSWER: A

25. Distribution objectives need to be stated from the point of view of the _____.
    a. chief executive officer
    b. Suppliers
    c. board of directors
    d. Customers
    e. sales force

    ANSWER: D

26. The _____ variables would be considered when selecting the optimal distribution structure.
    a. market variables
    b. product variables
    c. company variables
    d. external environmental variables
    e. all of the above

    ANSWER: E

27. The first step for motivation in the marketing channel would be _____.
    a. conducting a focus group interview
    b. developing the hypothesis
    c. learning about the needs and problems of channel members
    d. offering support to channel members to help meet their needs and solve their problems
    e. providing ongoing leadership

    ANSWER: C

28. Product strategy is often dependent on _____ strategy.
    a. Marketing
    b. Pricing
    c. Channel
    d. Promotion
    e. Motivation

    ANSWER: C

29. The term _____ describes logistical systems that emphasize close cooperation and comprehensive interorganizational management to integrate the logistical operations of the different firms in the channel.
    a. supply chain management
    b. horizontal integration
    c. marketing channel power
    d. transaction efficiency
    e. channel design

    ANSWER: A

Integrated Marketing Communications

CMBA Objective Correlations

- Given a specific promotional objective (building awareness, creating an image, reminding consumers of the product/service, generating excitement or involvement, encouraging trial, reducing post-purchase dissonance, protecting from competition
- Given a particular marketing communications execution, infer the underlying objective.

Sample Questions

1. Which one of the following is not an element, or tool, of marketing communication?
   a. Public relations
   b. Sales promotion
   c. Personal selling
   d. Advertising
   e. Word-of-mouth communications

   ANSWER: E

2. The marketing communications tool that consists of all marketing activities that attempt to stimulate quick buyer action is:
   a. advertising.
   b. publicity.
   c. sponsorship marketing.
   d. sales promotions.
   e. relationship marketing.

   ANSWER: D

3. Marketing communications includes all of the following tools except:
   a. point-of-purchase communications.
   b. personal selling.
   c. advertising.
   d. pricing.
   e. sales promotions.

   ANSWER: D

4. A morning television program featured an interview with the director of a newly released motion picture. The director used this opportunity to encourage viewers to see the movie. This is an illustration of:
   a. public relations.
   b. advertising.
   c. personal selling.
   d. sales promotions.
   e. word-of-mouth communications.

   ANSWER: A

5. Many companies sponsor Professional Golf Association (PGA) golf tournaments. Such sponsorships represent which form of marketing communications?
   a. Public relations
   b. Advertising
   c. Personal selling
   d. Sales promotions
   e. Event marketing

   ANSWER: E

6. The primary objective of integrated marketing communications is to:
   a. enhance brand equity.
   b. increase retailer traffic.
   c. motivate the sales force.
   d. reduce production expenditures.
   e. increase coupon redemption.

   ANSWER: A

7. Which of the following types of marketing communications is most important with a "pull" strategy?
   a. Trade-oriented sales promotions
   b. Consumer-oriented sales promotions
   c. Advertising
   d. Publicity
   e. Off-invoice allowances

   ANSWER: C

8. Which of the following statements is at least true regarding push and pull strategies?
   a. Personal selling is especially important with a push strategy.
   b. Advertising is especially important with a push strategy.
   c. Push and pull strategies are complementary rather than representing perfect substitutes for one another.
   d. A pull strategy involves encouraging consumer demand for a particular brand in order to obtain distribution for the brand in retail outlets.
   e. Advertising is especially important with a pull strategy.

   ANSWER: B

9. Intended market, nature of the product, product life-cycle stage, competitor actions, and available budget all are considerations for which of the following?
   a. Brand image
   b. Achieving synergy
   c. Determining whether a push or pull strategy will be more effective
   d. Selecting target markets
   e. Determining and managing an appropriate mix of integrated marketing communication tools

   ANSWER: E

10. A bicycle manufacturer has developed the new SPEEDY-100. The manufacturer hopes that this new product will create excitement among consumers. Because bicycle sales have been declining, retailers are reluctant to add new products to their existing inventory. In an effort to overcome this potential concern, the marketing manager for the bicycle manufacturer plans to utilize intensive personal selling and heavy trade allowances to gain retailer acceptance of the SPEEDY-100. What type of strategy is the manager using?
    a. pull strategy
    b. open strategy
    c. closed strategy
    d. push strategy
    e. competitive strategy

    ANSWER: D

11. Good (or effective) advertising satisfies all of the following considerations except:
    a. It takes the perspective of the company's needs and wants.
    b. It is persuasive.
    c. It finds a unique way to break through the clutter.
    d. It never promises more than it can deliver.
    e. It prevents the creative idea from overwhelming the strategy.

    ANSWER: A

12. The concept of "reach" in media strategy refers to which of the following?
    a. How often should the target audience be exposed to the advertisement?
    b. When are the best times to reach the target audience?
    c. What is the least expensive way to accomplish media strategy objectives?
    d. How long should an exposure episode last for optimal effect?
    e. What proportion of the target audience do we want to see (or read, or hear) the advertising message?

    ANSWER: E

13. Garden Dogs, a specialty manufacturer of vegetable-based hot dogs, has segmented its target market as people aged 18-49 who are outdoor oriented. These two segmentation variables (age and outdoor orientation) represent, respectively,
    a. geographic and demographic variables.
    b. both are product usage factors.
    c. both are psychographic variables.
    d. psychographic and geographic variables.
    e. demographic and psychographic variables.

    ANSWER: E

14. Garden Dogs, a specialty manufacturer of vegetable-based hot dogs, has decided to advertise in a magazine called *Health*. The marketing manager has concerns regarding the proportion of the target audience that will read a Garden Dogs advertisement placed in *Health*. Which of the following advertising objectives best reflects the manager's concern?
    a. reach
    b. average read rate
    c. gross read rate
    d. continuity
    e. frequency

    ANSWER: A

15. Garden Dogs, a specialty manufacturer of vegetable-based hot dogs, has decided to advertise in a magazine called *Health*. The marketing manager has concerns regarding how often the target audience will be exposed to advertisements for Garden Dogs that are placed in *Health* over a period of six consecutive months. Which of the following advertising objectives best reflects the manager's concern?
    a. reach
    b. average read rate
    c. gross read rate
    d. continuity
    e. frequency

    ANSWER: E

16. Sales promotions are designed to affect the behavior of
    a. retailers only.
    b. consumers only.
    c. wholesalers only.
    d. manufacturers only.
    e. consumers, retailers, and wholesalers.

    ANSWER: E

17. Sales promotions are best described as
    a. the basic benefits provided by the brand at the point of sale.
    b. tools for rewarding employees for doing a good job.
    c. the use of incentives by a manufacturer to induce the trade and/or consumers to buy a brand.
    d. a relatively permanent change in a brand's price.
    e. permanent benefits that replace a brand's normal benefits.

    ANSWER: C

18. Trade-oriented sales promotions are directed toward:
    a. wholesalers, retailers, and other marketing intermediaries.
    b. advertisers.
    c. consumers.
    d. direct marketers.
    e. manufacturers.

    ANSWER: A

19. Which of the following consumer-oriented sales promotions are capable of reinforcing a brand's image?
    a. refunds and rebates
    b. phone cards
    c. in-, on- and near-pack premiums
    d. coupons and sampling
    e. self liquidating premiums, contests, and sweepstakes

    ANSWER: E

20. Assume you are the marketing manager for Garden Dogs, a specialty manufacturer of vegetable-based hot dogs, and that you are attempting to gain retail distribution for a new, Mexican-flavored version of your hot dogs. In order to gain distribution, you likely will have to pay retailers a _____ allowance as incentive for their willingness to stock this new product.
    a. slotting
    b. off-invoice
    c. bill-back
    d. trial
    e. bill-forward

    ANSWER: A

21. Garden Dogs, a specialty manufacturer of vegetable-based hot dogs, sends out a news release to radio and television stations that includes the findings of a recent study regarding the health benefits of vegetable-based hot dogs compared to real meat "dogs." This is an example of
    a. campaign marketing.
    b. proactive marketing public relations.
    c. reactive marketing public relations.
    d. direct marketing.
    e. strike-while-the-iron-is-hot PR.

    ANSWER: B

22. Managing unanticipated marketplace developments such as product defects and failures is the domain of
    a. sales promotion.
    b. reactive marketing PR.
    c. personal selling.
    d. proactive marketing PR.
    e. market orientation.

    ANSWER: B

23. Sears, the large retail chain, was accused in the early 1990s of charging customers in California for automobile repair work that allegedly was never performed. The CEO of Sears immediately "hit the airways" to apologize and announce that nothing like this would happen in the future. The CEO's action represents
    a. proactive MPR.
    b. reactive MPR.
    c. rumor control.
    d. an executive-statement release.
    e. cause-oriented MPR.

    ANSWER: B

24. Supporting athletic events, underwriting rock concerts, and contributing to worthy causes such as efforts to generate funds for cancer research are all examples of
    a. consumer marketing.
    b. consumer sales promotion.
    c. sponsorship marketing.
    d. advertising.
    e. public relations.

    ANSWER: C

25. Garden Dogs, a specialty manufacturer of vegetable-based hot dogs, decides to put up a tent and distribute samples of Garden Dogs hot dogs to participants at the next Race for the Cure for breast cancer research. This is an example of
    a. cause-related marketing.
    b. health-related marketing.
    c. event marketing.
    d. strategic marketing.
    e. campaign marketing.

    ANSWER: C

26. More permanent point-of-purchase fixtures can achieve all of the following except
    a. compartmentalize and departmentalize a store area to achieve high product visibility.
    b. create long-term brand loyalty.
    c. facilitate customer self-service.
    d. help prevent stock-outs.
    e. help control inventory.

    ANSWER: B

Personal Selling and Sales Management

CMBA Objective Correlations

- Given specific numbers of sales accounts and phone calls and visits possible per day by a sales representative, calculate the total number of sales representatives needed in a market.

- Given a sales problem faced by a company, select the appropriate course of action.

Sample Questions

1. The primary purpose of personal selling is:
   a. to sell the firm's goods, services or ideas regardless of the prospect needs.
   b. only to communicate the background of the company.
   c. to explain how a firm's goods, services or ideas fit the prospect's needs.
   d. to get rid of the firm's goods, services or ideas.
   e. to sell more products than advertising does.

   ANSWER: C

2. Which of the following is a primary reason for utilizing personal selling?
   a. The averages sales call costs the organization just $113.96.
   b. One sales call in three is successful.
   c. Personal selling is the most expensive form of promotion.
   d. It is the only form of promotion that allows the firm to immediately respond to the needs of the prospect.
   e. Technology has improved the effectiveness of salespeople.

   ANSWER: D

3. Personal selling is best used when:
   a. buyers are relatively few in number.
   b. buyers are geographically dispersed.
   c. purchases are made in small quantities.
   d. the buying situation is low involvement.
   e. simple products are involved.

   ANSWER: A

4. Before utilizing personal selling as a form of promotion, a firm should ensure that its buyers:
   a. are geographically concentrated.
   b. are relatively few in number.
   c. purchase in large quantities.
   d. are highly involved in the buying situation.
   e. All of the above are correct.

   ANSWER: E

5. For which product would personal selling least likely be used to target consumers?
   a. Computers
   b. Vacation timeshares
   c. Automobiles
   d. Insurance
   e. Cleaning products

   ANSWER: E

6. Identifying customer needs and providing the best product to meet those needs
   a. results in a single transactional exchange.
   b. forces the customer to make a purchase.
   c. results in a long-term relationship with the customer.
   d. keeps the customer at a distance.
   e. is the least preferred method of selling.

   ANSWER: C

7. Eliciting customer needs and then taking the necessary steps to meets those needs in a manner that is in the best interest of the customer defines:
   a. customer-oriented selling.
   b. relationship selling.
   c. soft selling.
   d. role conflict.
   e. role ambiguity.

   ANSWER: A

8. The salesperson trait critical in building a relationship with a customer is
   a. customer orientation.
   b. self-motivation.
   c. competitiveness.
   d. goal orientation.
   e. adaptive selling skills.

   ANSWER: A

9. As a sales manager, you are responsible for hiring new sales representatives. Which of the following sets of traits would you most want in a new hire?
   a. driven, analytical, inflexible, self-managed, patient
   b. persistent, righteous attitude, dominating, aggressive, compulsive
   c. introverted, humble, pious, shy, timid, empathetic
   d. self-motivated, organized, enthusiastic, adaptive, competitive
   e. fast-talking, glib, ready smile, slick, high-pressure

   ANSWER: D

10. The three major selling environments are
    a. field selling, under the table, and telemarketing.
    b. over the counter, field selling, telemarketing.
    c. telemarketing, under the table, over the counter.
    d. media advertising, over the counter, field selling.
    e. field selling, media advertising, telemarketing.

    ANSWER: B

11. If you choose to shop at a store that is heavily oriented toward self-service, you are most likely to buy your products from a(n)
    a. order getter.
    b. order taker.
    c. suggestion seller.
    d. telemarketer.
    e. field seller.

    ANSWER: B

12. The salesperson who actively seeks to provide information to prospects, persuade prospective customers and close sales is called a(n):
    a. order taker.
    b. inbound telemarketer.
    c. suggestion seller.
    d. order getter.
    e. support salesperson.

    ANSWER: D

13. You go into a retail outlet to purchase some new running shoes. After you make your selection, the salesperson, who has been assisting you, picks up a package of sports socks, points out that the socks are currently on sale, and asks if you would like to purchase them. The salesperson is practicing:
    a. suggestion selling.
    b. order taking.
    c. field selling.
    d. retailing.
    e. store marketing.

    ANSWER: A

14. Field selling:
    a. is usually conducted as over-the-counter selling.
    b. involves calling on prospective customer in either their business or home locations.
    c. usually occurs in a retail outlet.
    d. utilizes the telephone for selling to customers.
    e. refers to those firms which have customers calling to place orders.

    ANSWER: B

15. Highly skilled salespeople who call on key customers' headquarter sites, or develop strategic plans for the accounts are known as:
    a. professional salespeople.
    b. order takers.
    c. missionary salespeople.
    d. national account managers.
    e. technical support salespeople.

    ANSWER: D

16. Before assigning a national account manager to a customer, a firm would want to be certain that the customer met all of the following criteria except:
    a. the customer has a large sales potential.
    b. the customer has complex buying behaviors.
    c. the customer has limited purchase requirements.
    d. the customer has multiple locations.
    e. the customer operates various units.

    ANSWER: C

17. The primary job of the support salesperson is:
    a. to persuade customer to place orders with wholesalers.
    b. to support the sales force.
    c. to develop strategic plans for the customer.
    d. to close a sale.
    e. to understand the complex buying behavior of key accounts.

    ANSWER: B

18. Support salespeople include all of the following except:
    a. individuals who set up product displays.
    b. individuals who handle order processing.
    c. individuals that sell to customers via telephone.
    d. individuals that provide technical advice.
    e. individuals that free the salesperson to spend more time with customers.

    ANSWER: C

19. Telemarketers are used by firms to:
    a. set up product displays in the customer's business.
    b. visit key customers at their headquarters.
    c. develop strategic plans for the customer.
    d. utilize the telephone for prospecting, selling, and following up with customers.
    e. make formal presentations to customers.

    ANSWER: D

20. Inbound telemarketing refers to:
    a. salespeople using the telephone to call customers.
    b. providing technical advice over the telephone.
    c. setting up displays in the customer's business.
    d. assisting with customers product decisions at the headquarters level.
    e. firms which have customers calling the vendor company to place orders.

    ANSWER: E

21. In hiring a sales representative, the sales manager should look for all of the following except a:
    a. match between the individual's values and goals and those of the firm.
    b. candidate that waits for the manager to set the interview appointment.
    c. candidate that demonstrates persistence.
    d. candidate that is a good listener.
    e. candidate that asks for the job.

    ANSWER: B

22. All of the following are methods by which sales territories may be organized except:
    a. product line
    b. customer orientation.
    c. customers.
    d. markets.
    e. geographical area

    ANSWER: B

23. An advantage of organizing sales territories around customers is that the salespersons:
    a. must call on customers representing many different industries.
    b. cannot become an expert in a particular industry.
    c. can develop a better understanding of customer problems.
    d. is prohibited from developing a close relationship with the customer.
    e. must sell to all customers within a geographic area.

    ANSWER: C

Pricing Strategies and Determination

CMBA Objective Correlations

- Describe demand elasticity.

- Given a retail price and channel margin structure, calculate the manufacturer's contribution margin.

- Given a retail price, channel margin structure, market size and marketing investment, calculate a break-even market share.

- Given specific market size, purchase cycle, average retail price, and market share information, forecast annual dollar sales for a company's product/service.

- Explain the conditions under which a particular pricing strategy is appropriate.

- Given a particular pricing strategy, infer the assumption(s) underlying the approach.

Sample Questions

1. Assume that the unit cost of making one doorstop is $1.32. For every unit sold, the firm wants 20% to represent profit. Applying the standard mark-up approach, what should the selling price be?
   a. $1.65
   b. $4.00
   c. $5.23
   d. $6.60
   e. $6.75

   ANSWER: A

2. If the unit cost of making one bike is $200 and the company wishes to obtain a 30% profit on each unit sold, what is the selling price?
   a. $275
   b. $286
   c. $356
   d. $450
   e. $667

   ANSWER: B

3. The Music Shop sells CDs for $15.00. If the cost per CD is $11.00, what is The Music Shop's markup on selling price?
   a. 22%
   b. 27%
   c. 66%
   d. 73%
   e. 80%

   ANSWER: B

4. The Music Shop sells CDs for $15.00. What is the cost per CD if the markup on selling price is 25%?
   a. $10.50
   b. $10.75
   c. $11.00
   d. $11.25
   e. $11.50

   ANSWER: D

5. A manufacturer has a fixed overhead of $4,000 and a variable cost of $3.00 per product. If there is an expected demand for 2750 of the product, what is the average total cost?
   a. $3.69
   b. $4.12
   c. $4.40
   d. $4.45
   e. $4.75

   ANSWER: D

6. The fixed overhead of a local theater production is $2,000, the rehearsal costs are $6,000, the performance costs are $4,000, and the variable cost is $2.00. The demand has always been 1100 tickets sold for the production. What is the average total cost?
   a. $2.10
   b. $8.56
   c. $10.91
   d. $11.75
   e. $12.91

   ANSWER: E

7. ODI Furniture sells premium quality desks for executive offices. Their average price for a desk is $2,500. Fixed costs are $200,000 per year and the cost of manufacturing each desk (including labor and materials) is $1550. What is the firm's breakeven point on these desks?
   a. 211
   b. 250
   c. 129
   d. 80
   e. 50

   ANSWER: A

8. The fixed overhead of a local theater production is $2,000, the rehearsal costs are $6,000, the performance costs are $4,000, and the variable cost is $2.00. The demand has always been 1100 tickets sold for the production. Using the target return pricing method, what should the selling price be if the desired profit is $3.00 per product?
    a. $10.91
    b. $12.91
    c. $14.91
    d. $15.91
    e. $17.91

    ANSWER: D

Scenario 1

Use the information below regarding demand for a breakfast cereal manufacturer to answer the questions that follow:

Price	Unit cost	Quantity (mil boxes)
2.49	1.57	19.1
2.39	1.57	21.9
2.29	1.57	23.1
2.19	1.57	24.4
2.09	1.57	26.9
1.99	1.57	29.2

These estimates are based upon past sales history and some experimentation. The quantity sold information is stated in terms of millions of boxes of cereals.

9. Refer to Scenario 1. At a price of $2.49, the manufacturer's unit contribution margin is:
    a. $1.57.
    b. $ 0.92.
    c. $17.57 million.
    d. 47%.
    e. 62%.

    ANSWER: B

10. Refer to Scenario 1. At a price of $2.19, total revenue for the company will be:
    a. $47.56 million.
    b. $52.34 million.
    c. $52.90 million.
    d. $53.44 million.
    e. $56.22 million.

    ANSWER: D

11. Refer to Scenario 1. Going from a price of $2.39 down to $2.29, marginal revenue is:
    a. $0.56 million.
    b. $0.54 million.
    c. $2.79 million.
    d. $3.79 million.
    e. $0.25 million.

    ANSWER: A

12. Refer to Scenario 1. Going from a price of $2.39 down to $2.29, marginal cost is:
    a. $3.93 million.
    b. $3.88 million.
    c. $2.04 million.
    d. $1.88 million.
    e. $1.01 million.

    ANSWER: D

13. Refer to Scenario 1. The profit-maximizing price is:
    a. $2.49.
    b. $2.39.
    c. $2.29.
    d. $2.19.
    e. $2.09.

    ANSWER: B

14. Refer to Scenario 1. The revenue-maximizing price is:
    a. $2.49.
    b. $2.39.
    c. $2.29.
    d. $2.19.
    e. $2.09.

    ANSWER: B

Scenario 2

Use the following scenario for answering the next set of questions. A retailer sells a particular line of batteries from Manufacturer XYZ. The average unit cost of these batteries is $23.62. The manufacturer has experimented with a series of different prices for the batteries and estimates that quantity demand for five different price points would be:

Price	Weekly Quantity
$45	96
$42	120
$39	165
$36	187
$33	203

15. Refer to Scenario 2. Going from a price of $39 down to $36, marginal revenue is:
    a. $297.
    b. $720.
    c. $1,019.
    d. $142.
    e. $1,395.

    ANSWER: A

16. Refer to Scenario 2. Going from a price of $39 down to $36, marginal cost is:
    a. $567.
    b. $378.
    c. $1,098.
    d. $520.
    e. $720.

    ANSWER: D

17. Refer to Scenario 2. The profit-maximizing price is:
    a. $45.
    b. $42.
    c. $39.
    d. $36.
    e. $32.

    ANSWER: C

18. Refer to Scenario 2. The revenue-maximizing price is:
    a. $45.
    b. $42.
    c. $39.
    d. $36.
    e. $32.

    ANSWER: D

19. The change in total revenue from price to price is:
    a. marginal cost.
    b. profit-maximization.
    c. demand elasticity.
    d. marginal revenue.
    e. sales revenue.

    ANSWER: D

20. By examining how revenues and costs change for a series of prices (for which a manager has estimates of demand), a manager can determine the:
    a. break even price.
    b. marginal profit price.
    c. profit-maximizing price.
    d. elastic price.
    e. revenue-satisficing price.

    ANSWER: C

21. If Mike's Burger Heaven makes 350 burgers per day, total costs are $1,350. If Mike's makes 351 burgers, their total costs are $1,353. The increase of $3.00 represents a:
    a. fixed cost.
    b. average cost.
    c. marginal cost.
    d. indigestion cost.
    e. average total cost.

    ANSWER: C

22. A company experiencing financial trouble may seek to just produce an acceptable cash flow to cover marginal costs. This pricing objective is known as:
    a. stabilization of price and margin.
    b. pricing to achieve a target ROI.
    c. market share target.
    d. survival.
    e. breakeven.

    ANSWER: D

23. In order to compete with a larger competitor who is rapidly gaining market share, a firm may drop their prices significantly, to the point of pricing at or near cost. This is known as the_____ pricing objective.
    a. stabilization of price and margin
    b. pricing to achieve a target ROI
    c. market share target
    d. survival
    e. breakeven

    ANSWER: D

24. For a product category, a choice between skimming and penetration strategies is most likely to be made in the
_____ stage of the product life cycle.
a. mature
b. introductory
c. growth
d. profit
e. decline

ANSWER: B

25. A skimming pricing policy works best when:
a. demand is inelastic.
b. demand is declining.
c. there are a number of large competitors.
d. demand is elastic.
e. the market is inefficient.

ANSWER: A

26. Which of the following pricing strategies is used when a company has developed a clearly differentiated product?
a. price penetration
b. odd-even pricing
c. high/low pricing
d. price skimming
e. inelastic demand pricing

ANSWER: D

27. When introducing an easily copied new product, a marketer would be likely to use a(n) _____ strategy.
a. price skimming
b. price penetration
c. high price
d. prestige price
e. odd-even price

ANSWER: B

28. A company introducing a new product should use a price penetration strategy if:
a. investment costs are low.
b. there is little threat of copy-cat competition.
c. the price elasticity of demand is inelastic.
d. more volume means lower production costs.
e. the product has a short life expectancy.

ANSWER: D

Organizational Behavior

Diversity and Individual Differences

CMBA Objective Correlations

- Explain the legal basis of sexual harassment.

- Specify the major equal employment laws and concepts.

- Specify the legal basis of employment discrimination.

- Analyze issues associated with gender discrimination in the workplace.

Sample Questions

1. Crude comments or sexual jokes and behaviors that disparage someone's sex or convey hostility is considered which type of sexual harassment?
   a. sexual coercion
   b. exploitation
   c. gender harassment
   d. sexual abuse

   ANSWER: C

2. The implicit or explicit demands for sexual favors by threatening negative job-related consequences or promising job-related rewards is considered:
   a. gender harassment
   b. biased sexual force
   c. sexual coercion
   d. sexual exploitation

   ANSWER: C

3. Which of the following would not be considered sexual harassment?
   a.   A male department head is propositioned by a female employee who has bid for a different job that carries a high rate of pay.
   b.   When congratulating employees for their good work, a male supervisor pats male workers on the shoulder and female workers on their behinds.
   c.   A female office employee frequently, in a joking fashion, suggests to certain male co-workers that they go to a motel during the lunch hour.
   d.   In trying to make an important point when issuing job instructions, a male supervisor puts his hand on the employee's shoulder. He does this with both male and female employees.

   ANSWER: D

4. The Americans with Disabilities Act defines disabled as:
    a. persons with permanent physical and mental problems
    b. anyone with a physical or mental impairment that substantially limits one or more major life activities
    c. individuals with physical impairments only
    d. those who cannot work

    ANSWER: B

5. The representation of individuals with disabilities in the workforce is expected to increase dramatically because:
    a. of EEO
    b. a larger portion of society has some type of disability
    c. of the Americans with Disabilities Act
    d. of companies like Pizza Hut and McDonald's

    ANSWER: C

6. Which statement regarding the glass ceiling is most correct?
    a. The glass ceiling has been recently found to apply equally to males and females.
    b. The glass ceiling is a barrier that has been traced to a lack of ability.
    c. The glass ceiling, like Cinderella's glass slipper, has resulted in a temporary movement of women into political leadership positions throughout the world.
    d. The glass ceiling is a transparent barrier that keeps women from rising above a certain level in organizations.

    ANSWER: D

7. With respect to the multiple roles assumed by women, which of the following statements is FALSE?
    a. Men have been favorably predisposed to adopt the sharing of domestic responsibilities.
    b. Working women often find themselves in the position of caring for the elderly parents.
    c. Arranging for child care is typically the woman's responsibility.
    d. Women have been quick to adopt the provider role.

    ANSWER: A

8. Corporations that shatter the glass ceiling have many practices in common, however, these practices DO NOT include:
    a. upper management support for the advancement of women
    b. women representation on committees that address strategic business issues
    c. targeting women for participation in executive education
    d. systems that identify women for advancement with certain quotas in place

    ANSWER: D

9. Assume you are the manager of a department with a diverse work group, but white males comprise the largest subgroup. Many of the white males resent having to work along side of female and minority employees who have less seniority and work experience but are paid the same. Several conflicts and incidents have taken place between the white males and others that have disrupted the workplace. Which of the following approaches would be more appropriate and effective in dealing with this situation?
    a. Fire the white male perpetrators.
    b. Extend preferential treatment to female and minority employees.
    c. Urge female and minority employees to take legal action against those who have caused problems.
    d. Indicate that discriminatory and other inappropriate behavior will not be tolerated and initiate a series of meetings to address the problems and encourage open and frank discussion of the issues.

    ANSWER: D

Motivation

CMBA Objective Correlations

- Analyze employee behavior in terms of cognitive bases of motivation.

Sample Questions

1. The meaning of the term "motivation" is closest to:
   a. job satisfaction
   b. organizational culture
   c. climate
   d. willingness to put forth effort

   ANSWER: D

2. Which of the following is NOT a component of expectancy theory?
   a. valence
   b. instrumentality
   c. expectancy
   d. reinforcement

   ANSWER: D

3. Expectancy theory was developed to explain:
   a. job satisfaction
   b. job commitment
   c. absenteeism
   d. motivation
   e. grievances

   ANSWER: D

4. Desire arises when:
   a. valence is high
   b. instrumentality is high
   c. expectancy is high
   d. both valence and instrumentality are high
   e. valence, instrumentality, and expectancy are high

   ANSWER: D

5. Desire would be zero when:
   a. valence is zero
   b. instrumentality is zero
   c. expectancy is zero
   d. either a or b
   e. either a, b, or c

   ANSWER: D

6. Effort arises when:
   a. valence is high
   b. instrumentality is high
   c. expectancy is high
   d. both valence and instrumentality are high
   e. valence, instrumentality, and expectancy are high

   ANSWER: E

7. Maslow's Hierarchy is a _____ theory.
   a. Needs
   b. Learning
   c. self-efficacy
   d. leadership
   e. personality

   ANSWER: A

8. According to Maslow, the last set of needs that an individual would seek to satisfy is:
   a. esteem
   b. love
   c. self-actualization
   d. physiological
   e. safety

   ANSWER: C

9. According to McClelland, people who are high in need for achievement prefer:
   a. Opportunities to take personal responsibility
   b. Personal credit for the consequences of their actions
   c. Clear and unambiguous feedback
   d. Both b and c
   e. all of the above

   ANSWER: E

292

10. If I am a manager shaping a subordinate's behavior, I should:
    a. reward the complete performance of a task
    b. reward successive approximations to a desired behavior
    c. punish failure in completing a task
    d. use extinction on all behaviors other than complete performance of a task

    ANSWER: B

11. The term that refers to increasing the likelihood that a person will engage in a particular behavior because the behavior has, in the past, been followed by a removal of something the person dislikes, is:
    a. extinction
    b. negative reinforcement
    c. positive reinforcement
    d. punishment

    ANSWER: B

12. Performance is enhanced when goals are:
    a. general and easy
    b. general and difficult
    c. specific and easy
    d. specific and difficult

    ANSWER: D

13. Specific and difficult goals lead to high performance when:
    a. when there is high commitment to achieving the goal
    b. regardless of the commitment to achieving the goal
    c. as long as there is at least some commitment to achieving the goal
    d. commitment is the result of participation in goal setting

    ANSWER: A

14. To increase subordinates' commitment to goals, managers should:
    a. involve subordinates in setting goals
    b. set goals only for subordinates with high needs for achievement
    c. encourage subordinates to set private goals
    d. make goals public

    ANSWER: D

15. Goal setting is *least* likely to enhance performance when:
    a. the task is simple and the means to accomplish it are clear
    b. workers are of high cognitive ability
    c. workers are fully trained and experienced in the task
    d. the task is complex and means to accomplish it are unclear

    ANSWER: D

Satisfaction and Stress in the Workplace

CMBA Objective Correlations

- Analyze interpersonal relations in a work environment based on the concept of organizational citizenship behavior.

- Understand issues associated with work stress in the organization.

Sample Questions

1. The key components of stress are:
   a. perceived challenge, importance of values, and uncertainty of resolution
   b. perceived challenge, personality, and uncertainty of resolution
   c. personality, uncertainty of resolution, and physiological reaction
   d. personality, physiological reaction, and need strength

   ANSWER: A

2. Stress is highest when:
   a. a person believes that he/she can readily cope with a challenge
   b. a person believes that there is no chance that he/she can cope with the challenge
   c. a person sees the perceived difficulty of the challenge as closely matching his/her perceived capacity to meet the demand
   d. no way to predict which of these situations has the highest stress

   ANSWER: C

3. The body's physiological reaction to stress includes all but one of the following. Which one?
   a. rise in blood pressure
   b. decrease in heart rate
   c. burst of energy
   d. blood fats are released

   ANSWER: B

4. The term that reflects the relationship between stress and symptoms is called:
   a. fight or flight
   b. general adaptation syndrome
   c. burnout
   d. exhaustion

   ANSWER: B

5. If stress continues unabated, a person is likely to suffer from:
   a. Burnout
   b. Exhaustion
   c. Fatigue
   d. high blood pressure

   ANSWER: A

6. Workers who hold jobs characterized by high stress are _____ than other workers to suffer high blood pressure.
   a. as likely as
   b. twice as likely as
   c. three times as likely as
   d. ten times as likely as

   ANSWER: C

7. Stress that is associated with positive challenge or opportunity is called:
   a. overchallenge
   b. eustress
   c. excessive opportunitism
   d. burnout

   ANSWER: B

8. Eustress is:
   a. what happens when a person continues to suffer from stress
   b. what is experienced by people who are not stress-prone
   c. stress associated with positive challenge or opportunity
   d. stress associated with other people

   ANSWER: C

9. Work-related stress tends to:
   a. increase workers' compensation costs
   b. increase absenteeism
   c. increase turnover
   d. decrease workers' commitment and citizenship
   e. all of the above

   ANSWER: E

10. The degree to which people identify with the organization that employs them is called:
    a. job satisfaction
    b. organization commitment
    c. citizenship
    d. corporate culture

    ANSWER: B

11. The tendency of some people to go beyond the formal requirements of their job is called:
    a. job satisfaction
    b. organizational commitment
    c. organizational citizenship behavior
    d. organizational climate

    ANSWER: C

12. Which of the following is NOT an example of an OCB?
    a. volunteering for assignments
    b. helping out new employees
    c. staying late to finish a job
    d. completing job requirements
    e. voicing an opinion

    ANSWER: D

13. Research has shown that stress symptoms are most frequent when:
    a. stress is high and social support is high
    b. stress is low and social support is high
    c. stress is high and social support is low
    d. stress is low and social support is low

    ANSWER: C

14. Which of the following is NOT a key factor in determining stress?
    a. physical strain
    b. task complexity
    c. task meaningfulness
    d. social contact

    ANSWER: D

15. Which of the following is NOT an action managers can take to *eliminate* dissatisfying or stressful work conditions?
    a. Training employees in time management
    b. Analyzing and clarifying employees' roles
    c. Providing physical exercise facilities for employees
    d. Letting people complain about problems and grievances
    e. Allowing participation in decision making

    ANSWER: C

Efficiency and Motivation in Work Design

CMBA Objective Correlations

- Analyze employee behavior in terms of environmental bases of work motivation.

Sample Questions

1. Factors that influence employee satisfaction are called:
   a. Motivators
   b. Hygiene factors
   c. Task factors
   d. Critical incidents

   ANSWER: A

2. Factors that influence employee dissatisfaction are called:
   a. Motivators
   b. hygiene factors
   c. task factors
   d. critical incidents

   ANSWER: B

3. Which of the following is an example of a motivator?
   a. Company policies
   b. Relationship with supervisor
   c. Recognition
   d. Status
   e. Salary

   ANSWER: C

4. Which of the following is an example of a hygiene factor?
   a. Recognition
   b. Achievement
   c. Responsibility
   d. Growth
   e. Status

   ANSWER: E

5. According to Herzberg's results, the strongest motivator is:
   a. advancement
   b. growth
   c. responsibility
   d. recognition
   e. achievement

   ANSWER: E

6. According to Herzberg's results, the strongest dissatisfier is:
   a. work conditions
   b. relationship with supervisor
   c. status
   d. company policy and administration
   e. salary

   ANSWER: D

7. In the Hackman-Oldham Model, which of the following is NOT a core job characteristic?
   a. Skill variety
   b. Task identity
   c. Autonomy
   d. Feedback from the job
   e. Social contact

   ANSWER: E

8. The degree to which a job results in the completion of a whole and identifiable piece of work is called:
   a. task identity
   b. autonomy
   c. experienced responsibility
   d. context satisfaction

   ANSWER: A

9. The task characteristics directly influence the extent to which employees experience:
   a. internal work motivation
   b. growth-need strength
   c. meaningfulness of work
   d. critical psychological states

   ANSWER: D

10. The degree to which a worker sees his/her job as having a useful and valuable outcome is:
    a. experienced meaningfulness of work
    b. knowledge of the actual results
    c. experienced responsibility for work
    d. high satisfaction with work
    e. task significance

    ANSWER: A

11. The type of intervention that is most likely to be successful in stimulating workforce motivation and satisfaction is:
    a. horizontal job enlargement
    b. vertical job enrichment
    c. horizontal job rotation
    d. methods that incorporate both a and b

    ANSWER: D

Performance, Assessment, and Compensation

CMBA Objective Correlations

- Analyze performance appraisals for manifestations of rating errors.

- Explain the benefits of performance appraisal.

- Analyze the rationale for multi-source (360-degree) assessments of performance.

- Explain the major organizational constraints on employee compensation.

- Analyze the components of a pay structure.

- Describe the administration of employee benefits systems.

Sample Questions

1. Performance appraisal is used for all of the following **except**:
   a. evaluating employee work behavior
   b. making promotion and other reward decisions
   c. identifying employee developmental needs
   d. selecting persons from a pool of job applicants

   ANSWER: D

2. The major function(s) of performance appraisal include:
   a. feedback on performance
   b. to identify developmental needs
   c. to make promotion and reward decisions
   d. all of the above

   ANSWER: D

3. If two supervisors evaluated an employee's performance using the same set of rating scales but arrived at different conclusions or results, the evaluation instrument is:
   a. invalid
   b. biased
   c. unreliable
   d. sufficient

   ANSWER: C

4. All of the following would be considered criticisms of forced ranking appraisal systems EXCEPT:
   a. they lead to scapegoating
   b. they encourage poor performers to leave the organization
   c. they discriminate against older workers
   d. they may penalize a good performer of a superstar team

   ANSWER: B

5. Performance feedback is more likely to lead to increased job performance when it is:
   a. constructive and specific
   b. provided in written form only
   c. not recorded
   d. one-way communication

   ANSWER: A

6. A key criticism of self-evaluations is:
   a. the decrease in commitment to organizational goals
   b. they have not been shown to lead to more satisfying and constructive evaluation interviews
   c. they have a low level of agreement with supervisory evaluations
   d. they have been shown to have no relationship to improving job performance

   ANSWER: C

7. The developmental aspect of a performance appraisal is most commonly done through:
   a. electronic performance monitoring
   b. self-evaluation
   c. coaching and counseling
   d. empathetic listening

   ANSWER: C

8. An effective performance appraisal system will contain or display all of the following except:
   a. reliability
   b. validity
   c. self-correcting behavior
   d. responsiveness

   ANSWER: C

9. The reliability of an effective performance appraisal system comes from:
   a. insuring the appropriate dimensions of performance are appraised
   b. insuring that the dimensions of performance that are measured are constructed in a valid way
   c. insuring that evaluations from multiple sources and at different times are captured over the course of the evaluation period
   d. insuring that when evaluations are conducted employees clearly understand what dimensions are being evaluated

   ANSWER: C

10. Traditional organizational reward systems in the United States place value on:
    a. entitlement
    b. group performance
    c. non-specific performance standards
    d. individual performance

    ANSWER: D

11. Reward allocation decisions involves:
    a. sequential decisions about which outcomes will be rewarded
    b. simultaneous decisions about which people to reward, how to reward them, and when to reward them
    c. a process of considering individual perceptions regarding instrumentalities and whether reward levels will be perceived equitable
    d. sequential decisions about which people to reward, how to reward them, and when to reward them

    ANSWER: D

12. The notion of entitlement at work is considered:
    a. to engender active, responsible, adult behavior
    b. to engender passive, irresponsible behavior
    c. to be necessary for developing expectations for high performance and appropriate rewards
    d. to define the consequence of rewarding high performance and developing achievement oriented behavior

    ANSWER: B

13. Which of the following is most correct regarding the meaning of entitlement and earning?
    a. The concept of entitlement in not different from the meaning of earning.
    b. Earning engenders passive, irresponsible behavior.
    c. The power of entitlement to rewards rests on a direct link between performance and rewards.
    d. Merit raises have come to be viewed entitlements and this has resulted in a reduction of their positive value.

    ANSWER: D

14. Which of the following laws is NOT an important consideration when an employer is deciding what benefits and services to provide his employees?
    a. Employee Pension Protection Act of 2001
    b. Health Insurance Portability and Accountability Act of 1996
    c. Pregnancy Discrimination Act of 1978
    d. Family and Medical Leave Act of 1993
    e. Economic Tax Recovery Act of 1981

    ANSWER: A

15. Which of the following statements about laws requiring employers to provide services and benefits to their employers is true?
    a. The first law that actually dealt with employee benefits was passed in 1972.
    b. The Pregnancy Discrimination Act requires employers to grant equal benefits for pregnancy as for other disabilities
    c. The Family and Medical Leave Act requires all employers to grant an employee up to twelve weeks unpaid leave annually.
    d. The Employee Retirement Income Security Act was designed to protect the interests of workers covered by private retirement plans.
    e. The Economic Recovery Tax Act gave employers tax credit for providing health benefits for their employees.

    ANSWER: D

16. Which of the following statements about private protection programs is true?
    a. The largest category of private protection plans is medical insurance.
    b. Private protection programs are required by law.
    c. Stock options are not a part of private protection plans.
    d. Private protection plans do not include any type of unemployment benefits.
    e. Private protection plans include retirement income plans and capital accumulation plans.

    ANSWER: E

17. A qualified retirement income plan:
    a. is only available to top management
    b. does not have to adhere to any strict tax regulations
    c. is regulated by the Department of Justice
    d. replaces Social Security in participating organizations
    e. receives favorable tax treatment

    ANSWER: E

18. To further control the cost of providing health care for their employees, a company might employ the strategy of:
    a. a hospital utilization program
    b. case management
    c. cost sharing with employees
    d. incentives to improve health
    e. any of the above

    ANSWER: E

Managing Human Resources

CMBA Objective Correlations

- Explain the costs and benefits of various systems of employee recruitment.

- Analyze major methods of personnel selection on the basis of staffing needs.

- Explain the benefits of training needs analyses.

- Describe the legal basis of occupational health and safety.

- Define employee rights affecting the employment relationship.

- Explain the process of unionization.

Sample Questions

1. Our organization has adopted a strategy of increasing market share by offering the lowest cost services. Which of the following is NOT a recruiting and retention objective?
   a. retain current talent as company grows
   b. recruiting plans may call for preparation of lateral transfers
   c. low cost strategy puts pressure on compensation and benefits, so need to be creative in our programs
   d. continuously improve efficiency of recruitment practices
   e. need to predict rate of growth and translate into needed increases in workforce

   ANSWER: B

2. What is the best recruiting and retention strategy given the company objective of "increase return on investment by offering innovative products and maintaining high margins"
   a. best talent not likely to be looking so we will have to go get them
   b. develop layoff plans
   c. recruiting plans may call for preparation of lateral transfers
   d. retain current talent as company grows
   e. none of these are appropriate strategies

   ANSWER: A

3. Which of the following is <u>not</u> a cost of high turnover?
   a. lost knowledge
   b. excessive hours for remaining employees
   c. more errors
   d. increased litigation
   e. opportunities missed

   ANSWER: D

4. _____ is the process of obtaining and using information about job applicants in order to determine who should be hired for long- or short-term positions.
    a. Placement
    b. Selection
    c. Prospecting
    d. Hiring
    e. Qualifying

    ANSWER: B

5. More expensive procedures for measuring a job candidate's appropriateness for a position are justified when:
    a. labor costs are variable and rise with productivity gains
    b. labor markets are tight
    c. tenure in the job is expected to be relatively short
    d. incremental increases in performance reap large rewards for the organization
    e. there are only a few applicants to choose from

    ANSWER: D

6. Which of the following statements about the steps in the selection process is true?
    a. The first step is to assess the job demands and organizational needs to establish the criteria of interest.
    b. Valid predictors are chosen after the selection process has been designed.
    c. Synthesis of information collected is the first step of the process.
    d. The development of the criteria of interest occurs once the employer sees the applicant pool.
    e. The first step is to establish the predictors to be used for inferring the type of person needed for the open job.

    ANSWER: A

7. Which of the following statements about how job demands and organizational needs are assessed during the selection process is true?
    a. A systematic job analysis is conducted for all jobs in the organization.
    b. Systematic job analyses are more likely to be conducted for lower-level and midlevel jobs than for top positions.
    c. Job analysis for positions near the top of the organization tend to be quantitative.
    d. The criteria of interest are linked to how well the individual will adapt to the organizational culture, not to the elements of the job performance.
    e. Job analyses for positions near the top of an organization tend to be very systematic.

ANSWER: B

8. Without a(n) _____, an organization cannot guarantee the right training will be provided to the right trainee.
    a. human resource analysis
    b. organizational appraisal
    c. social audit
    d. formal needs assessment
    e. training control system

    ANSWER: D

9. A properly executed organizational needs analysis:
    a. results in a clear statement of training goals
    b. includes an assessment of the organizational climate
    c. identifies available resources and constraints
    d. begins with an analysis of short and long term strategy
    e. is accurately described by all of the above

    ANSWER: E

10. A job-needs analysis:
    a. examines the ethics of each employee in the organization
    b. uses information gathered from job analysis and competency modeling
    c. includes an assessment of how each employee adds to the organizational culture
    d. should be performed after a person-needs analysis
    e. is accurately described by all of the above

    ANSWER: B

11. A person-needs analysis:
    a. is performed before a job-needs analysis
    b. focuses on the generic job incumbent, not the current employee
    c. identifies gaps between a person's current capabilities and those identified as necessary for a particular job
    d. is derived from job analysis and competency modeling
    e. is accurately described by all of the above

    ANSWER: C

12. The Occupational Safety and Health Act of 1970:
    a. calls for safety and health inspections of all organizations, no matter how big or small
    b. requires all employers to record occupational accidents and illnesses
    c. made OSHA responsible for establishing and enforcing occupational safety and health standards
    d. does not require employers to record minor employee injuries that require only first aid and don't involve medical treatment
    e. is accurately described by all of the above

    ANSWER: E

13. According to OSHA, communication is the key to reducing occupational accidents and illnesses. Effective communication of information that will protect employees from possible danger should include:
    a. proper procedures for determining the presence of chemicals
    b. protective measures and equipment that should be used
    c. the location of written hazard communication programs
    d. the Hazard Communication Standard's requirements for workplace operations that use hazardous chemicals
    e. all of the above

    ANSWER: E

14. During the first stage of the union certification process, employers must be careful not to:
    a. misrepresent the facts about the union
    b. threaten employees with pay reductions if they support a union
    c. allow solicitation by union activists
    d. make unscheduled changes in wages, benefits, or hours
    e. spy on employees' union activities

    ANSWER: E

15. A useful acronym for remembering prohibited management activities in the face of a union organizing campaign is SPIT. As in, "You can't SPIT." The S stands for no spying or surveillance on union activities, the I stands for no interrogation of sympathetic employees, and the T stands for no threats or terminations because of union sympathy. What does the P stand for?
    a. do not promulgate a riot
    b. provide anti-union materials to employees
    c. do not promise or promote
    d. do not allow picketing
    e. no pre-election influencing

    ANSWER: C

16. What happens once the union begins the campaign to collect authorization cards?
    a. If the union gets 75 percent or more of the qualified employees to sign the cards, the employer must accept the union as a bargaining agent.
    b. If the union gets at least 50 percent or more of the qualified employees to sign the cards, the NRLB must conduct an election.
    c. The union needs 30 percent or more of the qualified employees to sign the cards in order to petition the NLRB for an election.
    d. The employer usually resists the union's card-signing campaign.
    e. The employer typically supports the union's card-signing campaign in order to reduce disruption in the workplace during the campaign.

    ANSWER: C

17. If an employee has the right to a safe working environment, the employer has
    a. the right to expect the employee to assist in providing it.
    b. an obligation to provide a safe workplace.
    c. the right to demand compliance with all necessary rules.
    d. the responsibility to compensate the employee for any workplace injury.

    ANSWER: B

18. The _____ nature of rights and responsibilities suggests that both parties to an employment relationship should regard the other as having equal rights and should treat the other with respect.
    a. adversarial
    b. contractual
    c. legal
    d. reciprocal

    ANSWER: D

19. Employees' _____ are the result of specific laws passed by federal, state, or local governments.
    a. statutory rights
    b. responsibilities
    c. contractual obligations
    d. contractual rights

    ANSWER: A

20. An employee's _____ are based on a specific agreement with an employer.
    a. reciprocal rights
    b. legal rights
    c. contractual rights
    d. statutory rights

    ANSWER: C

21. An agreement in which an employee who is being terminated agrees not to sue the employer in exchange for specific benefits is called a(n)
    a. employment contract.
    b. separation agreement.
    c. employment-at-will understanding.
    d. reciprocal agreement.

    ANSWER: B

22. Provisions stating that if the individual leaves the organization intellectual property and trade secrets remain, are contained in a(n)
    a. non-compete covenant.
    b. contractual right.
    c. separation agreement.
    d. employment contract.

    ANSWER: D

Roles, Socialization, and Communication

CMBA Objective Correlations

- Explain the basis of the socialization process.

- Analyze issues associated with justice and fairness in the workplace.

Sample Questions

1. The term that refers to basic rules of behavior is:
   a. roles
   b. expectations
   c. critical incidents
   d. norms

   ANSWER: D

2. The difference between a pivotal and a peripheral norm is that pivotal norms are _____ and peripheral norms are _____.
   a. required, optional
   b. optional, required
   c. required of everyone, required only of some people
   d. optional, required of some people

   ANSWER: A

3. People who choose to accept both pivotal and peripheral norms are exhibiting:
   a. creative individualism
   b. subversive rebellion
   c. open rebellion
   d. conformity

   ANSWER: D

4. When individuals accept peripheral norms but reject pivotal ones, they are exhibiting:
   a. creative individualism
   b. subversive rebellion
   c. open rebellion
   d. conformity

   ANSWER: B

5. When individuals accept pivotal norms but reject peripheral ones, they are exhibiting:
   a. creative individualism
   b. subversive rebellion
   c. open rebellion
   d. conformity

   ANSWER: A

6. When individuals reject both peripheral and pivotal norms, they are exhibiting:
    a. creative individualism
    b. subversive rebellion
    c. open rebellion
    d. conformity

    ANSWER: C

7. The procedure through which people acquire the social knowledge and skills to assume new roles is called:
    a. Norming
    b. Socialization
    c. Orientation
    d. training and development

    ANSWER: B

8. Socialization occurs:
    a. when a person joins a group or organization
    b. when a person moves into a new role within an organization
    c. when a person is promoted
    d. all of the above

    ANSWER: D

9. To try to create members with a custodial response, which type of socialization program should an organization adopt?
    a. collective
    b. random
    c. disjunctive
    d. investiture

    ANSWER: A

10. Putting people in groups to go through a socialization experience is an example of _____ socialization.
    a. serial
    b. disjunctive
    c. investiture
    d. collective
    e. divestiture

    ANSWER: D

11. A military boot camp is an example of _____ socialization.
    a. serial
    b. disjunctive
    c. investiture
    d. collective
    e. sequential

    ANSWER: D

Organizational Behavior   309

12. Mentoring programs are an example of _____ socialization.
   a. serial
   b. disjunctive
   c. investiture
   d. collective
   e. divestiture

   ANSWER: A

13. If the goal of a socialization program is to change the organization, then one should adopt a program that is:
   a. individual, random, disjunctive, investiture
   b. individual, sequential, serial, investiture
   c. collective, sequential, disjunctive, divestiture
   d. collective, sequential, serial, divestiture

   ANSWER: A

14. The theory that people make judgments about fairness in relationships by making comparisons about inputs and outputs of other people is called:
   a. distributive justice theory
   b. procedural justice theory
   c. interactive justice theory
   d. equity theory

   ANSWER: D

15. Which of the following would be likely to be considered an input under equity theory?
   a. personal appearance
   b. status symbols
   c. pay
   d. working conditions

   ANSWER: A

16. Which of the following would be likely to be considered an output under equity theory?
   a. status symbols
   b. job effort
   c. health
   d. training

   ANSWER: A

17. The term that refers to judgments that people make about whether the rewards they get from their jobs are fair, is:
   a. distributive justice
   b. procedural justice
   c. interactional justice
   d. trust

   ANSWER: A

18. The term that refers to perceptions of fairness of the manner in which a decision was reached, is:
    a. distributive justice
    b. procedural justice
    c. interactional justice
    d. trust

    ANSWER: B

19. The term that refers to perceptions of the interpersonal nature of the implementation of decisions, is:
    a. distributive justice
    b. procedural justice
    c. interactional justice
    d. trust

    ANSWER: C

Group Dynamics and Team Effectiveness

CMBA Objective Correlations

- Analyze group dynamics as a function of dimensions of team interaction.

Sample Questions

1. The stages of group development are, in order:
   a. initiation, differentiation, integration, maturity
   b. initiation, integration, differentiation, maturity
   c. initiation, integration, maturity, differentiaton
   d. integration, initiation, differentiation, maturity
   e. integration, differentiation, initiation, maturity

   ANSWER: A

2. Members are most uncertain and anxious in the _____ stage of group development.
   a. Maturity
   b. Differentiation
   c. Integration
   d. Initiation

   ANSWER: D

3. Members often disagree about the purpose or goals of the group in the _____ stage of group development.
   a. Maturity
   b. Differentiation
   c. Integration
   d. Initiation

   ANSWER: B

4. Members create norms and roles in the _____ stage of group development.
   a. Maturity
   b. Differentiation
   c. Integration
   d. Initiation

   ANSWER: B

5. Groups reach consensus on the purpose and goals in the _____ stage of group development.
   a. Maturity
   b. Differentiation
   c. Integration
   d. Initiation

   ANSWER: C

6. Group roles and norms may become formalized in the _____ stage of group development.
   a. Maturity
   b. Differentiation
   c. Integration
   d. Initiation

   ANSWER: A

7. Which of the following is NOT a characteristic of a group?
   a. members identify with each other
   b. members share common norms
   c. members are highly interdependent
   d. members feel that their membership is rewarding
   e. members stick together against outside forces

   ANSWER: C

8. Which of the following differentiates a team from a group?
   a. teams use work flow grouping
   b. teams are comprehensively interdependent
   c. teams have members that are not interchangeable
   d. both a and b
   e. all of the above

   ANSWER: E

9. Teams with members with different skills or backgrounds are high in:
   a. functional homogeneity
   b. functional heterogeneity
   c. personal homogeneity
   d. personal heterogeneity

   ANSWER: B

10. Heterogeneity in personality is helpful for a team:
    a. for all dimensions of personality
    b. for dimensions of personality such as conscientiousness
    c. for dimensions of personality such as extroversion
    d. never

    ANSWER: C

11. Which of the following types of teams is most likely to exhibit low performance?
    a. a team that is highly culturally heterogeneous
    b. a team that is highly culturally homogeneous
    c. a team with a moderate level of cultural heterogeneity
    d. this cannot be predicted

    ANSWER: C

Leadership in Groups and Organizations

CMBA Objective Correlations

- Describe the basis of leadership in organizations.

Sample Questions

1. The model of leadership that encompasses all of the other specific theories of leadership is the:
   a. traits model
   b. behavior model
   c. power model
   d. tranformational model
   e. transactional model

   ANSWER: E

2. Leadership is an outcome of which of the following forces?
   a. the leader him/herself
   b. followers
   c. situations
   d. all of the above

   ANSWER: D

3. Universal theories of leadership focus on which aspect of leadership?
   a. the leader him/herself
   b. followers
   c. situations
   d. a and b together
   e. a and c together

   ANSWER: A

4. A leader who works with a group to help members come to their own decisions is:
   a. authoritarian
   b. democratic
   c. laissez-faire
   d. charismatic

   ANSWER: B

5. McClelland suggested that successful leaders will exhibit:
   a. high need for achievement
   b. high need for power, low need for affiliation, and high self-control
   c. high need for power and high need for achievement
   d. high need for power, affiliation, and achievement
   e. either a or b

   ANSWER: E

6. The leadership motivation pattern is:
   a. high need for achievement, power, and affiliation, and high self-control
   b. high need for achievement and power, and high self-control, but low for need for affiliation
   c. high need for achievement, but low need for affiliation
   d. high need for achievement, low need for affiliation, and high self-control

   ANSWER: D

7. The theory that suggests that leaders do behave differently with different subordinates is:
   a. Managerial Grid
   b. McClelland's LMP
   c. Transformational Leadership
   d. Vertical Dyad

   ANSWER: D

8. According to Vertical Dyad Theory, workers in the out-group are more likely to:
   a. be assigned more routine tasks
   b. exhibit more OCB's
   c. be highly committed
   d. rate their leaders more positively

   ANSWER: A

9. The leadership model that focuses on followers' maturity is:
   a. Managerial Grid
   b. Vertical Dyad
   c. Transformational Leadership
   d. Life-Cycle Model

   ANSWER: D

10. According to the Life-Cycle Model, when subordinates are very low in maturity, leaders should adopt a:
    a. telling style
    b. selling style
    c. participating style
    d. delegating style

    ANSWER: A

11. According to Fiedler's Contingency Theory, the effectiveness of any leader behavior is contingent upon the:.
    a. maturity of the subordinate
    b. favorableness of the situation
    c. formality of the organization
    d. intrinsic motivation in the task

    ANSWER: B

12. The Vroom-Yetton Decision Tree Model focuses on the _____ dimension of leader behavior.
    a. relationship orientation
    b. task orientation
    c. participation in decision making
    d. charisma

    ANSWER: C

Power, Politics, and Conflict

CMBA Objective Correlations

- Analyze the bases of social power.

Sample Questions

1. The point of view that judges the appropriateness of use of power in terms of the consequences of its use is:
   a. utilitarianism
   b. moral rights perspective
   c. social justice perspective
   d. relativism

   ANSWER: A

2. The question, "Does using power provide the greatest good for the greatest number of people?" reflects:
   a. utilitarianism
   b. moral rights perspective
   c. social justice perspective
   d. relativism

   ANSWER: A

3. The point of view that judges the appropriateness of use of power in terms of whether any individual's rights or freedoms are sacrificed is:
   a. utilitarianism
   b. moral rights perspective
   c. social justice perspective
   d. relativism

   ANSWER: B

4. Looking out for the rights of the minority is a concern of the _____ perspective.
   a. utilitarianism
   b. moral rights perspective
   c. social justice perspective
   d. relativism

   ANSWER: B

5. The point of view that judges the appropriateness of use of power in terms of treating all people equitably is:
   a. utilitarianism
   b. moral rights perspective
   c. social justice perspective
   d. relativism

   ANSWER: C

6. Which of the following is NOT an interpersonal source of power?
   a. expert
   b. reward
   c. legitimate
   d. visibility
   e. referent

   ANSWER: D

7. If I have control over outcomes you want, I have _____ power over you.
   a. coercive
   b. reward
   c. expert
   d. referent
   e. legitimate

   ANSWER: B

8. If I have the right to tell you what to do , I have _____ power over you.
   a. coercive
   b. reward
   c. expert
   d. referent
   e. legitimate

   ANSWER: E

9. Compliance is likely to result from:
   a. expert power
   b. reward power
   c. referent power
   d. legitimate power

   ANSWER: B

10. Identification is likely to result from:
    a. expert power
    b. reward power
    c. coercive power
    d. referent power

    ANSWER: D

11. The kind of power that derives from being able to cope with critical problems and contingencies is:
    a. uncertainty reduction
    b. substitutability
    c. centrality
    d. visibility

    ANSWER: A

Structuring the Organization

CMBA Objective Correlations

- Specify the benefits of various organizational structures.

- Define the concepts of job analysis and job evaluation.

Sample Questions

1. The form of organization which governs through written rules and standards is called:
    a. undifferentiated structure
    b. simple differentiated structure
    c. bureaucratic structure
    d. virtual structure

    ANSWER: C

2. Which of the following is NOT an example of a bureaucratic structure?
    a. divisional
    b. multi-unit
    c. functional
    d. modular
    e. matrix

    ANSWER: D

3. The key difference between bureaucratic structures and pre-bureacratic structures is:
    a. the use of mutual adjustment
    b. the use of direct supervision
    c. the use of standardization
    d. the absence of direct supervision
    e. the absence of mutual adjustment

    ANSWER: C

4. The primary strength of the functional structure is:
    a. focus on products
    b. focus on customers
    c. focus on geographical areas
    d. focus on efficiency

    ANSWER: D

5. A functional structure can coordinate the work of an organization effectively in all but one of the following situations. Which one?
   a. makes only one type of product
   b. has three types of customers
   c. manufactures in four geographical locations
   d. operates in a relatively stable environment

   ANSWER: C

6. Most often, functional structures rely on standardization of:
   a. outcomes
   b. norms
   c. behaviors
   d. skills

   ANSWER: C

7. Divisional structures rely on standardization of:
   a. behaviors
   b. outputs
   c. skills
   d. all of the above

   ANSWER: D

8. The primary strength of a divisional organization is:
   a. focus on a product or customer type, or geographic area
   b. focus on efficiency
   c. focus on flexibility
   d. both a and c
   e. all of the above

   ANSWER: D

9. Structures that use both functional and divisional departmentalization are called:
   a. pre-bureaucratic
   b. post-bureaucratic
   c. matrix
   d. virtual
   e. modular

   ANSWER: C

10. In a matrix structure:
    a. everyone has two bosses
    b. most people have two bosses
    c. some people have two bosses
    d. only one person has two bosses

    ANSWER: C

11. A unit within a matrix organization is called a:
    a. cell
    b. module
    c. division
    d. department

    ANSWER: A

12. The primary coordination mechanism used at the top level in matrix structures is:
    a. standardization
    b. bureaucracy
    c. mutual adjustment
    d. direct supervision

    ANSWER: C

13. Beneath the upper level of each cell of a matrix, the primary coordination mechanism is:
    a. standardization
    b. formalization
    c. mutual adjustment
    d. direct supervision

    ANSWER: A

14. The type of structure that decouples divisions to achieve high flexibility is:
    a. modular
    b. virtual
    c. multi-unit
    d. matrix

    ANSWER: C

15. The type of organization that consists of a collection of autonomous cells connected by a computerized intranet is called:
    a. virtual structure
    b. modular structure
    c. multi-unit structure
    d. matrix structure

    ANSWER: B

16. The type of organization that is formed from a network of allied companies that bands together to exploit a business opportunity quickly is called:
    a. virtual structure
    b. modular structure
    c. multi-unit structure
    d. matrix structure

    ANSWER: A

Culture, Change, and Organization Development

CMBA Objective Correlations

- Explain the basis of organizational culture.

- Analyze the rationale for organizational resistance to change.

Sample Questions

1. The *formal* organization includes all but one of the following. Which one?
   a. job design
   b. rules and procedures
   c. culture
   d. structure

   ANSWER: C

2. The term that describes the mutual understanding of organizational members of what goes around them is:
   a. commitment
   b. organizational citizenship
   c. culture
   d. climate

   ANSWER: C

3. Which of the following is NOT a function of culture?
   a. gives members identity
   b. facilitates commitment
   c. promotes stability
   d. helps people make sense of what goes on
   e. promotes productivity

   ANSWER: E

4. Fundamental norms and values that are expressed and passed from one person to another are called:
   a. surface elements
   b. philosophic bases
   c. symbols
   d. deep elements

   ANSWER: A

5. A rite that is repeated on a regular basis is a:
   a. ritual
   b. ceremony
   c. myth
   d. saga

   ANSWER: A

6. The idea that managers can influence deep cultural norms and elements by influencing surface elements, is called:
   a. social information processing
   b. symbolic management
   c. impression management
   d. organization development

   ANSWER: B

7. Managers who consciously choose to do specific things that will strengthen a culture are engaging in:
   a. social information processing
   b. symbolic management
   c. impression management
   d. organization development

   ANSWER: B

8. The idea that managers can influence culture by helping members to examine current culture and decide what new culture to adopt, is called:
   a. social information processing
   b. symbolic management
   c. impression management
   d. organization development

   ANSWER: D

9. Scheduling a retreat at which managers identify gaps between the current culture and a desired situation is called:
   a. social information processing
   b. symbolic management
   c. impression management
   d. organization development

   ANSWER: D

10. The process of planning, implementing, and stabilizing the results of organizational change is called:
    a. social information processing
    b. symbolic management
    c. impression management
    d. organization development

    ANSWER: D

11. OD research focuses on:
    a. matching an organization's structure to its environment
    b. job analysis
    c. hiring and staffing processes
    d. developing and assessing change techniques

    ANSWER: D

12. Which of the following is NOT a feature of OD?
    a. OD emphasizes reactionary change
    b. OD focuses on multiple levels of an organization
    c. OD has a long-term orientation
    d. OD is guided by a change agent

    ANSWER: A

13. OD is characterized by:
    a. short-term time orientation
    b. top management as change agents
    c. focused change
    d. planned change

    ANSWER: D

14. A diagnostic technique for visualizing the situation surrounding a possible change is:
    a. intervention technique
    b. force field analysis
    c. action research
    d. symbolic management

    ANSWER: B

15. Which of the following is NOT a way to overcome resistance to change?
    a. education
    b. involvement
    c. bargaining
    d. symbolic management
    e. coercion

    ANSWER: D

16. When change is being undermined by inaccurate information, managers should adopt _____ as a way of managing resistance.
    a. bargaining
    b. persuasion
    c. coercion
    d. education
    e. involvement

    ANSWER: D

17. When information required to implement change is dispersed among many people, managers should adopt _____ as a way of managing resistance.
   a. bargaining
   b. persuasion
   c. coercion
   d. education
   e. involvement

   ANSWER: E

18. When people are having trouble making personal adjustments to change, managers should adopt _____ as a way of managing resistance.
   a. support
   b. persuasion
   c. coercion
   d. education
   e. involvement

   ANSWER: A

19. When a group with power to block a change is likely to lose out from the change, managers should adopt _____ as a way of managing resistance.
   a. bargaining
   b. persuasion
   c. coercion
   d. education
   e. involvement

   ANSWER: A

20. When other approaches such as education and negotiation are too expensive, managers should adopt _____ as a way of managing resistance.
   a. bargaining
   b. selective persuasion
   c. coercion
   d. education
   e. involvement

   ANSWER: B

21. When speed is essential and the people resisting change hold considerable power, managers should adopt _____ as a way of managing resistance.
   a. bargaining
   b. persuasion
   c. coercion
   d. education
   e. involvement

   ANSWER: C

The International Context

CMBA Objective Correlations

- Analyze the factors that differentiate national cultures.

Sample Questions

1. Piece-rate pay plans fit best with cultures that are:
   a. high in power distance
   b. Individualistic
   c. short-term oriented
   d. Feminine

   ANSWER: B

2.. Patrimonialism is consistent with cultures with:
   a. individualism and high power distance
   b. collectivism and masculinity
   c. collectivism and high power distance
   d. masculinity and high power distance

   ANSWER: C

3. National cultures that are highly supportive of change tend to be characterized by:
   a. low power distance
   b. collectivism
   c. uncertainty avoidance
   d. femininity
   e. masculinity

   ANSWER: A

4. U.S. managers are least likely to have to reconfigure their management practices when managing in:
   a. Canada
   b. China
   c. Russia
   d. Japan

   ANSWER: A

5. When managing in a stronger uncertainty avoidance culture, managers should be prepared for:
   a. fewer rules
   b. more emphasis on individual performance
   c. greater anxiety
   d. more time spent in planning

   ANSWER: D

6. Rituals serve as ways to reduce anxiety in _____ cultures.
   a. collectivist
   b. individualistic
   c. high power distance
   d. low uncertainty avoidance
   e. high uncertainty avoidance

   ANSWER: E

7. Managers working in cultures that favor less uncertainty avoidance than their own culture should:
   a. expect to be stressed out by rules and red tape
   b. expect to find people to be "laid back"
   c. expect traditional approaches to problems
   d. expect participate in many rituals

   ANSWER: B

8. When managing in masculine culture, a female manager should:
   a. expect to get more respect
   b. seek out male mentors
   c. emphasize work-life balance issues
   d. all of the above

   ANSWER: B

9. When managing in a feminine culture, a male manager should:
   a. expect to be shown deference
   b. control their aggressive tendencies
   c. act as mentors to many females
   d. expect reliance on team work

   ANSWER: B

10. Females and males are most likely to be treated equally in:
    a. individualistic cultures
    b. collectivist cultures
    c. feminine cultures
    d. masculine cultures

    ANSWER: C

11. Managers who move into cultures that are more individualistic than their own are more likely to feel:
    a. independent
    b. rootless
    c. constrained
    d. stressed

    ANSWER: B

12. Managers who work in cultures that are more collectivist than their own must learn to:
    a. accept equal sharing
    b. refrain from complimenting individuals
    c. praise group performance
    d. all of the above

    ANSWER: D

13. Managers working in cultures that favor lower power distance than their own should:
    a. learn to be more participatory
    b. focus on group performance
    c. work independently
    d. centralize decision making

    ANSWER: A

14. Managers working in cultures that favor higher power distance than their own should:
    a. learn to be more participatory
    b. empower employees
    c. compliment individuals on their work
    d. become more authoritarian

    ANSWER: D

15. Managers working in cultures that favor short-term orientation more than their own should:
    a. pay more attention to past successes and failures
    b. pay more attention to the future
    c. reject traditional approaches
    d. foster creative problem solving

    ANSWER: A

16. Managers working in cultures that favor long-term orientation more than their own should:
    a. focus on past mistakes
    b. rely on tradition
    c. encourage creativity
    d. learn about the history of the organization

    ANSWER: C

Operations

Product, Process, and Service Design

CMBA Objective Correlations

- From a list of processes, identify a process by a primary characteristic.

- Match a process to the characteristics of the markets for its products.

- Given several charts and a verbal description of their purpose, identify a Pareto chart.

Sample Questions

1. Process planning and design uses which of the following sources of information:
    a. product/service information
    b. production system information
    c. operations strategy
    d. All of the alternatives are correct.

ANSWER: D

2. Which of the following is an input to process planning and design:
    a. facility layout
    b. selection of equipment
    c. personnel requirements
    d. None of the alternatives is correct.

ANSWER: D

3. In a very complex organization situation, the department that does the process planning is:
    a. the manufacturing engineering department
    b. the plant engineering department
    c. the production department
    d. Many departments will be involved.

ANSWER: D

4. Which of the following is a type of study usually conducted during process planning and design:
    a. degree of vertical integration study
    b. material flow study
    c. feasibility study
    d. efficiency study

ANSWER: A

5. The choice of which production process design to employ is affected by which of the following factors:
    a. product quality
    b. degree of vertical integration
    c. nature of product demand
    d. All of the alternatives are correct.

ANSWER: D

6. One of the factors affecting process design decisions is:
    a. facility location
    b. nature of product/service demand
    c. degree of horizontal integration
    d. facility layout

ANSWER: B

7. The amount of the production and distribution chain, from suppliers of components to the delivery of finished products/services to customers, that is brought under the ownership of a company is known as:
    a. horizontal integration
    b. forward integration
    c. vertical integration
    d. backward integration

ANSWER: C

8. When demand is subject to peaks and valleys and when it is impractical to inventory products in anticipation of customer demand, it is necessary to employ the concept of:
    a. volume flexibility
    b. horizontal integration
    c. product flexibility
    d. forward integration

ANSWER: A

9. Automation usually cannot be justified based only on:
    a. labor cost savings
    b. improved product/service quality
    c. product flexibility
    d. volume flexibility

ANSWER: A

10. The common types of production processing organizations are
    a. produce-to-stock, produce-to-order, and group technology/cellular manufacturing
    b. automated, produce-to-stock, and process-focused
    c. process-focused, product-focused, and group technology/cellular manufacturing
    d. None of the alternatives is correct.

ANSWER: C

11. A form of production processing in which production departments are organized according to the type of product/service being produced is:
    a. process-focused
    b. product-focused
    c. customer-focused
    d. None of the alternatives is correct.

ANSWER: B

12. Product-focused production is also called
    a. production line
    b. continuous production
    c. discrete unit manufacturing
    d. All of the alternatives are correct.

ANSWER: D

13. Ways to describe a process-focused form of production are all of the following EXCEPT:
    a. all production operations that have similar technological processes are grouped together to form a department
    b. production is performed at a steady pace on all products
    c. operations are intermittent and products move from department to department in batches
    d. products follow irregular stop-and-go, zigzag routes with sidetracking or backtracking

ANSWER: B

14. An advantage common to a process-focused production system is:
    a. the ability to produce a large amount of products of the same type
    b. the product flexibility is very high
    c. the start-up and stop costs are low
    d. planning and control is kept at a minimum

ANSWER: C

15. Characteristics of group technology/cellular manufacturing include all of the following EXCEPT:
    a. parts with similar characteristics are grouped together in part families
    b. numerous part families are assigned to a production line
    c. the shop floor is arranged into manufacturing cells
    d. determination of how to route parts through production is done through use of the parts' identification code

ANSWER: B

16. What would be the best reason why a company would prefer cellular manufacturing to a job shop?
    a. fewer machine changeovers
    b. improved product quality
    c. reduced in-process inventory levels
    d. greater product flexibility

ANSWER: D

17. All of the following are advantages claimed for cellular manufacturing over job shops EXCEPT:
    a. employees perform a number of tasks thus eliminating employee boredom
    b. shorter routes through production reduces the amount of handling costs and control necessary
    c. parts spend less time waiting, in-process inventory levels are reduced, and machine changeovers between batches of parts are simplified
    d. quality control is improved

ANSWER: A

18. The inventory policy that is generally used when producing a large quantity of highly standardized products is:
    a. product-focused
    b. process-focused
    c. produce-to-stock
    d. produce-to-order

ANSWER: C

19. When a process-focused, produce-to-order production system is used, the product manufactured usually is:
    a. of relatively simple design
    b. highly customized
    c. of inconsistent quality
    d. a commodity

ANSWER: B

20. A way often used to compare alternative processing plans for the production of products is:
    a. the concept of operating leverage
    b. break-even analysis
    c. financial analysis
    d. All of the alternatives are correct.

ANSWER: D

21. The main difference between an assembly chart and a process chart is:
    a. assembly charts are good for comparing alternative methods of performing operations whereas process charts are not
    b. assembly charts are beneficial when looking for flaws in the production process and process charts look only for inefficiencies in the steps used to manufacture a product
    c. assembly charts are good for an in-depth look at the processes whereas a process chart is good for the whole picture
    d. assembly charts provide a macro-view of the processes used to finish products and process charts are somewhat more specific

ANSWER: D

Facility Planning and Capacity

CMBA Objective Correlations

- Given a scenario, calculate the capacity cushion of a process.

- Given a scenario, calculate the capital costs of increasing the capacity of a process made up of a series of linked activities.

Sample Questions

1. Facility planning does NOT include:
   a. how much long-range production capacity is needed
   b. where the production facilities should be located
   c. the layout and characteristics of the facility
   d. the quality control methods used in the facility

ANSWER: D

2. Which of the following activities is NOT involved in capacity planning decisions:
   a. estimating the capacities of the present facilities
   b. identifying internal production controls
   c. predicting the long-range future capacity needs for all products and services
   d. selecting from among the alternative sources of capacity

ANSWER: B

3. In general, the term "production capacity" means:
   a. the approximate physical size of the productive area of a facility
   b. the maximum production rate of an organization
   c. average production in one shift
   d. total production divided by man-hours worked

ANSWER: B

4. Which of the following factors underlying the concept of capacity makes its use and understanding somewhat complex:
   a. day-to-day variations combine to make the output rate of facilities uncertain
   b. production rates of different products and services are not the same
   c. what level of capacity is being discussed
   d. All of the alternatives are correct.

ANSWER: D

5. All of the following are ways to measure capacity EXCEPT:
   a. aggregate unit rate
   b. input rate
   c. percentage of utilization
   d. least average unit cost

ANSWER: D

6. Which of the following is an example of an aggregate unit of capacity among diverse products:
   a. cubic yards of cement
   b. tons per hour
   c. minutes per completed unit
   d. revenue per salesman

ANSWER: B

7. The lead time for capacity planning decisions is typically:
   a. days to weeks
   b. weeks to months
   c. quarters
   d. years

ANSWER: D

8. Ford, General Motors, and Chrysler are companies that are in an industry with:
   a. too much capacity
   b. too little capacity
   c. just the right amount of capacity
   d. idle factories

ANSWER: A

9. Which of the following methods can be used to change long-range capacity:
   a. mothball facilities
   b. phase in new products
   c. acquire other companies
   d. All of the alternatives are correct.

ANSWER: C

10. Declining costs that result from fixed costs being spread over more and more units is called:
    a. diseconomies of scale
    b. diminishing returns
    c. economies of scope
    d. economies of scale

ANSWER: D

11. "Diseconomies of scale" refers to:
    a. the large fixed cost that often exists in old manufacturing facilities
    b. the cost acceleration that occurs past the best operating level for a facility
    c. the decrease in revenues that occurs late in the life cycle of a product
    d. the effects of a downturn in the business cycle on an individual plant

ANSWER: B

12. Falling average cost per unit of output is an indication of:
    a. poor product quality
    b. diseconomies of scale
    c. best operating level
    d. None of the alternatives is correct.

ANSWER: D

13. At the best operating level, this condition exists:
    a. economies of scale
    b. total fixed cost equals total variable cost
    c. minimum average unit costs
    d. None of the alternatives is correct.

ANSWER: C

14. The use of subcontractor and supplier networks allows a company to:
    a. build large facilities with great productive capacity
    b. avoid the problems of centralization
    c. rely less on backward vertical integration
    d. create simplified management information systems

ANSWER: C

15. Advantages of developing subcontractor and supplier networks include all of the following EXCEPT:
    a. companies can better offer lifetime-employment policies to their workforces
    b. companies can operate with less capacity within their own facilities
    c. they achieve the best operating level
    d. None of the alternatives is correct; they all are advantages.

ANSWER: D

16. Which of the following techniques is NOT used to analyze long-range capacity decisions:
    a. decision trees
    b. linear programming
    c. computer simulation
    d. None of the alternatives is correct; they all can be used.

ANSWER: D

Service Operations Planning and Scheduling

CMBA Objective Correlations

- Describe the relationship between the degree of customer contact and the efficiency of a service.

- Identify situations where waiting line analysis can be useful.

- Identify the inputs to a waiting line problem.

- Given several call center scenarios, (in a table) rank the scenarios in terms of efficiency.

Sample Questions

1. Which of the following is NOT a characteristic of service operations:
   a. intangible outputs that cannot be inventoried
   b. close customer contact
   c. short lead times
   d. low labor costs relative to capital costs

ANSWER: D

2. Which of the following is NOT a dimension of service design:
   a. amount of customer contact
   b. standard or custom service
   c. mix of skilled and unskilled workers
   d. mix of goods and services

ANSWER: C

3. Service firms consist of what type of production processes?
   a. quasi-manufacturing
   b. customer-as-participant
   c. customer-as-product
   d. All of the alternatives are correct.

ANSWER: D

4. Which of the following characteristics makes planning and controlling day-to-day service activities challenging:
   a. services are increasingly being automated
   b. the pattern of demand is inconsistent and unpredictable
   c. there is always high customer contact
   d. None of the alternatives is correct.

ANSWER: D

5. Which of the following is a way to make service systems more flexible:
   a. part-time personnel
   b. subcontractors
   c. assigning personnel to critical duties during peak demand periods
   d. All of the alternatives are correct.

ANSWER: D

6. A personnel factor that influences a service firm's ability to maintain or increase market share is:
   a. selection and hiring
   b. training
   c. supervising and evaluating
   d. All of the alternatives are correct.

ANSWER: D

7. In service operations waiting lines are used to:
   a. help establish priorities
   b. buffer the difference between customer demand and system capacity
   c. vary the system capacity
   d. All of the alternatives are correct.

ANSWER: B

8. Which of these conditions contributes to the formation of waiting lines:
   a. irregular arrival patterns
   b. irregular service times
   c. inflexible service center capacities
   d. All of the alternatives are correct.

ANSWER: D

9. In queuing models, what are "channels"?
   a. the walking paths through service systems
   b. service phases
   c. the number of waiting lines in a system
   d. external sources from which customers originate

ANSWER: C

10. Rules that determine the order in which arrivals are sequenced through the service system are called:
   a. queuing theory
   b. line formations
   c. queue discipline
   d. channels

ANSWER: C

11. The arrival rate in queuing formulas is expressed as:
    a.   a fraction of the service rate
    b.   arrivals per unit of time
    c.   total number of arrivals
    d.   average time between arrivals

ANSWER: B

12. The number of steps in servicing arrivals is called:
    a.   queue discipline
    b.   phases
    c.   channels
    d.   service rate

ANSWER: B

13. Which of the following variables is ordinarily NOT an output of waiting line analysis:
    a. n_1
    b. λ
    c. P_n
    d. t_s

ANSWER: B

14. Which of the following can NOT be found by queuing formulas:
    a.   the average number of units waiting
    b.   the maximum time a unit is in the system
    c.   the average time a unit spends in the system
    d.   the percentage of time the system is empty

ANSWER: B

15. The probability distribution that is most often used to model the service rate in queuing models is:
    a.   normal
    b.   poisson
    c.   hypergeometric
    d.   negative exponential

ANSWER: B

16. A one-lane automatic car wash is an example of what kind of queuing situation?
    a.   single channel, constant service rate
    b.   multiple channel, Poisson service rate
    c.   multiple channel, constant service rate
    d.   single channel, normal service rate

ANSWER: A

17. What queuing discipline is assumed by the standard queuing formulas?
    a. shortest processing time
    b. first-come first-served
    c. longest processing time
    d. No discipline is assumed.

ANSWER: B

18. What objective is achieved when service companies use questionnaires for feedback from customers?
    a. dissatisfied customers can be identified and given special attention
    b. valuable information is provided for continuous improvement of operations
    c. employees who perform poorly on customer satisfaction can be properly disciplined
    d. All of the alternatives are correct.

ANSWER: B

Project Management

CMBA Objective Correlations

- Understand the relationships between activities in a critical path diagram.

- Given information about the activities that comprise a project, identify the project's critical path.

- Given information about the activities that comprise a project, calculate the amount of slack time for an activity not on the project's critical path.

- Given information about the activities that comprise a project, identify the most cost-effective way to complete the project at an earlier date than planned.

Sample Questions

1. Scheduling and control charts:
    a. serve as a planning device
    b. serve as a scheduling device
    c. are used to compare actual project progress with planned project progress
    d. All of the alternatives are correct.

ANSWER: D

2. In project control charts, the horizontal bars are shaded to indicate:
    a. work completed
    b. work to be done
    c. tasks that are understaffed
    d. None of the alternatives is correct.

ANSWER: A

3. When using a horizontal bar chart for project control, an in-progress activity that is on schedule is shown by:
    a. shaded bar ending at present date
    b. open bar ending at present date
    c. shaded bar beyond present date
    d. None of the alternatives is correct.

ANSWER: A

4. Horizontal bar chart status dates are represented by:
    a. a horizontal line
    b. a vertical line
    c. an asterisk
    d. shading in activities

ANSWER: B

5. An activity:
    a. is a milestone accomplishment
    b. consumes no time
    c. shows precedence between events
    d. is an effort required to complete part of the project

ANSWER: D

6. In CPM, a critical activity is one that:
    a. is preventing another activity from being started
    b. has no room for schedule slippage
    c. must be started immediately
    d. represents a milestone event

ANSWER: B

7. A dummy activity:
    a. can be delayed
    b. consumes no time but shows precedence
    c. is used to account for any slack in the schedule
    d. signals event completion

ANSWER: B

8. Status reports from planning and control charts allow managers to do which of the following:
    a. observe the progress of the project's activities
    b. identify problem areas
    c. develop corrective actions to bring the project back on target
    d. All of the alternatives are correct.

ANSWER: D

9. Bar charts can be used for planning and control of:
    a. cash acquisition
    b. personnel usage
    c. material acquisition
    d. All of the alternatives are correct.

ANSWER: E

10. Inputs to CPM include:
    a. the estimated duration of the project
    b. identification of the critical activities
    c. each activity's duration time
    d. All of the alternatives are correct.

ANSWER: D

11. Outputs to CPM include:
    a. predecessor relationships between activities
    b. each activity's duration time
    c. identification of critical activities
    d. All of the alternatives are correct.

ANSWER: C

12. For a CPM activity, its duration plus the sum of all preceding activity durations is its:
    a. latest finish (LF)
    b. earliest finish (EF)
    c. earliest start (ES)
    d. None of the alternatives is correct.

ANSWER: D

13. In CPM, for activities with more than one immediate predecessor activity, which of the following is used to compute its earliest finish (EF) time:
    a. largest EF among the immediate predecessors
    b. smallest LF among the immediate predecessors
    c. smallest EF among the immediate predecessors
    d. average of EFs among the immediate predecessors

ANSWER: A

14. In CPM, which of the following is always true about critical activities:
    a. LS = LF
    b. EF = LF
    c. ES = LS
    d. EF = LF and ES = LS

ANSWER: D

15. Activities with zero slack:
    a. can be delayed
    b. must be completed first
    c. lie on the critical path
    d. must be delayed

ANSWER: C

16. In CPM, the duration of the project:
    a. is determined by managers
    b. is equal to the duration of the critical path
    c. is unpredictable using CPM
    d. is based on delay estimates

ANSWER: B

17. The main difference between CPM and PERT is:
   a. PERT is probabilistic
   b. CPM is best for longer projects
   c. CPM requires 3 duration estimates for each activity
   d. None of the alternatives is correct.

ANSWER: A

18. CPM and PERT differ because of:
   a. network diagrams
   b. activity precedence relationships
   c. activity time estimates
   d. internal calculations

ANSWER: C

19. In PERT, which activity duration time is used to calculate the earliest finish time?
   a. optimistic
   b. most likely
   c. pessimistic
   d. mean

ANSWER: D

20. For a PERT path, its variance is:
   a. the sum of the variances of the activities on the path
   b. the square of $[(t_p - t_o)/6]$
   c. assumed to be normal
   d. None of the alternatives is correct.

ANSWER: A

21. In PERT, which of the following is true concerning the critical path:
   a. it is the path with the longest expected duration
   b. it is the path subject to the greatest uncertainty
   c. it is the path with the greatest probability of completing the project on time
   d. it is the path with the shortest expected duration

ANSWER: A

22. The most frequent use of PERT/CPM is in:
   a. production planning and control
   b. maintenance planning and control
   c. project planning and control
   d. cost planning and control

ANSWER: C

23. PERT and CPM do NOT help operations managers to:
   a. assign responsibilities for activities
   b. plan and control time performance
   c. establish cost estimates
   d. identify corrective actions that must be taken

ANSWER: C

Production Planning and Aggregate Planning

CMBA Objective Correlations

- Identify basic aggregate planning strategies.

- Identify the bottleneck in a diagram of linked activities.

Sample Questions

1. Aggregate planning:
   a. is short-range production planning
   b. the process of developing a plan for production capacity to meet demand over a medium-range horizon
   c. involves the master production schedule and purchase material schedule
   d. done at the shop-floor level of the organization

ANSWER: B

2. Short-range production plans:
   a. are also called aggregate production plans
   b. are driven by the master production schedule
   c. usually span from several days to a few weeks
   d. None of the alternatives is correct.

ANSWER: B

3. Short-range plans develop all of the following EXCEPT:
   a. production schedules of parts and assemblies
   b. schedules of purchased materials
   c. work-force schedules
   d. aggregate inventory plans

ANSWER: D

4. In process-focused production, capacity may be determined by:
   a. the bottleneck operation
   b. the last assembly operation
   c. labor standards
   d. the gateway operation

ANSWER: A

5. Which of the following is NOT a variable that can be utilized to change medium-range production capacity:
   a. straight-time labor
   b. inventory
   c. subcontracting
   d. None of the alternatives is correct.

ANSWER: D

6. Level capacity is a traditional form of
    a. aggregate planning
    b. capacity requirements planning
    c. long-range planning
    d. short-range planning

ANSWER: A

7. A production plan that uses a fluctuating work force to meet aggregate demand is called a:
    a. level-capacity plan
    b. matching-capacity plan
    c. Just-in-Time plan
    d. None of the alternatives is correct.

ANSWER: B

8. The difference between a level production rate and varying demand can be made up with which of the following:
    a. inventory
    b. backlog
    c. overtime
    d. All of the alternatives are correct.

ANSWER: D

9. Finished-goods inventory serves as a buffer between production capacity and demand in:
    a. Level-capacity planning and produce-to-order production systems
    b. Matching-capacity planning and produce-to-stock production systems
    c. Level-capacity planning and produce-to-stock production system
    d. Matching-capacity planning and produce-to-order production system

ANSWER: C

10. Operations managers like level capacity buffered with inventory for all of the following reasons EXCEPT:
    a. operating costs tend to be low
    b. quality of outputs tends to be high and consistent
    c. production rates are usually dependable
    d. None of the alternatives is correct.

ANSWER: D

11. Which of the following serves to buffer the difference between production capacity and demand in a produce-to-order system:
    a. finished-goods inventory
    b. level capacity planning
    c. a backlog of customer orders
    d. revised forecasts

ANSWER: C

12. Aggregate planning may be more difficult in produce-to-order firms because:
    a. of the large number of nonstandard product designs
    b. backlogs do not buffer the variation in demand
    c. of large lot sizes
    d. All of the alternatives are correct.

ANSWER: A

13. Aggregate planning for services that supply standardized services to customers:
    a. is more difficult than for manufacturing
    b. is simpler than for manufacturing
    c. uses only level capacity planning
    d. uses only matching capacity planning

ANSWER: B

14. When performing aggregate planning for custom-designed services the first step is to:
    a. develop plans for each customer
    b. develop a plan that can be constantly adjusted as demand changes
    c. only include the standard services
    d. develop demand forecasts in homogeneous units of measure

ANSWER: D

15. Which of the following is NOT a standby resource that provides service operations managers, using a near-level capacity aggregate plan, with the extra capacity needed to respond to surges in demand:
    a. on-call workers
    b. subcontractors
    c. finished-goods inventory
    d. machines and buildings that can be activated if needed

ANSWER: C

16. Which of the following is NOT considered a mathematical model for aggregate planning:
    a. linear programming
    b. linear decision rules
    c. rough-cut capacity planning
    d. computer search

ANSWER: C

17. If an aggregate planning problem is formulated as a linear programming problem, the decision variables represent:
    a. the amount of straight-time and over-time labor available in each period
    b. the amount of machine hours available in each period
    c. the amount of each product to produce in each period with each type of labor
    d. the amount of inventory to carry in each period

ANSWER: C

18. Which of the following is NOT a production planning and control technique that focuses on bottlenecks:
    a. optimized production technology
    b. Just-in-Time
    c. general theory of constraints
    d. synchronous manufacturing

ANSWER: B

19. A key part of the philosophy of the Theory of Constraints is:
    a. continuous improvement of production performance
    b. bottlenecks can become an advantage
    c. computer simulations of the production process
    d. statistical process control

ANSWER: A

Inventory Management

CMBA Objective Correlations

- Select the correct definition for an inventory management term.

- Identify the EOQ formula from a list of several similar formulas.

- Identify the nature of the basic lot-sizing trade-off made by the EOQ formula.

- From a list of terms, identify those which are costs or benefits associated with carrying inventory.

Sample Questions

1. Which of the following is not a type of inventory:
    a. in-process
    b. safety stock
    c. backlogged demand
    d. None of the alternatives is correct.

ANSWER: C

2. Why are in-process inventories necessary?
    a. to keep all machines full utilized
    b. to create production slack
    c. to uncouple the stages of production and increase flexibility
    d. in product-focused systems large in-process inventories reduce per unit costs

ANSWER: C

3. Which of the following costs is reduced when more inventory is held:
    a. ordering costs
    b. stockout costs
    c. startup quality costs
    d. All of the alternatives are correct.

ANSWER: D

4. Holding more inventory causes which one of the following costs to increase:
    a. carrying costs
    b. ordering costs
    c. backlogging costs
    d. acquisition costs

ANSWER: A

5. What fundamental issue underlies all inventory planning?
    a. how to balance ordering costs and shortage costs
    b. how much to order of each material
    c. when to place the orders
    d. how much to order of each material and when to place the orders

ANSWER: D

6. A feasible EOQ is one where:
    a. the supplier accepts your purchase order
    b. the EOQ is greater than demand during lead time
    c. the EOQ fits in the quantity range for the acquisition cost
    d. None of the alternatives is correct.

ANSWER: C

7. Which of the following costs are NOT ordering costs:
    a. processing purchase requisitions
    b. expediting
    c. quality inspection of incoming orders
    d. None of the alternatives is correct; they are all ordering costs

ANSWER: D

8. Stockout costs include:
    a. financing charges
    b. profits foregone through lost sales
    c. annual acquisition costs
    d. inspection costs

ANSWER: B

9. Which of the following is a fixed order quantity system?
    a. base stock model
    b. single-period model
    c. economic order quantity
    d. optional replenishment model

ANSWER: C

10. A two-bin inventory system is an example of a:
    a. fixed order quantity system
    b. fixed order period system
    c. EOQ with gradual deliveries
    d. EOQ with quantity discounts

ANSWER: A

11. A perpetual inventory system is assumed in:
    a. fixed order period systems
    b. fixed order quantity systems
    c. two-bin systems
    d. produce-to-order firms

ANSWER: B

12. An assumption of the basic economic order quantity model is:
    a. stockout costs are balanced with ordering costs
    b. quantity discounts do not exist
    c. safety stock is set at a uniform level
    d. materials with higher ordering costs are ordered less frequently

ANSWER: B

13. A firm is presently using the basic EOQ model and is considering switching to the EOQ for production lots model. If everything else stays the same, what change should the firm expect?
    a. EOQ decreases
    b. annual carrying costs increase
    c. average inventory level decreases
    d. maximum inventory level increases

ANSWER: C

14. An important difference between the Basic EOQ model and EOQ for production lots model is:
    a. the amount of safety stock required
    b. the opportunity for a quantity discount
    c. the resulting minimum inventory level
    d. the rate at which inventory is replenished

ANSWER: D

15. Which inventory method is best suited for planning the lot size for in-house production of products?
    a. basic EOQ
    b. EOQ with gradual deliveries
    c. EOQ with quantity discounts
    d. fixed order period system

ANSWER: B

16. For the case of the EOQ with quantity discounts model:
    a. price breaks apply incrementally rather than to all units ordered
    b. the feasible EOQ is always the optimal order quantity
    c. the sum of annual carrying, ordering, and acquisition costs is minimized
    d. All of the alternatives are correct.

ANSWER: C

17. For the EOQ with quantity discounts model, all of the following are true EXCEPT:
    a. TMC is greater than TSC
    b. annual carrying cost can exceed annual ordering cost
    c. the EOQ is the quantity that minimizes TMC
    d. None of the alternatives is correct; they are all true.

ANSWER: D

18. The variation in demand during lead time for a material is due to:
    a. daily demand for the material is subject to variation
    b. uncertainty of stockouts
    c. replenishment lead time is subject to variation
    d. daily demand for the material and replenishment lead time are subject to variation

ANSWER: D

19. When there is insufficient inventory to cover demand for a material during lead time, what occurs?
    a. safety stock is increased
    b. a stockout
    c. order quantity is increased
    d. safety stock and order quantity are increased

ANSWER: B

20. Management sets a service level at 95% for a material. This means that:
    a. 95% of all customer orders for the material will be filled
    b. 5% of all customer orders for the material will be filled
    c. there is a 5% probability of a stockout on the material
    d. there is a 5% probability that a portion of safety stock will be used

ANSWER: C

21. If one assumes a constant lead time and a normal distribution for demand per day in setting safety stock levels, then demand during lead time (DDLT) is:
    a. normally distributed
    b. exponentially distributed
    c. constant
    d. certain

ANSWER: A

22. The only true test of an order point (OP) is:
    a. to try different methods until a minimum OP is found
    b. whether the safety stock gives the level of stockout protection desired
    c. whether safety stock is ever needed
    d. whether the EOQ is feasible

ANSWER: B

Resource Requirement Planning

CMBA Objective Correlations

- Given a bill a materials, be able to identify end items or components, which characterize dependent or independent demand.

- Given a bill of materials, calculate the number of component items needed to produce an end item.

Sample Questions

1. A main element of resource requirements planning systems is:
    a. capacity requirements planning (CRP)
    b. inventory status files
    c. material requirements planning (MRP)
    d. capacity requirements planning (CRP) and material requirements planning (MRP)

ANSWER: D

2. Material requirements planning (MRP) is:
    a. a procedure to forecast demand for end items
    b. a work center loading technique
    c. the next step after aggregate production planning
    d. a computer based system

ANSWER: D

3. Which of these materials would ordinarily have independent demand:
    a. a raw material
    b. a component
    c. an assembly
    d. an end item

ANSWER: D

4. MRP systems are based on the philosophy that:
    a. parts are interchangeable
    b. the MPS can be changed at any point
    c. raw materials, parts, and assemblies should arrive at the right time to produce end items
    d. the bills of material is the key ingredient for the inventory status file

ANSWER: C

5. Which of the following drives the material requirements planning (MRP) system:
    a. inventory status file
    b. capacity requirements planning (CRP)
    c. master production schedule (MPS)
    d. bills of material (BOM)

ANSWER: C

6. Which of the following is NOT an input into the MRP:
    a. bills of material file
    b. inventory status file
    c. master production schedule
    d. planned order schedule

ANSWER: D

7. Inputs into the MRP system include:
    a. MPS, bills of material, inventory status file
    b. bills of material, MPS, planned order schedule
    c. planned order schedule, BOMs, exception schedule
    d. MPS, planning reports, planned order schedule

ANSWER: A

8. A bills of material (BOM) file includes:
    a. invoices for materials that must be paid in this period
    b. a list of materials and quantities required to produce one unit of an end item
    c. accounts payable for materials
    d. invoices for materials that must be paid in this period and accounts payable for materials

ANSWER: B

9. The bills of material (BOM) file is:
    a. part of the inventory status file
    b. never changed because it would interfere with the MRP
    c. a list of materials and quantities required to produce one unit of an end item
    d. exploded into the MRP to get the MPS

ANSWER: C

10. Parts, subassemblies, and assemblies carried as end items supplied to customers as replacement parts are:
    a. included in the MPS
    b. fed directly into the inventory status file
    c. part of the bills of material file
    d. not a part of the MRP system

ANSWER: B

11. In MRP systems, a bucket is:
    a. part of a bill of material
    b. a standard-size container for parts
    c. sufficient safety stock to cover one week
    d. a measure of time

ANSWER: D

12. A primary output of MRP is the:
    a. planned order schedule
    b. exception report
    c. inventory transaction data
    d. performance report

ANSWER: A

13. A secondary output of MRP is the:
    a. planned order schedule
    b. inventory status file
    c. inventory transaction data
    d. performance report

ANSWER: D

14. Which of the following is NOT an appropriate lot-sizing technique for materials with lumpy demand:
    a. part-period balancing
    b. period order quantity
    c. lot-for-lot
    d. economic order quantity

ANSWER: D

15. Capacity requirements planning (CRP):
    a. gets most of its information from MRP schedules
    b. develops labor and machine load schedules
    c. prevents overloading or underloading of the factory
    d. All of the alternatives are correct.

ANSWER: D

CMBA Objective Correlations

- Given a scenario, identify the job sequence resulting from a shortest operating time job priority rule.

- Identify the job priority rule that always results in the shortest average waiting time for a single-machine.

- Identify the effects of "balance delay" in assembly line layout.

Sample Questions

1. The finite loading approach to assigning jobs to work centers:
    a. eliminates the need for dispatching lists
    b. is a form of backward scheduling
    c. is used when the capacities of work centers are allocated among a list of jobs
    d. assumes excess production capacity exists

ANSWER: C

2. When backward scheduling is used to determine to which time slots jobs are assigned within work centers, which of the following does NOT apply:
    a. jobs are assigned to the earliest unassigned time slots in work centers
    b. jobs are assigned to the latest possible time slots in work centers
    c. accurate lead times are required
    d. the starting point for planning is the promised delivery date to the customer

ANSWER: A

3. Which of the following is NOT an order sequencing rule:
    a. earliest due date
    b. least changeover cost
    c. part-period balancing
    d. critical ratio

ANSWER: C

4. The critical ratio is calculated by which of following:
    a. (time to due date)/(total remaining processing time)
    b. (time to due date)/(task time)
    c. (task time)/(time to due date)
    d. (due date)/(current date)

ANSWER: A

5. Which of the following is NOT a criterion for evaluating sequencing rules:
   a. average flow time
   b. average number of jobs in the system
   c. changeover cost
   d. sum of task times

ANSWER: D

6. When sequencing jobs in process-focused manufacturing, the flow time for a job is computed by:
   a. summing the flow time for the preceding job and the production time of the present job
   b. summing the flow time for the present job and the production time of the preceding job
   c. adding all the production times together and dividing by the total number of jobs
   d. first determining the critical ratio for each job

ANSWER: A

7. If a job is late, then its lateness is the:
   a. difference between its flow time and its production time
   b. difference between its flow time and its time to promised delivery
   c. sum of the flow times divided by its production time
   d. critical ratio multiplied by its production time

ANSWER: B

8. With regard to actual applications, what generalization can be said about sequencing rules?
   a. first-come first-served is best for manufacturing, critical ratio is best for service
   b. first-come first-served is the best all-around rule
   c. critical ratio is best for manufacturing, earliest due date is best for service
   d. no single rule is best for all situations

ANSWER: D

9. Which of these sequencing rules ordinarily scores best on average job lateness:
   a. shortest processing time
   b. first-come first-served
   c. critical ratio
   d. None of the alternatives is correct.

ANSWER: C

10. Which of these sequencing rules performs poorly on most evaluation criteria:
    a. critical ratio
    b. longest processing time
    c. earliest due date
    d. first-come first-served

ANSWER: D

11. What is the major advantage of a first-come first-served priority system as compared to other priority systems?
    a.   best average flow time
    b.   smallest average number of jobs in the system
    c.   sense of fair play
    d.   minimal job lateness

ANSWER: C

12. The chief disadvantage of the shortest processing time rule is:
    a.   average job completion times are excessive
    b.   average number of jobs in the system is excessive
    c.   long duration jobs may have excessive completion times
    d.   average job lateness is excessive

ANSWER: C

13. If a print shop has five major jobs that can be printed on any one of its five presses, which of the following techniques would be used to indicate which press should handle which job:
    a.   Johnson's rule
    b.   shortest processing time rule
    c.   assignment method
    d.   run-out method

ANSWER: D

14. When a soft drink bottling company uses one filling line for making six different kinds of soft drinks, an approach that they might use to develop a production schedule is:
    a.   Finite loading
    b.   run-out method
    c.   input-output control
    d.   Gantt chart

ANSWER: B

15. The line-of-balance method is useful in situations where:
    a.   actual product deliveries should match with the planned delivery schedule
    b.   workload among machines should be approximately equal
    c.   numbers of employees across shifts should be made approximately equal
    d.   a number of jobs should be assigned to an equal number of machines

ANSWER: A

16. The line-of-balance method is used to:
    a.   schedule and control upstream production steps
    b.   schedule personnel to match demand
    c.   share production capacity between connecting departments
    d.   determine the required capacity of all departments in the production system

ANSWER: A

Quality Control

CMBA Objective Correlations

- Understand how charting is useful in managing quality in a process.

- Understand the use of control charts.

- Understand the relationship of statistical variance to six-sigma quality measurements.

Sample Questions

1. In the context of quality control, the flow of products is broken into discrete batches called:
    a. lots
    b. samples
    c. runs
    d. shipments

ANSWER: A

2. Which of the following is a statistical concept in quality control:
    a. inspecting
    b. sorting
    c. sampling
    d. testing

ANSWER: C

3. The primary purpose of control charts is to:
    a. indicate when production processes have changed sufficiently to affect quality
    b. determine the cause of a quality problem
    c. assist in the development of quality standards
    d. allow management to evaluate how well workers are doing in terms of quality

ANSWER: A

4. Compared to the population standard deviation, the standard error of the sampling distribution is:
    a. equal
    b. larger
    c. smaller
    d. None of the alternatives is correct.

ANSWER: C

5. What is needed to construct a control chart for attributes?
    a. center line
    b. upper limit
    c. lower limit
    d. All of the alternatives are correct.

ANSWER: D

6. In what way is the center line for a control chart determined, particularly for new processes?
    a. using the expert knowledge of a supervisor
    b. a target that we want to attain
    c. the average number over some trial period
    d. All of the alternatives are correct.

ANSWER: D

7. What is the difference between control charts for attributes and control charts for variables?
    a. attributes measure the percent defective; variables measure sample means and ranges
    b. attributes have 2-sigma control limits; variables have 3-sigma control limits
    c. attributes require single samples; variables require sequential samples
    d. attributes require a smaller sample size; variables require a larger sample size

ANSWER: A

8. If the percent defectives in a sample goes below the lower limit of a control chart, what should be done:
    a. ignore it; it indicates improvement
    b. decrease the lower limit
    c. investigate the cause
    d. decrease the sample size

ANSWER: C

9. When sample sizes increase, the control limits in p charts:
    a. remain the same distance apart
    b. move closer together
    c. move farther apart
    d. you cannot determine from the information given

ANSWER: B

10. When using 3 standard deviation control chart limits, what percentage of sample points would fall inside the limits when the process is in control?
    a. 95%
    b. 97.5%
    c. more than 99%
    d. 100%

ANSWER: C

11. Which of the following are variables:
    a. p and X-bar
    b. X-bar and R
    c. n and c
    d. producer's risk and consumer's risk

ANSWER: B

12. R charts monitor:
    a. variation among items within samples
    b. variation among sample means
    c. variation within lots
    d. variation among attributes

ANSWER: A

13. Which control chart uses TWO factors from control chart table to determine the control limits?
    a. p chart
    b. X-bar chart
    c. R chart
    d. s chart

ANSWER: C

14. When X-bar and R charts are used together to control variables, we would ordinarily expect the charts' trends to be:
    a. equal
    b. directly related
    c. inversely related
    d. not necessarily related

ANSWER: D

15. When data points are trending outside the control limits in control charts:
    a. the sample mean does not represent the population
    b. the control limits need to be extended
    c. the underlying process is changing
    d. the sample size should be increased

ANSWER: C

Employee Productivity

CMBA Objective Correlations

- Identify the trade-offs between job enrichment, operational flexibility and workforce training.

Sample Questions

1. Productivity can be increased by which of the following:
    - a. increasing production using a smaller amount of resources
    - b. reducing the amount of resources while keeping the same production
    - c. decreasing production but also decreasing the amount of resources used even more
    - d. All of the alternatives are correct.

    ANSWER: D

2. What is the payoff to companies that have satisfied employees?
    - a. reduced turnover and absenteeism
    - b. higher product quality
    - c. higher productivity
    - d. All of the alternatives are correct.

    ANSWER: D

3. Why should management worry about satisfaction of workers needs?
    - a. satisfied workers are going to be less demanding
    - b. satisfied workers are more willing to work overtime
    - c. satisfied workers are more likely to produce high quality products
    - d. satisfied workers don't ask for raises

    ANSWER: C

4. Which of the following is a proposal to modify specialized jobs to provide for a broader range of needs satisfaction:
    - a. lifetime employment
    - b. team production
    - c. wage restructuring
    - d. job security

    ANSWER: B

5. Job enlargement is:
    - a. adding additional similar tasks to workers' jobs
    - b. attempts to design jobs that adjust production technology to the needs of workers
    - c. adding more planning, inspecting and other management functions to workers jobs
    - d. training workers to perform several jobs so they can be moved from job to job

    ANSWER: A

6. What is a disadvantage of labor specialization?
   a. it takes a long time to train workers
   b. workers are not motivated to produce high quality products
   c. productivity tends to be low
   d. wage rates are high

ANSWER: B

7. What type of chart shows how one or more workers work together and/or with machines?
   a. operation chart
   b. multiactivity chart
   c. motion economy chart
   d. cycle time chart

ANSWER: B

8. What is the universal unit of measure in work measurement?
   a. foot-pounds per hour
   b. worker-minutes per unit of output
   c. calories per minute
   d. labor hours

ANSWER: B

9. The main goal of work measurement is:
   a. higher productivity
   b. to determine quotas
   c. to develop labor standards
   d. both higher productivity and to develop labor standards

ANSWER: D

10. What would the appropriate work measurement technique be for a job performed by a single worker in a fixed location, where the job involves repetitive short cycles and this pattern is expected to continue for a long time?
    a. work sampling
    b. time study
    c. predetermined time study
    d. repetitive motion study

ANSWER: B

11. When the learning by workers causes the labor hours per unit to fall as the number of units produced increases, it is called:
    a. learning by doing
    b. learning curve
    c. continuous improvement
    d. natural improvement

ANSWER: B

12. The concept of learning curves is based upon the idea that:
    a. the more simple the job, the greater the rate of learning
    b. the area under the curve represents improvement
    c. a ratio exists between errors and the time on the job
    d. the rate of learning can be sufficiently regular to be predictive

ANSWER: D

13. Which approach to learning curve problems is the simplest?
    a. learning curve tables
    b. logarithmic analysis
    c. arithmetic analysis
    d. learning curve coefficients

ANSWER: C

14. Learning curve theory is important in job shops and custom service operations because:
    a. there is a need to complete orders quickly
    b. learning rates vary among workers
    c. training is costly
    d. batches tend to be small

ANSWER: D

Quantitative Methods

Introduction to Probability

CMBA Objective Correlations

- Given a scenario with a historical data distribution, identify the probability of a specified event.

- Given a scenario with normal distribution (mean and SD given) and a value, calculate the probability that corresponds to the specified value.

- Given a scenario with normal distribution (mean and SD given) and the percentile, calculate the value that corresponds to the specified probability.

Sample Questions

1. Which of the following is not a valid representation of a probability?
   a. 35%
   b. 0
   c. 1.04
   d. 3/8

   ANSWER: C

2. Which of the following is not a proper sample space when all undergraduates at a university are considered?
   a. S = {in-state, out-of-state}
   b. S = {freshmen, sophomores}
   c. S = {age under 21, age 21 or over}
   d. S = {a major within business, no business major}

   ANSWER: B

3. In the set of all past due accounts, let the event A mean the account is between 31 and 60 days past due and the event B mean the account is that of a new customer. The union of A and B is
   a. all new customers.
   b. all accounts fewer than 31 or more than 60 days past due.
   c. all accounts from new customers and all accounts that are from 31 to 60 days past due.
   d. all new customers whose accounts are between 31 and 60 days past due.

   ANSWER: C

4. In the set of all past due accounts, let the event A mean the account is between 31 and 60 days past due and the event B mean the account is that of a new customer. The intersection of A and B is
   a. all new customers.
   b. all accounts fewer than 31 or more than 60 days past due.
   c. all accounts from new customers and all accounts that are from 31 to 60 days past due.
   d. all new customers whose accounts are between 31 and 60 days past due.

   ANSWER: D

5. The probability of an event
   a. is the sum of the probabilities of the sample points in the event.
   b. is the product of the probabilities of the sample points in the event.
   c. is the maximum of the probabilities of the sample points in the event.
   d. is the minimum of the probabilities of the sample points in the event.

   ANSWER: A

6. If $P(A \cap B) = 0$
   a. A and B are independent events.
   b. $P(A) + P(B) = 1$
   c. A and B are mutually exclusive events.
   d. either $P(A) = 0$ or $P(B) = 0$.

   ANSWER: C

7. If $P(A|B) = .4$, then
   a. $P(B|A) = .6$
   b. $P(A)*P(B) = .4$
   c. $P(A) / P(B) = .4$
   d. None of the above is true.

   ANSWER: D

8. If $P(A|B) = .2$ and $P(B^c) = .6$, then $P(B|A)$
   a. is .8
   b. is .12
   c. is .33
   d. cannot be determined.

   ANSWER: D

The following information applies to Questions 9-11.

There are two more assignments in a class before its end, and if you get an A on at least one of them, you will get an A for the semester. Your subjective assessment of your performance is

Event	Probability
A on paper and A on exam	.25
A on paper only	.10
A on exam only	.30
A on neither	.35

9. What is the probability of getting an A on the paper?
   a. is .35
   b. is .25
   c. is .20
   d. cannot be determined.

ANSWER: A

10. What is the probability of getting an A on the exam?
   a. is .35
   b. is .25
   c. is .20
   d. is .55

ANSWER: D

11. What is the probability of getting an A in the course?
   a. is .35
   b. is .65
   c. is .20
   d. is .55

ANSWER: B

12. Super Cola sales breakdown as 80% regular soda and 20% diet soda. While 60% of the regular soda is purchased by men, only 30% of the diet soda is purchased by men. If a woman purchases Super Cola, what is the probability that it is a diet soda?
   a. is .30453
   b. is .63303
   c. is .30435
   d. cannot be determined

ANSWER: C

The following information applies to Questions 13-14.

A medical research project examined the relationship between a subject's weight and recovery time from a surgical procedure, as shown in the table below.

	Underweight	Normal weight	Overweight
Less than 3 days	6	15	3
3 to 7 days	30	95	20
Over 7 days	14	40	27

13. What is the probability a patient will recover in fewer than 3 days?
    a. .096
    b. .400
    c. .066
    d. cannot be determined

    ANSWER: A

14. Given that recovery takes over 7 days, what is the probability the patient is overweight?
    a. .76
    b. .42
    c. .73
    d. None of the above is true.

    ANSWER: C

15. The Ambell Company uses batteries from two different manufacturers. Historically, 60% of the batteries are from manufacturer 1, and 90% of these batteries last for over 40 hours. Only 75% of the batteries from manufacturer 2 last for over 40 hours. A battery in a critical tool fails at 32 hours. What is the probability it was from manufacturer 2?
    a. .750
    b. .675
    c. .320
    d. .625

    ANSWER: D

16. Consider a quality control experiment, where parts are inspected. There are four events that can occur. The event where a part is truly defective is designated as Event D. The event where a part is truly good is called Event G. The event where the results of the inspection indicate that the part is good is designated as Event Q. The event that the part fails the inspection is designated as Event N. The probability (G|N) is the probability that:

a. we say the part is good when it is in fact bad.
b. we say the part is bad when it is in fact good.
c. we say the part is good when it is in fact good.
d. we say the part is bad when it is in fact bad.
e. none of these are correct.

ANSWER: B

17. A physics professor has decided, after grading an exam, to curve the raw scores to bring them more in line with students' expectations. The mean raw score is 58 with a standard deviation of 9. His curve function is $Y = aS + b$, where S is the raw score random variable, and a is 1.1 and b is 12. The Mean and Standard deviation for the random variable Y representing curved scores are

a. 72.8 and 20.6
b. 75.8 and 9.9
c. 78.3 and 13.7
d. 63.6 and 20.8
e. 69.6 and 9

ANSWER: B

18. Given the following Probability Table, the probability represented as $P(T|R)$ equals:

	S	T
Q	.25	.05
R	.15	.55

a. 0.55
b. 0.8572
c. 0.9167
d. 0.7857
e. 0.8182

ANSWER: D

Probability Distributions

CMBA Objective Correlations

- Given a scenario with probabilities and quantitative outcomes, calculate the expected value.

- Given a scenario with two small (five numbers each) sets of data (with same average and different SD's), identify the managerial impact of having the larger SD.

- Given a scenario with normal distribution (mean and SD given), calculate parameters for the aggregated (or disaggregated) normal distribution.

- Given a scenario including sample size, average and SD, differentiate SE from SD.

- Given a scenario, choose appropriate distribution for a random variable.

- Given a scenario including sample size, average and SD; calculate the 95% confidence interval for the population average.

- Given a scenario including sample size, average, and standard deviation, determine statistical significance from the average in question and managerial implications

Sample Questions

1. A numerical description of the outcome of an experiment is
   a. a normal variable.
   b. a discrete variable.
   c. a random variable.
   d. an experimental variable.

   ANSWER: C

2. Which of the following are continuous random variables?

   I.   the weight of an elephant
   II.   the time to answer a questionnaire
   III.   the number of floors in a skyscraper
   IV.   the square feet of countertop in a kitchen

   a. I and II only
   b. III and IV only
   c. I, II and IV
   d. I, II, II, and IV

   ANSWER: C

3. A statement that matches the values of a random variable with the probabilities of those values is
   a. the expected value.
   b. the variation of the random variable.
   c. an experiment.
   d. a probability distribution.

   ANSWER: D

4. In order to measure the dispersion of a random variable, look at its
   a. standard deviation.
   b. mean.
   c. expected value.
   d. average.

   ANSWER: A

5. Experiments with repeated independent trials will be described by the binomial distribution if
   a. the trials are continuous.
   b. each trial result influences the next.
   c. the time between trials is constant.
   d. each trial has exactly two outcomes whose probabilities do not change.

   ANSWER: D

6. In a Poisson probability problem, the rate of errors is one every two hours. To find the probability of three defects in four hours,
   a. $\lambda = 1, x = 4$
   b. $\lambda = 2, x = 3$
   c. $\lambda = 3, x = 2$
   d. $\lambda = 3, x = 6$

   ANSWER: B

7. A probability density function
   a. gives the probability that the random variable equals a specific value of x.
   b. is used for discrete random variables.
   c. describes the graph whose underlying area represents probability over an interval.
   d. each of the above is true.

   ANSWER: C

8. The uniform distribution defined over the interval from 25 to 40 has the probability density function
   a. $f(x) = 1/40$ for all x
   b. $f(x) = 5/8$ for $25 = x = 40$ and $f(x) = 0$ elsewhere
   c. $f(x) = 1/25$ for $0 = x = 25$ and $f(x) = 1/40$ for $26 = x = 40$
   d. $f(x) = 1/15$ for $25 = x = 40$ and $f(x) = 0$ elsewhere

   ANSWER: D

9. If x is normally distributed with mean 12 and standard deviation 2, then P(x = 9) is
   a. $P(z = 9/10)$
   b. $P(z = -3/2)$
   c. $P(z = 2/3)$
   d. $P(z = -3/4)$

   ANSWER: B

10. When the exponential distribution probability is given as

    $$P(x \leq 9) = 1 - e^{-9/18}$$

    the average value for x is
    a. 18
    b. 9
    c. 9/18
    d. 1/2

    ANSWER: A

The following information applies to Questions 11-13.

The high school GPA of applicants for admission to a college program are recorded and relative frequencies are calculated for the categories.

GPA	F(x)
x < 2.0	.08
2.0 = x < 2.5	.12
2.5 = x < 3.0	.35
3.0 = x < 3.5	.30
3.5 = x	

11. Complete the table to make this a valid probability distribution.
    a. $f(x) = .12$ for 3.5 = x
    b. $f(x) = .18$ for 3.5 = x
    c. $f(x) = .20$ for 3.5 = x
    d. $f(x) = .15$ for 3.5 = x

    ANSWER: D

12. What is the probability an applicant's GPA will be below 3.0?
    a. .57
    b. .50
    c. .45
    d. .55

    ANSWER: D

13. What is the probability an applicant's GPA will be 2.5 or above?
    a. .80
    b. .20
    c. .70
    d. .78

    ANSWER: A

The following information applies to Questions 14-16.

A calculus instructor uses computer aided instruction and allows students to take the midterm exam as many times as needed until a passing grade is obtained. Following is a record of the number of students in a class of 20 who took the test each number of times.

Students	Number of tests
10	1
7	2
2	3
1	4

14. Find the expected value of the number of tests taken.
    a. .71
    b. 1.7
    c. 1.2
    d. 1.4

    ANSWER: B

15. Compute the variance.
    a. 1.7
    b. .71
    c. .74
    d. .82

    ANSWER: B

16. Compute the standard deviation.
    a. .8457
    b. .8246
    c. .8426
    d. .8626

    ANSWER: C

The following information applies to Questions 17-20.

A video rental store has two video cameras available for customers to rent. Historically, demand for cameras has followed this distribution. The revenue per rental is $40. If a customer wants a camera and none is available, the store gives a $15 coupon for tape rental.

Demand	Relative Frequency	Revenue	Cost
0	.35	0	0
1	.30	40	0
2	.20	80	0
3	.10	80	15
4	.05	80	30

17. What is the expected demand?
    a. 1.2
    b. 1.8
    c. 1.3
    d. 1.6

    ANSWER: A

18. What is the expected revenue?
    a. 40
    b. 50
    c. 70
    d. 80

    ANSWER: A

19. What is the expected cost?
    a. 15
    b. 5
    c. 3
    d. 8

    ANSWER: C

20. What is the expected profit?
    a. 25
    b. 45
    c. 47
    d. 37

    ANSWER: D

The following information applies to Questions 21-23.

Scores on an endurance test for cardiac patients are normally distributed with $\mu = 182$ and $\sigma = 24$.

21. What is the probability a patient will score above 190?
    a. .3607
    b. .3077
    c. .3567
    d. .3707

    ANSWER: D

22. What percentage of patients score below 170?
    a. .3072
    b. .3077
    c. .3087
    d. .3085

    ANSWER: D

23. What score does a patient at the 75th percentile receive?
    a. 187
    b. 198
    c. 189
    d. 192

    ANSWER: B

Decision Analysis

CMBA Objective Correlations

- Given a scenario including probabilities and end values, use the principles of decision analysis to identify the range of probabilities under which a course of action would be chosen.

Sample Questions

1. The options from which a decision maker chooses a course of action are
   a. called the decision alternatives.
   b. under the control of the decision maker.
   c. not the same as the states of nature.
   d. each of the above is true.

   ANSWER: D

2. States of nature
   a. can describe uncontrollable natural events such as floods or freezing temperatures.
   b. can be selected by the decision maker.
   c. cannot be enumerated by the decision maker.
   d. each of the above is true.

   ANSWER: A

3. A payoff
   a. is always measured in profit.
   b. is always measured in cost.
   c. exists for each pair of decision alternative and state of nature.
   d. exists for each state of nature.

   ANSWER: C

4. Making a good decision
   a. requires probabilities for all states of nature.
   b. requires a clear understanding of decision alternatives, states of nature, and payoffs.
   c. implies that a desirable outcome will occur.
   d. each of the above is true.

   ANSWER: B

5. A decision tree
    a. presents all decision alternatives first and follows them with all states of nature.
    b. presents all states of nature first and follows them with all decision alternatives.
    c. alternates the decision alternatives and states of nature.
    d. arranges decision alternatives and states of nature in their natural chronological order.

ANSWER: D

6. Sensitivity analysis considers
    a. how sensitive the decision maker is to risk.
    b. changes in the number of states of nature.
    c. changes in the values of the payoffs.
    d. changes in the available alternatives.

ANSWER: C

7. If $P(high) = .3$, $P(low) = .7$, $P(favorable \mid high) = .9$, and $P(unfavorable \mid low) = .6$, then $P(favorable) =$
    a. .10
    b. .27
    c. .30
    d. .55

ANSWER: D

8. A payoff table is given as

	s_1	s_2	s_3
d_1	10	8	6
d_2	14	15	2
d_3	7	8	9

If the probabilities of s_1, s_2, and s_3 are .2, .4, and .4, respectively, then what decision should be made under expected value?

    a. d_1
    b. d_2
    c. d_3
    d. a three way tie

ANSWER: D

9. A payoff table is given as

	s_1	s_2	s_3
d_1	250	750	500
d_2	300	-250	1200
d_3	500	500	600

If the probabilities of d_1, d_2, and d_3 are .2, .5, and .3, respectively, then what choice should be made under expected value?

a. d_1
b. d_2
c. d_3
d. a three way tie

ANSWER: A

The following information applies to Questions 10-11.

Choice/Event	Event 1	Event 2
A	0	20
B	8	0

10. If p is the probability of Event 1 and (1-p) is the probability of Event 2, for what values of p would you choose A? Values in the table are payoffs.

a. p = .5
b. p = .2
c. p = .4
d. p = .6

ANSWER: A

11. If p is the probability of Event 1 and (1-p) is the probability of Event 2, for what values of p would you choose C? Values in the table are payoffs.

a. p = .5
b. p = .7
c. p = .8
d. p = .9

ANSWER: C

The following information applies to Questions 12-13.

Dollar Department Stores has received an offer from Harris Diamonds to purchase Dollar's store on Grove Street for $120,000. Dollar has determined probability estimates of the store's future profitability, based on economic outcomes, as: P($80,000) = .2, P($100,000) = .3, P($120,000) = .1, and P($140,000) = .4.

12. Should Dollar sell the store on Grove Street?

    a.   no, don't sell the store
    b.   yes, sell the store
    c.   insufficient information to decide
    d.   either a or b

ANSWER: B

13. Dollar can have an economic forecast performed, costing $10,000, that produces indicators I_1 and I_2, for which $P\left(I_1|80,000\right) = .1$; $P\left(I_1|100,000\right) = .2$; $P\left(I_1|120,000\right) = .6$; $P\left(I_1|140,000\right) = .3$. Should Dollar purchase the forecast?

    a.   No, don't purchase the forecast
    b.   Yes, purchase the forecast
    c.   insufficient information to decide
    d.   either a or b

ANSWER: A

Investor I

An investor is considering 4 investments, A, B, C, and leaving his money in the bank. The payoff from each investment is a function of the economic climate over the next 2 years. The economy can expand or decline. The following payoff matrix has been developed for the decision problem.

	A	B	C	D
1		Payoff Matrix		
2				
3		Economy		
4	Investment	Decline	Expand	
5	A	0	85	
6	B	25	65	
7	C	40	30	
8	Bank	10	10	
	Payoffs			

14. Refer to Investor I. What decision should be made according to the maximax decision rule?
    a. A
    b. B
    c. C
    d. Bank

    ANSWER: A

15. Refer to Investor I. What decision should be made according to the maximin decision rule?
    a. A
    b. B
    c. C
    d. Bank

    ANSWER: C

16. Refer to Investor I. What decision should be made according to the minimax regret decision rule?
    a. A
    b. B
    c. C
    d. Bank

    ANSWER: B

Investor III

An investor is considering 4 investments, A, B, C and leaving his money in the bank. The payoff from each investment is a function of the economic climate over the next 2 years. The economy can expand or decline. The following payoff matrix has been developed for the decision problem. The investor has estimated the probability of a declining economy at 70% and an expanding economy at 30%.

	A	B	C	D
1		Payoff Matrix		
2				
3		Economy		
4	Investment	Decline	Expand	EMV
5	A	-10	90	
6	B	20	50	
7	C	40	45	
8	Bank	15	20	
9				
10	Probability	0.7	0.3	
	Payoffs			

17. Refer to Investor III. What decision should be made according to the expected monetary value decision rule?
    a. A
    b. B
    c. C
    d. Bank

    ANSWER: C

18. Refer to Investor III. What is the expected monetary value of Investment A?
    a. 34.
    b. 30.
    c. 20.
    d. 15.

    ANSWER: C

19. Refer to Investor III. What decision should be made according to the expected regret decision rule?
    a. A
    b. B
    c. C
    d. Bank

    ANSWER: C

Expected Value

	A	B	C	D	E
1		Payoff Matrix			
2					
3		Economy			
4	Investment	Decline	Expand	EMV	
5	A	0	80		
6	B	30	70		
7	C	50	35		
8	Bank	20	20		
9					
10	Probability	0.7	0.3		
11					
12	Payoff of decision made with perfect information:				
13					
14			EVPI:		

EVPI

20. Refer to Expected Value. What is the expected value of perfect information for the investor?
    a. 13.5
    b. 20
    c. 45.5
    d. 59

    ANSWER: A

21. Refer to Expected Value. What is the expected value with perfect information for the investor?
    a. 13.5
    b. 45.5
    c. 59
    d. 80

    ANSWER: C

Forecasting

CMBA Objective Correlations

- Given a scenario with monthly data, demonstrate an understanding of the moving average method.

- Understand how to generate a forecast with data that exhibits a long-term trend and seasonal variation.

- Given historical data, determine whether or not to include an outlier in generating a prediction.

Sample Questions

1. Time series methods
   a. discover a pattern in historical data and project it into the future.
   b. include cause-effect relationships.
   c. are useful when historical information is not available.
   d. each of the above is true.

   ANSWER: A

2. Gradual shifting of a time series over a long period of time is called
   a. periodicity.
   b. cycle.
   c. regression.
   d. trend.

   ANSWER: D

3. Seasonal components
   a. cannot be predicted.
   b. are regular repeated patterns.
   c. are long runs of observations above or below the trend line.
   d. reflect a shift in the series over time.

   ANSWER: B

4. Short-term, unanticipated, and nonrecurring factors in a time series provide the random variability known as
   a. uncertainty.
   b. the forecast error.
   c. the residuals.
   d. the irregular component.

   ANSWER: D

5. The focus of smoothing methods is to smooth
    a. the irregular component.
    b. wide seasonal variations.
    c. significant trend effects.
    d. long range forecasts.

    ANSWER: A

6. Forecast errors
    a. are the difference in successive values of a time series
    b. are the differences between actual and forecast values
    c. should all be nonnegative
    d. should be summed to judge the goodness of a forecasting model

    ANSWER: B

7. To select a value for α for exponential smoothing
    a. use a small α when the series varies substantially.
    b. use a large α when the series has little random variability.
    c. use any value between 0 and 1
    d. each of the above is true.

    ANSWER: D

8. Linear trend is calculated as $T_t = 28.5 + .75t$. The trend projection for period 15 is
    a. 11.25
    b. 28.50
    c. 39.75
    d. 44.25

    ANSWER: C

10. Causal models
    a. should avoid the use of regression analysis.
    b. attempt to explain a time series' behavior.
    c. do not use time series data.
    d. each is true.

    ANSWER: B

384

Honest Al's – Moving Averages

Honest Al's Used Cars wants to predict how many cars are sold each month. He has collected data for 12 months. He needs your help in analyzing this data using moving averages.

	A	B	C
1		**Number of**	**4-Month**
2	**Time Period**	**Cars Sold**	**Moving Avg.**
3	1	70	
4	2	80	
5	3	66	
6	4	74	
7	5	64	
8	6	76	71.00
9	7	72	70.00
10	8	82	71.50
11	9	82	73.50
12	10	76	78.00
13	11	84	78.00
14	12	80	81.00
15			
16		MSE	40.59

11. Refer to Honest Al's Moving Average. What is the 4-month moving average forecast for month 5?
    a. 71
    b. 72.5
    c. 74
    d. 75

    ANSWER: B

12. Refer to Honest Al's Moving Average. What would be the forecasted values for time periods 13 and 13?
    a. 81.00 and 79.50
    b. 78.00 and 78.00
    c. 80.50 and 80.13
    d. 80.50 and 80.00

    ANSWER: C

Honest Al's – Weighted Moving Averages

Honest Al's Used Cars wants to predict how many cars are sold each month. He has collected data for 12 months. He needs your help in analyzing this data using weighted moving averages.

	A	B	C	D	E	F
1			**2-Month Weighted**			
2	**Time Period**	**Number of Cars Sold**	**Moving Avg.**		**Weights**	
3	1	70			w1	0.244
4	2	80			w2	0.756
5	3	66			sum	1.000
6	4	74	76.59			
7	5	64	67.95			
8	6	76	71.56			
9	7	72	66.93			
10	8	82	75.02			
11	9	82	74.44			
12	10	76	82.00			
13	11	84	80.54			
14	12	80	77.95			
15						
16		MSE	26.72			

13. Refer to Honest Al's Weighted Averages. What is the 2-month weighted moving average forecast for month 3 using the weight in the spreadsheet?
    a. 72.44
    b. 75.00
    c. 76.59
    d. 77.56

    ANSWER: A

14. Refer to Honest Al's Weighted Averages. What would be the forecasted value for time period 13?
    a. 83.024.
    b. 80.796.
    c. 79.245.
    d. 79.908.

    ANSWER: A

Joe's Sporting Goods – Additive Seasonal Method

Joe's Sporting Goods wants to forecast quarterly sales figures using the additive seasonal method. The store has collected 12 quarters of data and needs your help to analyze the data.

	A	B	C	D	E	F	G	H	I	J
1			Time	Actual	Base	Seasonal	Predicted			
2	Year	Qtr	Period	Sales	Level	Factor	Sales			
3	1991	1	1	284	331.25	-47.250			alpha	0.764
4		2	2	184	331.25	-147.250			beta	1.0
5		3	3	365	331.25	33.750				
6		4	4	492	331.25	160.750				
7	1992	1	5	485	484.85	0.146	284.00			
8		2	6	277	438.54	-161.541	337.60			
9		3	7	606	540.72	65.279	472.29			
10		4	8	722	556.41	165.591	701.47			
11	1993	1	9	763	714.17	48.827	556.56			
12		2	10	593	745.02	-152.022	552.63			
13		3	11	912	822.74	89.260	810.30			
14		4	12	1145	942.47	202.534	988.33			
15										
16							17688.777			

15. Refer to Joe's Sporting Goods - Additive Seasonal Model. What are predicted sales for time period 13 using the data in the spreadsheet?
   a. 915 ≤ predicted sales < 916
   b. 916 ≤ predicted sales < 917
   c. 991 ≤ predicted sales < 992
   d. 1045 ≤ predicted sales < 1046

   ANSWER: C

Multiplicative Seasonal Effects Model

A store wants to predict quarterly sales. The owner has collected 3 years of sales data and wants your help in analyzing the data using the multiplicative seasonal effects model.

	A	B	C	D	E	F	G	H	I	J
1			Time	Actual		Seasonal				
2	Year	Qtr	Period	Sales	Level	Factor	Forecast			
3	1994	1	1	368	462.50	0.796			alpha	0.332167
4		2	2	168	462.50	0.363			beta	1
5		3	3	530	462.50	1.146				
6		4	4	784	462.50	1.695				
7	1995	1	5	770	630.32	1.222	368.00			
8		2	6	354	744.66	0.475	228.96			
9		3	7	1012	790.65	1.280	853.34			
10		4	8	1244	771.79	1.612	1340.26			
11	1996	1	9	1326	875.98	1.514	942.82			
12		2	10	986	1273.96	0.774	416.43			
13		3	11	1624	1272.25	1.276	1630.62			
14		4	12	2090	1280.35	1.632	2050.66			
15										
16							85564.040			

16. Refer to Multiplicative Seasonal Effects Model. What are predicted sales for time period 13 using the data in the spreadsheet?
    a. $1259 \leq$ predicted sales < 1260
    b. $1938 \leq$ predicted sales < 1939
    c. $2090 \leq$ predicted sales < 2091
    d. $2187 \leq$ predicted sales < 2188

    ANSWER: C

Double Moving Average Model

A store wants to predict quarterly sales. The owner has collected 3 years of sales data and wants your help in analyzing the data using the double moving average model with $k=4$.

	A	B	C	D	E	F	G	H	I
1			Time	Actual	Moving	Dbl Moving			
2	Year	Qtr	Period	Sales	Ave	Ave	Level	Trend	Forecast
3	1994	1	1	368					
4		2	2	168					
5		3	3	530					
6		4	4	784	462.50				
7	1995	1	5	770	563.00				
8		2	6	354	609.50				
9		3	7	1012	730.00	591.25	868.75	92.50	
10		4	8	1244	845.00	686.88	1003.13	105.42	961.25
11	1996	1	9	1326	984.00	792.13	1175.88	127.92	1108.54
12		2	10	986	1142.00	925.25	1358.75	144.50	1303.79
13		3	11	1624	1295.00	1066.50	1523.50	152.33	1503.25
14		4	12	2090	1506.50	1231.88	1781.13	183.08	1675.83
15	1997	1	13						
16		2	14						

17. Refer to Double Moving Average Model. What are predicted sales for time period 16 using the data in the spreadsheet?
    a. $1964 \leq$ predicted sales < 1965
    b. $2147 \leq$ predicted sales < 2148
    c. $2330 \leq$ predicted sales < 2331
    d. $2513 \leq$ predicted sales < 2513

    ANSWER: D

Holt's Forecast

Joe's Sporting Goods wants to forecast quarterly sales figures using Holt's method. The store has collected 12 quarters of data and needs your help to analyze the data.

	A	B	C	D	E	F	G	H	I	J
1			Time	Actual	Base		Predicted			
2	Year	Qtr	Period	Sales	Level	Trend	Sales			
3	1991	1	1	284					alpha	0.5
4		2	2	184					beta	0.5
5		3	3	365	287.0	14.0	209.0			
6		4	4	492	396.5	61.8	301.0			
7	1992	1	5	485	471.6	68.4	458.3			
8		2	6	277	408.5	2.7	540.1			
9		3	7	606	508.6	51.4	411.2			
10		4	8	722	641.0	91.9	560.0			
11	1993	1	9	763	747.9	99.4	732.9			
12		2	10	593	720.2	35.8	847.3			
13		3	11	912	834.0	74.8	756.0			
14		4	12	1145	1026.9	133.9	908.8			
15										
16							31877.0			

18. Refer to Holt's Forecast. What are predicted sales for time period 2 using the data in the spreadsheet?
    a. $208.5 \le$ predicted sales < 209.5
    b. $233.5 \le$ predicted sales < 234.5
    c. $283.5 \le$ predicted sales < 284.5
    d. $300.5 \le$ predicted sales < 301.5

    ANSWER: C

19. Refer to Holt's Forecast. What are predicted sales for time period 13 using the data in the spreadsheet?
    a. $908 \le$ predicted sales < 909
    b. $1026 \le$ predicted sales < 1027
    c. $1144 \le$ predicted sales < 1146
    d. $1160 \le$ predicted sales < 1161

    ANSWER: D

Linear Forecast

Joe's Sporting Goods wants to forecast quarterly sales figures using a linear trend model. The store has collected 12 quarters of data and needs your help to analyze the data. The relevant regression output is in the following table.

Regression Statistics	
	Coefficients
Intercept	114.136
X Variable	69.979

	A	B	C	D	E
1			Time	Actual	Linear
2	Year	Qtr	Period	Sales	Trend
3	1991	1	1	284	
4		2	2	184	254.1
5		3	3	365	324.1
6		4	4	492	394.1
7	1992	1	5	485	464.0
8		2	6	277	534.0
9		3	7	606	604.0
10		4	8	722	674.0
11	1993	1	9	763	743.9
12		2	10	593	813.9
13		3	11	912	883.9
14		4	12	1145	953.9
15					
16					

20. Refer to Linear Forecast. What are predicted sales for the fourth quarter of 1994?
    a. $1020 \leq$ predicted sales < 1025
    b. $1090 \leq$ predicted sales < 1095
    c. $1160 \leq$ predicted sales < 1165
    d. $1230 \leq$ predicted sales < 1235

ANSWER: D

Quadratic Forecast

Joe's Sporting Goods wants to forecast quarterly sales figures using a quadratic trend model. The store has collected 12 quarters of data and needs your help to analyze the data. The relevant regression output is in the following table.

Regression Statistics	
	Coefficients
Intercept	263.4545
X Variable 1	5.985514
X Variable 2	4.922577

	A	B	C	D	E	F
			Time		Actual	Quadratic
1			**Time**		**Actual**	**Quadratic**
2	Year	Qtr	Period	Time^2	Sales	Trend
3	1991	1	1	1	284	
4		2	2	4	184	295.1
5		3	3	9	365	325.7
6		4	4	16	492	366.2
7	1992	1	5	25	485	416.4
8		2	6	36	277	476.6
9		3	7	49	606	546.6
10		4	8	64	722	626.4
11	1993	1	9	81	763	716.1
12		2	10	100	593	815.6
13		3	11	121	912	924.9
14		4	12	144	1145	1044.1

21. Refer to Quadratic Forecast. What are predicted sales for the fourth quarter of 1994?
    a. $1170 \leq$ predicted sales < 1175
    b. $1310 \leq$ predicted sales < 1315
    c. $1460 \leq$ predicted sales < 1465
    d. $1615 \leq$ predicted sales < 1620

    ANSWER: C

Regression Analysis

CMBA Objective Correlations

- Given a scenario, regression output, and values for the independent variables, predict range of a value.

- Given a scenario and regression output, determine the significant coefficients.

- Given a scenario and regression output, determine the managerial interpretation of coefficients.

- Given a scenario and regression output, explain managerial implications of a dummy variable.

- Given a scenario and regression output, determine how much a coefficient might vary.

- Given a scenario including three groups with their averages, sample sizes, and SD's, along with the p-value of an ANOVA, determine the managerial impact if the group means are statistically significantly different.

Sample Questions

1. Regression analysis is a modeling technique
   a. that assumes all data is normally distributed.
   b. for analyzing the relationship between dependent and independent variables.
   c. for examining linear trend data only.
   d. for capturing uncertainty in predicted values of Y.

   ANSWER: B

2. Why do we create a scatter plot of the data in regression analysis?
   a. To compute the error terms.
   b. Because Excel calculates the function from the scatter plot.
   c. To check for a relationship between X and Y.
   d. To estimate predicted values.

   ANSWER: C

3. Which of the following represents a regression model?
   a. $\hat{Y} = f(X_1, X_2, ..., X_k)$
   b. $\hat{Y} = f(X_1, X_2, ..., X_k) + \varepsilon$
   c. $Y = f(X_1, X_2, ..., X_k)$
   d. $Y = f(X_1, X_2, ..., X_k) + \varepsilon$

   ANSWER: D

4. The term ε in the regression model represents
   a. the slope of the regression model.
   b. a random error term.
   c. a correction for mistakes in measuring X.
   d. a correction for the fact that we are taking a sample.

   ANSWER: B

5. The regression line denotes the _____ between the dependent and independent variables.
   a. unsystematic variation
   b. systematic variation
   c. random variation
   d. average variation

   ANSWER: B

6. The regression function indicates the
   a. average value the dependent variable assumes for a given value of the independent variable.
   b. actual value the independent variable assumes for a given value of the dependent variable.
   c. average value the dependent variable assumes for a given value of the independent variable.
   d. actual value the independent variable assumes for a given value of the dependent variable.

   ANSWER: A

7. Based on the following regression output, what is the equation of the regression line.

Regression Statistics					
Multiple R	0.917214				
R Square	0.841282				
Adjusted R Square	0.821442				
Standard Error	9.385572				
Observations	10				
ANOVA					
	df	SS	MS	F	Significance F
Regression	1	3735.306	3735.306	42.40379	0.000186
Residual	8	704.7117	88.08896		
Total	9	4440.017			
	Coefficients	Standard Error	t Stat	P-value	Lower 95%
Intercept	31.62378	10.44297	3.028236	0.016353	7.542233
X Variable 1	1.131661	0.173786	6.511819	0.000186	0.73091

a. $\hat{Y}_1 = 1.131661 + 31.62378\, X_{1i}$

b. $\hat{Y}_1 = 31.62378 + 1.131661\, X_{1i}$

c. $\hat{Y}_1 = 3.028236 + 6.511819\, X_{1i}$

d. $\hat{Y}_1 = 7.542233 + 0.73091\, X_{1i}$

ANSWER: B

8. Based on the following regression output, what proportion of the total variation in Y is explained by X?

Regression Statistics					
Multiple R	0.917214				
R Square	0.841282				
Adjusted R Square	0.821442				
Standard Error	9.385572				
Observations	10				
ANOVA					
	df	SS	MS	F	Significance F
Regression	1	3735.306	3735.306	42.40379	0.000186
Residual	8	704.7117	88.08896		
Total	9	4440.017			
	Coefficients	Standard Error	t Stat	P-value	Lower 95%
Intercept	31.62378	10.44297	3.028236	0.016353	7.542233
X Variable 1	1.131661	0.173786	6.511819	0.000186	0.73091

a. 0.917214
b. 0.841282
c. 0.821442
d. 9.385572

ANSWER: B

9. Based on the following regression output, what conclusion can you reach about β_1?

Regression Statistics					
Multiple R	0.917214				
R Square	0.841282				
Adjusted R Square	0.821442				
Standard Error	9.385572				
Observations	10				
ANOVA					
	df	SS	MS	F	Significance F
Regression	1	3735.306	3735.306	42.40379	0.000186
Residual	8	704.7117	88.08896		
Total	9	4440.017			
	Coefficients	Standard Error	t Stat	P-value	Lower 95%
Intercept	31.62378	10.44297	3.028236	0.016353	7.542233
X Variable 1	1.131661	0.173786	6.511819	0.000186	0.73091

a. $\beta_1 = 0$, with P-value = 0.016353
b. $\beta_1 \neq 0$, with P-value = 0.016353
c. $\beta_1 = 0$, with P-value = 0.000186
d. $\beta_1 \neq 0$, with P-value = 0.000186

ANSWER: D

10. Based on the following regression output, what conclusion can you reach about β_0?

Regression Statistics					
Multiple R	0.917214				
R Square	0.841282				
Adjusted R Square	0.821442				
Standard Error	9.385572				
Observations	10				
ANOVA					
	df	SS	MS	F	Significance F
Regression	1	3735.306	3735.306	42.40379	0.000186
Residual	8	704.7117	88.08896		
Total	9	4440.017			
	Coefficients	Standard Error	t Stat	P-value	Lower 95%
Intercept	31.62378	10.44297	3.028236	0.016353	7.542233
X Variable 1	1.131661	0.173786	6.511819	0.000186	0.73091

a. $\beta_0 = 0$, with P-value = 0.016353

b. $\beta_0 \neq 0$, with P-value = 0.016353

c. $\beta_0 = 0$, with P-value = 0.000186

d. $\beta_0 \neq 0$, with P-value = 0.000186

ANSWER: B

11. Based on the following regression output, what is the equation of the regression line?

Regression Statistics					
Multiple R	0.99313				
R Square	0.98630				
Adjusted R Square	0.98238				
Standard Error	2.94802				
Observations	10				
ANOVA					
	df	SS	MS	F	Significance F
Regression	2	4379.182	2189.591	251.943	0.0000
Residual	7	60.836	8.691		
Total	9	4440.017			
	Coefficients	Standard Error	t Stat	P-value	Lower 95%
Intercept	14.169	3.856	3.674	0.008	5.050
X Variable 1	0.985	0.114	8.607	0.000	0.714
X Variable 2	0.995	0.057	17.498	0.000	0.860

a. $\hat{Y}_i = 14.169 + 0.985\ X_{1i} + 0.995\ X_{2i}$

b. $\hat{Y}_i = 14.169 + 0.995\ X_{1i} + 0.985\ X_{2i}$

c. $\hat{Y}_i = 0.995 + 14.169\ X_{1i} + 0.985\ X_{2i}$

d. $\hat{Y}_i = 3.856 + 0.114\ X_{1i} + 0.057\ X_{2i}$

ANSWER: A

12. An analyst has identified 3 independent variables (X_1, X_2, X_3) which might be used to predict Y. He has computed the regression equations using all combinations of the variables and the results are summarized in the following table. Which combination of variables provides the best regression results?

Independent Variable in the Model	R^2	Adjusted-R^2	S_e	Parameter Estimates
X_1	0.00089	-0.124	23.548	$b_0=93.7174, b_1=0.922$
X_2	0.3870	0.3104	18.448	$b_0 = 57.0803, b_2= 1.545$
X_1 and X_2	0.3910	0.2170	19.654	$b_0 = 50.2927, b_1= 1.952, b_2 = 1.554$
X_3	0.8413	0.8214	9.3858	$b_0=31.6238, b_3=1.132$
X_1 and X_3	0.8413	0.7960	10.033	$b_0 = 31.133, b_1= 0.148, b_3 = 1.132$
X_2 and X_3	0.9863	0.9824	2.948	$b_0 = 14.169, b_2= 0.985, b_3 = 0.995$
All three	0.9871	0.9807	3.085	$b_0 = 11.113, b_1= 0.899, b_2 = 0.990, b_3 = 0.993$

a. X_1
b. All three
c. X_1 and X_2
d. X_2 and X_3

ANSWER: D

13. An analyst has identified 3 independent variables (X_1, X_2, X_3) which might be used to predict Y. He has computed the regression equations using all combinations of the variables and the results are summarized in the following table. Why is the R^2 value for the X_3 model the same as the R^2 value for the X_1 and X_3 model, but the Adjusted R^2 values differ?

Independent Variable in the Model	R^2	Adjusted-R^2	S_e	Parameter Estimates
X_1	0.00089	-0.124	23.548	$b_0=93.7174, b_1=0.922$
X_2	0.3870	0.3104	18.448	$b_0 = 57.0803, b_2 = 1.545$
X_1 and X_2	0.3910	0.2170	19.654	$b_0 = 50.2927, b_1 = 1.952, b_2 = 1.554$
X_3	0.8413	0.8214	9.3858	$b_0=31.6238, b_3=1.132$
X_1 and X_3	0.8413	0.7960	10.033	$b_0 = 31.133, b_1 = 0.148, b_3 = 1.132$
X_2 and X_3	0.9863	0.9824	2.948	$b_0 = 14.169, b_2 = 0.985, b_3 = 0.995$
All three	0.9871	0.9807	3.085	$b_0 = 11.113, b_1 = 0.899, b_2 = 0.990, b_3 = 0.993$

a.   The standard error for X_1 is greater than the standard error for X_3.
b. X_1 does not reduce ESS enough to compensate for its addition to the model.
c. X_1 does not reduce TSS enough to compensate for its addition to the model.
d. X_1 and X_3 represent similar factors so multicollinearity exists.

ANSWER: B

Linear Programming

CMBA Objective Correlations

- Given a scenario including cost and sales data, write the objective function for the appropriate Linear Programming model.

- Given a scenario including RHS and coefficients, write a constraint for the appropriate Linear Programming model.

- Given a scenario including LP Output, determine the most critical resource to relieve.

- Given a scenario including correlation coefficient (r) and graphs, match the correlation coefficient to appropriate graphs.

- Given a scenario, determine managerial interpretation of slope and intercept coefficients.

Sample Questions

1. A greater than or equal to constraint can be expressed as
   a. $f(X_1, X_2, \ldots, X_n) <= b$.
   b. $f(X_1, X_2, \ldots, X_n) >= b$.
   c. $f(X_1, X_2, \ldots, X_n) = b$.
   d. $f(X_1, X_2, \ldots, X_n) <> b$.

ANSWER: B

2. A production optimization problem has 4 decision variables and resource b_1 limits how many of the 4 products can be produced. Which of the following constraints reflects this fact?
   a. $f(X_1, X_2, X_3, X_4) <= b_1$
   b. $f(X_1, X_2, X_3, X_4) >= b_1$
   c. $f(X_1, X_2, X_3, X_4) = b_1$
   d. $f(X_1, X_2, X_3, X_4) <> b_1$

ANSWER: A

3. A production optimization problem has 4 decision variables and a requirement that at least b_1 units of material b_1 are consumed. Which of the following constraints reflects this fact?
   a. $f(X_1, X_2, X_3, X_4) <= b_1$
   b. $f(X_1, X_2, X_3, X_4) >= b_1$
   c. $f(X_1, X_2, X_3, X_4) = b_1$
   d. $f(X_1, X_2, X_3, X_4) <> b_1$

ANSWER: B

4. Which of the following is the general format of an objective function?
    a. $f(X_1, X_2, \ldots, X_n) <= b$
    b. $f(X_1, X_2, \ldots, X_n) >= b$
    c. $f(X_1, X_2, \ldots, X_n) = b$
    d. $f(X_1, X_2, \ldots, X_n)$

ANSWER: D

5. Linear programming problems have
    a. linear objective functions, non-linear constraints.
    b. non-linear objective functions, non-linear constraints.
    c. non-linear objective functions, linear constraints.
    d. linear objective functions, linear constraints.

ANSWER: D

6. The first step in formulating a linear programming problem is:
    a. Identify any upper or lower bounds on the decision variables.
    b. State the constraints as linear combinations of the decision variables.
    c. Understand the problem.
    d. Identify the decision variables.
    e. State the objective function as a linear combination of the decision variables.

ANSWER: C

7. The second step in formulating a linear programming problem is:
    a. Identify any upper or lower bounds on the decision variables.
    b. State the constraints as linear combinations of the decision variables.
    c. Understand the problem.
    d. Identify the decision variables.
    e. State the objective function as a linear combination of the decision variables.

ANSWER: D

8. The third step in formulating a linear programming problem is:
    a. Identify any upper or lower bounds on the decision variables.
    b. State the constraints as linear combinations of the decision variables.
    c. Understand the problem.
    d. Identify the decision variables.
    e. State the objective function as a linear combination of the decision variables.

ANSWER: E

9. The following linear programming problem has been written to plan the production of two products. The company wants to maximize its profits.

X_1 = number of product 1 produced in each batch
X_2 = number of product 2 produced in each batch

MAX: $150 X_1 + 250 X_2$
Subject to: $2 X_1 + 5 X_2 \leq 200$
              $3 X_1 + 7 X_2 \leq 175$
              $X_1, X_2 \geq 0$

How much profit is earned per product 2 unit produced?
a. 150
b. 175
c. 200
d. 250

ANSWER: D

10. The following linear programming problem has been written to plan the production of two products. The company wants to maximize its profits.

X_1 = number of product 1 produced in each batch
X_2 = number of product 2 produced in each batch

MAX: $150 X_1 + 250 X_2$
Subject to: $2 X_1 + 5 X_2 \leq 200$ - resource 1
              $3 X_1 + 7 X_2 \leq 175$ - resource 2
              $X_1, X_2 \geq 0$

How many units of resource 1 are consumed by each product 1 unit produced?
a. 1
b. 2
c. 3
d. 5

ANSWER: B

11. The following linear programming problem has been written to plan the production of two products. The company wants to maximize its profits.

X$_1$ = number of product 1 produced in each batch
X$_2$ = number of product 2 produced in each batch

MAX: 150 X$_1$ + 250 X$_2$
Subject to: 2 X$_1$ + 5 X$_2$ ≤ 200
               3 X$_1$ + 7 X$_2$ ≤ 175
               X$_1$, X$_2$ ≥ 0

How much profit is earned if the company produces 10 units of product 1 and 5 units of product 2?
a. 750
b. 2500
c. 2750
d. 3250

ANSWER: C

12. A company uses 4 pounds of resource 1 to make each unit of X$_1$ and 3 pounds of resource 1 to make each unit of X$_2$. There are only 150 pounds of resource 1 available. Which of the following constraints reflects the relationship between X$_1$, X$_2$ and resource 1?
a. 4 X$_1$ + 3 X$_2$ ≥ 150
b. 4 X$_1$ + 3 X$_2$ ≤ 150
c. 4 X$_1$ + 3 X$_2$ = 150
d. 4 X$_1$ ≤ 150

ANSWER: B

13. A diet is being developed which must contain at least 100 mg of vitamin C. Two fruits are used in this diet. Bananas contain 30 mg of vitamin C and Apples contain 20 mg of vitamin C. The diet must contain at least 100 mg of vitamin C. Which of the following constraints reflects the relationship between Bananas, Apples and vitamin C?
a. 20 A + 30 B ≥ 100
b. 20 A + 30 B ≤ 100
c. 20 A + 30 B = 100
d. 20 A = 100

ANSWER: A

14. The constraint for resource 1 is 5 X$_1$ + 4 X$_2$ ≤ 200. If X$_1$ = 20, what it the maximum value for X$_2$?
a. 20
b. 25
c. 40
d. 50

ANSWER: B

15. The constraint for resource 1 is $5 X_1 + 4 X_2 \geq 200$. If $X_2 = 20$, what it the minimum value for X_1?
    a. 20
    b. 24
    c. 40
    d. 50

ANSWER: B

16. The constraint for resource 1 is $5 X_1 + 4 X_2 \leq 200$. If $X_1 = 20$ and $X_2 = 5$, how much of resource 1 is unused?
    a. 0
    b. 80
    c. 100
    d. 200

ANSWER: B

17. The constraint for resource 1 is $5 X_1 + 4 X_2 \geq 200$. If $X_1 = 40$ and $X_2 = 20$, how much additional units, if any, of resource 1 are employed?
    a. 0
    b. 20
    c. 40
    d. 80

ANSWER: D

18. The objective function for a LP model is $3 X_1 + 2 X_2$. If $X_1 = 20$ and $X_2 = 30$, what is the value of the objective function?
    a. 0
    b. 50
    c. 60
    d. 120

ANSWER: D

19. As long as the slope of the objective function stays between the slope of the binding constraints
    a. the value of the objective function won't change.
    b. there will be alternative optimal solutions.
    c. the values of the dual variables won't change.
    d. there will be no slack in the solution.

ANSWER: C

20. Which of the following is a valid objective function for a linear programming problem?
    a. Max $5xy$
    b. Min $4x + 3y + (2/3)z$
    c. Max $5x^2 + 6y^2$
    d. Min $(x_1 + x_2)/x_3$

ANSWER: B

21. Which of the following statements is NOT true?
    a.   A feasible solution satisfies all constraints.
    b.   An optimal solution satisfies all constraints.
    c.   An infeasible solution violates all constraints.
    d.   A feasible solution point does not have to lie on the boundary of the feasible region.

ANSWER: C

22. A marketing research application uses the variable HD to represent the number of homeowners interviewed
    during the day. The objective function minimizes the cost of interviewing this and other categories and there is
    a constraint that HD $\geq$ 100. The solution indicates that interviewing another homeowner during the day will
    increase costs by 10.00. What do you know?
    a.   the objective function coefficient of HD is 10.
    b.   the dual price for the HD constraint is 10.
    c.   the objective function coefficient of HD is -10.
    d.   the dual price for the HD constraint is -10.

ANSWER: D

23. The dual price for a constraint that compares funds used with funds available is .058. This means that
    a.   the cost of additional funds is 5.8%.
    b.   if more funds can be obtained at a rate of 5.5%, some should be.
    c.   no more funds are needed.
    d.   the objective was to minimize.

ANSWER: B

24. Let M be the number of units to make and B be the number of units to buy. If it costs $2 to make a unit and $3
    to buy a unit and 4000 units are needed, the objective function is
    a.   Max 2M + 3B
    b.   Min 4000 (M + B)
    c.   Max 8000M + 12000B
    d.   Min 2M + 3B

ANSWER: D

25. If P_{ij} = the production of product i in period j, then to indicate that the limit on production of the company's
    three products in period 2 is 400,
    a. $P_{21} + P_{22} + P_{23} \leq 400$
    b. $P_{12} + P_{22} + P_{32} \leq 400$
    c. $P_{32} \leq 400$
    d. $P_{23} \leq 400$

ANSWER: B

26. Let P_{ij} = the production of product i in period j. To specify that production of product 1 in period 3 and in period 4 differs by no more than 100 units,
    a. $P_{13} - P_{14} \leq 100$; $P_{14} - P_{13} \leq 100$
    b. $P_{13} - P_{14} \leq 100$; $P_{13} - P_{14} \geq 100$
    c. $P_{13} - P_{14} \leq 100$; $P_{14} - P_{13} \geq 100$
    d. $P_{13} - P_{14} \geq 100$; $P_{14} - P_{13} \geq 100$

ANSWER: A

27. Let A, B, and C be the amounts invested in companies A, B, and C. If no more than 50% of the total investment can be in company B, then
    a. $B \leq 5$
    b. $A - .5B + C \leq 0$
    c. $.5A - B - .5C \leq 0$
    d. $-.5A + .5B - .5C \leq 0$

ANSWER: D

28. Let x_1 and x_2 be 0 - 1 variables whose values indicate whether projects 1 and 2 are not done or are done. Which answer below indicates that project 2 can be done only if project 1 is done?
    a. $x_1 + x_2 = 1$
    b. $x_1 + x_2 = 2$
    c. $x_1 - x_2 \leq 0$
    d. $x_1 - x_2 \geq 0$

ANSWER: D

29. Let x_1 , x_2 , and x_3 be 0 - 1 variables whose values indicate whether the projects are not done or are done. Which answer below indicates that at least two of the projects must be done?
    a. $x_1 + x_2 + x_3 \geq 2$
    b. $x_1 + x_2 + x_3 \leq 2$
    c. $x_1 + x_2 + x_3 = 2$
    d. $x_1 - x_2 = 0$

ANSWER: A

Simulation

CMBA Objective Correlations

- Given a list of situations, identify those in which simulation would be a viable approach (contain random variables.)

- Given a scenario including simulation output, determine the course of action for two alternatives with means that are not significantly different.

Sample Questions

1. A simulation model uses the mathematical expressions and logical relationships of the
    a. real system.
    b. computer model.
    c. performance measures.
    d. estimated inferences.

ANSWER: A

2. Values for the probabilistic inputs to a simulation
    a. are selected by the decision maker.
    b. are controlled by the decision maker.
    c. are randomly generated based on historical information.
    d. are calculated by fixed mathematical formulas.

ANSWER: C

3. A quantity that is difficult to measure with certainty is called a
    a. risk analysis.
    b. project determinant.
    c. probabilistic input.
    d. profit/loss process.

ANSWER: C

4. A value for probabilistic input from a discrete probability distribution
    a. is the value given by the RAND() function.
    b. is given by matching the probabilistic input with an interval of random numbers.
    c. is between 0 and 1.
    d. must be non-negative.

ANSWER: B

5. The number of units expected to be sold is uniformly distributed between 300 and 500. If r is a random number between 0 and 1, then the proper expression for sales is
    a. 200(r)
    b. r + 300
    c. 300 + 500(r)
    d. 300 + r(200)

ANSWER: D

6. When events occur at discrete points in time
    a. a simulation clock is required.
    b. the simulation advances to the next event.
    c. the model is a discrete-event simulation.
    d. each of these is correct.

ANSWER: D

7. If customer 2 has a service time of 1.6, and if customer 3 has an interarrival time of 1.1 and a service time of 2.3, when will customer 3's service be completed?
    a. 5.0
    b. 3.9
    c. 3.4
    d. There is not enough information to answer.

ANSWER: D

8. Common features of simulations--generating values from probability distributions, maintaining records, recording data and summarizing results--led to the development of
    a. Excel and Lotus.
    b. BASIC, FORTRAN, PASCAL, and C.
    c. GPSS, SIMSCRIPT, SIMAN, and SLAM.
    d. LINDO and The Management Scientist

ANSWER: C

9. In order to verify a simulation model
    a. compare results from several simulation languages.
    b. be sure that the procedures for calculations are logically correct.
    c. confirm that the model accurately represents the real system.
    d. run the model long enough to overcome initial start-up results.
ANSWER: B

10. Simulation
    a. does not guarantee optimality.
    b. is flexible and does not require the assumptions of theoretical models.
    c. allows testing of the system without affecting the real system.
    d. each of these is correct.

ANSWER: D

11. The most frequent use of simulation models is in the analysis of a company's production operations. This is because:
   a. the company has a need to continuously improve production processes, and needs to evaluate changes that they are considering before implementing the changes in the production facility.
   b. the company might want to evaluate new processes.
   c. the company might want to evaluate new operations strategies.
   d. the company needs to model the production process where the durations of various jobs are uncertain and scheduling is complex.
   e. all of the above are correct.

ANSWER: E

12. Simulation modeling is an important tool because it
   a. develops the optimal solution to help managers make good decisions.
   b. graphs the response surface between two distribution functions to help the manager communicate with his team.
   c. "fills in" missing information about the manager's problem to improve the analysis.
   d. allows the manager to play "what if" and to see the impact of his decision before he implements it.
   e. none of these is correct.

ANSWER: D

13. The interval rule for simulating the toss of a fair coin for the chart shown below would be

14. Interval	15. Showing Face
16. *f*	17. Heads
18. *g*	19. Tails

   a. $f = 0.5, g = 0.5$
   b. $f = 0.0, g = 0.5$
   c. $f = 0.0 - 0.5, g = 0.5 - 1.0$
   d. $f = 1.0 - 0.5, g = 0.5 - 0.0$
   e. $f = 0.5, g = 0.0$

ANSWER: C

14. If one were to simulate the rolling of a standard die, how many intervals would be required, and what would be the width of each interval?
   a. 4, 0.1667
   b. 5, 0.2
   c. 6, 0.25
   d. 6, 0.1667
   e. 4, 0.25

ANSWER: D

15. Consider a random number drawn according to a uniform distribution. Which of these values is more likely to be drawn?
    a.   1.0
    b.   0.25
    c.   0.50
    d.   0.75
    e.   all of these values are equally likely.

ANSWER: E

16. If a random number 0.8032 is drawn, the very next random number is more likely to be
    a.   between 1.0 and 0.8032.
    b.   smaller than 0.8032.
    c.   larger than 0.8032.
    d.   between 0.0 and 0.8032.
    e.   it is not known what the next number will be.

ANSWER: E

17. In any simulation model, the questions of interest are likely to be centered about the distribution of the random variable in question. If the random variable were to be profit (P), then all but which of the following questions would be of interest?
    a.   What is the shape of the probability density function of P?
    b.   What is the probability that P will exceed some given amount?
    c.   What is the probability that P will be less than some given amount?
    d.   What is the expected value and standard deviation of P
    e.   All of these questions would be of interest.

ANSWER: E

18. A simulation model should never be used when
    a.   a simpler solution methodology is available.
    b.   there are many random variables interacting, and guessing the outcome of a scenario is nearly impossible.
    c.   one cannot verify the results by implementing each tested scenario.
    d.   to build the model, one has to guess about or estimate some of the distributions and parameters to use within the model.
    e.   all of these are true.

ANSWER: A

Strategy

The Strategic Management Process

CMBA Objective Correlations

- Identify the key elements of strategy.

- Identify the attributes of a good strategy.

- Identify the key levels of strategy.

- Distinguish between vision and mission.

- Distinguish between different perspectives on strategy.

- Describe the various steps in the assessment of a strategy.

Sample Questions

1. The purpose of strategy in business organizations is:
   a. To integrate effort
   b. To set direction
   c. To set the tone
   d. All of the above

ANSWER: D

2. Why does an articulated strategy matter to business organizations?
   a. Improved efficiency
   b. Improved effectiveness
   c. Survival
   d. All of the above

ANSWER: D

3. What is the purpose of the SW in SWOT analysis?
   a. Internal assessment
   b. External assessment
   c. Off set the OT
   d. Define opportunities

ANSWER: A

4. What is the purpose of OT in SWOT analysis?
   a. Internal assessment
   b. External assessment
   c. Offset the SW
   d. Define weaknesses

ANSWER: B

5. Competitive advantage can lead to:
   a. Greater profitability
   b. Survival
   c. Increased cash flow
   d. All of the above

ANSWER: D

6. Goals are used to:
   a. Communicate what has to be done
   b. Focus effort
   c. Both A & B
   d. Neither A or B

ANSWER: C

7. SWOT analysis is used as a tool to:
   a. Develop strategic alternatives
   b. Analyze opportunities
   c. Develop evaluations of current strategy
   d. All of the above

ANSWER: D

8. Single business firms have different management concerns than multibusiness firms because:
   a. They are less focused
   b. They have fewer markets to follow
   c. Risk concerns are lower
   d. All of the above

ANSWER: D

9. The industry environment in which business competition occurs is know as:
   a. Terrain
   b. Climate
   c. Culture
   d. Strategy

ANSWER: A

10. The aspect of direction setting for a firm that is the broadest in scope is:
    a. Mission
    b. Goals
    c. Vision
    d. Objectives

ANSWER: C

11. Strategy is an attempt to match:
    a. Industry and company strengths
    b. Competition and industry
    c. Economic development and strategy
    d. Structure and personnel

ANSWER: A

12. Mission is:
    a. The essence of strategy
    b. A statement of what business the firm is in
    c. A statement of the CEO's vision
    d. None of the above

ANSWER: B

13. The purpose of goals and objectives is to:
    a. Provide direction
    b. Create time limitations
    c. Create strategic focus
    d. All of the above

ANSWER: D

14. Which of the following is *not* a part of the strategic management process?
    a. Formulation
    b. Implementation
    c. Development
    d. Analysis

ANSWER: C

15. Business strategy is characterized by:
    a. A multi-division company
    b. A focus strategy
    c. A strategy that is in one line of business
    d. The development of diversified firm

ANSWER: C

16. Who generally carries the responsibility for strategic management?
    a. Management
    b. All employees
    c. Strategic managers
    d. Top managers

ANSWER: D

17. Which of the following is *not* a stakeholder of a business firm?
    a. The community
    b. Shareholders
    c. Employees of competing firms
    d. Employees

ANSWER: C

18. Fiduciary responsibility refers to:
    a. Making ethical decisions
    b. Making unethical decisions
    c. Making decisions in the best interest of the company
    d. Making decisions in the best interest of specific employees

ANSWER: C

19. Corporate managers are responsible for:
    a. The corporation
    b. The management of the corporate portfolio
    c. The management of specific SBUs
    d. The development of the firm's strategy

ANSWER: B

The Competitive Environment: Assessing Industry Attractiveness

CMBA Objective Correlations

- Describe how you would use the Porter 5 forces framework to do a structural analysis of an industry.

- Define the various ways in which an industry can be defined.

- Describe strategic groups and identify how they are useful in industry analysis.

- Describe the various stages of industry evolution.

- Describe various industry structures and their implications for strategy.

- Describe Porter's generic strategies.

Sample Questions

1. Strategic groups are:
   a. Groups of strategic managers
   b. Groups of firms
   c. Strategically similar groups of firms
   d. Teams inside business organizations

ANSWER: C

2. The industry environment includes which of the following:
   a. Competition
   b. Technological product/service changes
   c. Suppliers
   d. All of the above

ANSWER: D

3. Exit barriers are:
   a. Walls in buildings
   b. Impediments to competition
   c. Restraints on leaving an industry
   d. All of the above

ANSWER. C

4. Environmental scanning is used to:
    a. Formulate strategies
    b. Implement strategies
    c. Change strategies
    d. All of the above

ANSWER: A

5. The five forces model of the industry environment are used for:
    a. Competitive analysis
    b. Supplier analysis
    c. Buyer analysis
    d. All of the above

ANSWER: D

6. Barriers to entry are:
    a. Costs associated with industry entry
    b. Walls and doors
    c. Competitive advantages
    d. All of the above

ANSWER: A

7. Economies of scale occur when:
    a. Assets increase
    b. Variable costs increase
    c. Volume decreases
    d. Volume increases

ANSWER: D

8. Which of the following is a technique utilized to monitor changes in the environment?
    a. Competitive intelligence gathering
    b. Strategic grouping
    c. Retaliation
    d. All of the above

ANSWER: A

9. Industry rivalry is the center of the five forces model. What does it represent?
    a. Suppliers
    b. Buyers
    c. Competition
    d. Substitutes

ANSWER: C

10. Supplier power influences the cost structure of:
    a. Substitute products
    b. Buyers
    c. Non-competitors
    d. Competitors

ANSWER: D

11. The elements of the five forces model should be good predictors of:
    a. Environmental scanning
    b. Switching costs
    c. Industry profitability
    d. All of the above

ANSWER: C

12. The power of substitute products on a firm's current strategy is harder to understand when:
    a. Suppliers are powerful
    b. Buyers are powerful
    c. Technology is changing fast
    d. All of the above

ANSWER: C

13. The following are a part of the general environment:
    a. Demographic trends
    b. Political environment
    c. Social/cultural trends
    d. All of the above

ANSWER: D

14. The political environment contains:
    a. Government regulation
    b. New laws and bills
    c. Enforcement agencies and their policies
    d. All of the above

ANSWER: D

15. The social/cultural environment is characterized by *all but which* of the following:
    a. Values
    b. Corporate culture
    c. Beliefs
    d. Ideals

ANSWER: B

16. Large technological developments in a firm's industry usually cause a firm's existing strategy to be:
    a. More profitable
    b. Less profitable
    c. More viable
    d. More logical

ANSWER: B

17. Which of the following is *not* a key indicator of industry attractiveness?
    a. Level of competition
    b. Ease of entry
    c. Strategic groups
    d. Existence of substitute products

ANSWER: C

18. Which of the following is *not* an example of entry barriers?
    a. Brand identity
    b. Economies of scale
    c. Product differentiation
    d. Competitive strategy

ANSWER: D

19. The level of industry rivalry is characterized by *all but which* of the following?
    a. Strength of the industry leader
    b. The number of competitors
    c. Fast paced industry growth
    d. Exit barriers

ANSWER: C

20. Strategic groups are defined by *all but which* of the following:
    a. Similar technology
    b. Similar strategy
    c. Markets served
    d. Level of competition

ANSWER: D

21. Competition within strategic groups is often more heated than:
    a. Competition in other parts of the industry
    b. Between strategic groups
    c. With other industries
    d. The industry's suppliers or buyers

ANSWER: B

22. The PC industry is a good example to analyze using the five forces model because:
    a. The level of competition in the industry
    b. The low level of supplier power
    c. The lack of substitute products
    d. The low level of buyer power

ANSWER: A

23. Environmental scanning involves:
    a. Assessment of the external environment
    b. Assessment of competitors
    c. Intelligence gathering of moves by competitors
    d. All of the above

ANSWER: D

24. Industries that have just a few suppliers tend to:
    a. Have lower levels of profitability
    b. Have increased rivalry
    c. Have increased buyer power
    d. Have higher rates of return

ANSWER: A

25. Industries that have many buyers tend to:
    a. Have lower levels of profitability
    b. Have increased rivalry
    c. Have increased buyer power
    d. Have higher rates of return

ANSWER: D

26. Michael Porter argues that competitive advantage in international markets comes from having the:
    a. cheapest product.
    b. cheapest labor.
    c. best natural resources.
    d. best innovation.

ANSWER: D

27. Factors of production in Porter's model of international competitive advantage include all of the following EXCEPT:
    a. labor.
    b. capital.
    c. infrastructure.
    d. quality of demand.

ANSWER: D

Strategy   421

28. The four aspects of Porter's model of international competitive advantage include all of the following <u>EXCEPT</u>:
   a. factors of production.
   b. demand conditions.
   c. substitute products.
   d. related and supporting industries.

ANSWER: C

29. In addition to the four basic dimensions of Porter's "diamond" model, _____ may also contribute to the success or failure of firms.
   a. management skill
   b. educational requirements
   c. government policy
   d. national pride

ANSWER: C

Firm Capabilities: Assessing Strengths and Weaknesses

CMBA Objective Correlations

- Distinguish between economies of scale and scope.

- Distinguish between core competence and distinctive competence.

- Describe key components of a value chain and value system.

- Define value as commonly used in strategic management.

- Describe vulnerability analysis.

Sample Questions

1. The value chain is:
   a. Used to analyze activities that create value for a firm
   b. Made of steel
   c. Another name for a SWOT analysis
   d. None of the above

ANSWER: A

2. Downstream activities could include:
   a. Fishing
   b. Wholesaling
   c. Retailing
   d. Procurement

ANSWER: C

3. Competitive advantage creates:
   a. Capability drivers
   b. Primary activities
   c. Support activities
   d. Increased market share

ANSWER: D

4. First mover advantage entails:
   a. Early R & D
   b. Innovation
   c. Early market entry
   d. Vertical integration

ANSWER: C

5. Distinctive competence is important to the development of competitive advantages because:
   a. It is what competitive advantages are based on
   b. They are different
   c. It provides the capital needed
   d. It assures higher profits

ANSWER: D

6. Product development has an especially powerful effect on:
   a. Primary activities
   b. Capability drivers
   c. Distinctive competence
   d. First mover advantage

ANSWER: D

7. The experience curve can lead to sustainable:
   a. Profits
   b. Cash flow
   c. Competitive advantage
   d. Distinctive competence

ANSWER: C

8. Vertical integration involves the acquisition of:
   a. Buyers
   b. Competitors
   c. Substitute products
   d. Securities

ANSWER: A

9. The concept of leverage is most relevant to which of the following ratios?
   a. Return on assets
   b. Total asset turnover
   c. Debt to equity
   d. Fixed asset turnover

ANSWER: C

10. Comparative financial analysis for firms must be conducted:
    a. Using audited financial statements
    b. By CPAs
    c. Across multiple time periods
    d. At the end of the fiscal year

ANSWER: C

11. Of the return ratios, which is likely to be most important to shareholders?
    a. Return on assets
    b. Fixed asset turnover
    c. Return on equity
    d. Return on sales

ANSWER: C

12. Which of the following ratios measures liquidity?
    a. Current ratio
    b. Debt to asset
    c. Total asset turnover
    d. Return on sales

ANSWER: A

13. Relatedness between business units can be termed a:
    a. Capability driver
    b. Good thing
    c. Learning curve effect
    d. None of the above

ANSWER: A

14. Value added is the extent to which:
    a. A firm is valuable
    b. It increases stock value
    c. The value of the business system
    d. A firm's products are improved

ANSWER: D

15. Primary activities include:
    a. Procurement
    b. Operations
    c. Human resource management
    d. Technology development

ANSWER: B

16. The extent to which a firm can hold its place in its industry is affected by:
    a. Capability drivers
    b. Competitive advantage
    c. Distinctive competence
    d. All of the above

ANSWER: D

17. Which of the following is *not* a support activity?
    a. Procurement
    b. Information technology
    c. Personnel
    d. Web development

ANSWER: D

18. Which of the following is *not* a source of first-mover advantage?
    a. Patents
    b. Location
    c. Government laws
    d. Licenses

ANSWER: C

19. Reengineering is the process by which a company:
    a. Decides what to do strategically
    b. Changes what its people do daily
    c. Reinvents how its business operates
    d. Develop an understanding of their competitors

ANSWER: C

20. Which of the following is *not* a capability driver?
    a. First mover advantage
    b. Scale of operation
    c. Security
    d. Experience

ANSWER: C

21. Which of the following is an activity ratio?
    a. Current Ratio
    b. Debt-to-Equity Ratio
    c. Inventory Turnover
    d. Return on Equity

ANSWER: C

Opportunities for Distinction: Building Competitive Advantage

CMBA Objective Correlations

- Distinguish between vertical and horizontal differentiation.

- Describe the factors that contribute to competitive advantage.

- Describe the factors that affect sustainability of competitive advantage.

- Identify various levels of uncertainty and ways of dealing with the same.

- Identify the elements of parenting advantage.

- Describe critical success factors.

Sample Questions

1. A shorter product life cycle would have the following effect on strategic decision making:
   a. Slow down
   b. Speed up
   c. No effect
   d. None of the above

ANSWER: B

2. A just-in-time inventory system has the following effects on business firms:
   a. Increase costs
   b. Increase buyer/supplier interactions
   c. Decrease flexibility
   d. Increase inventory

ANSWER: B

3. Modular product designs are characterized by:
   a. Difficult development
   b. More product failure
   c. Multiple products based on similar parts
   d. Higher R&D costs

ANSWER: C

4. The ability to produce small numbers of a product at low costs that approximate those of companies with high economies of scale is called:
   a. Low-cost leadership
   b. Batch production
   c. Mass customization
   d. Magic

ANSWER: C

5. Focus strategies are:
   a. Strategies focused toward a particular market segment
   b. Strategies focused toward everyone
   c. Not segment specific
   d. Used to address broad market categories

ANSWER: A

6. Quality is:
   a. What the customer thinks it is
   b. More important in service industries
   c. A specific measurement that can be performed by a firm
   d. Not important when using a low-cost leadership strategy

ANSWER: A

7. Low-cost leadership is one of the three:
   a. Distinctive competencies
   b. Generic strategies
   c. Competitive advantages
   d. General strategies

ANSWER: B

8. The product life cycle consists of all the following steps *except*:
   a. Introductory
   b. Growth
   c. Maturity
   d. Death

ANSWER: D

9. Competitive advantage is most often developed at which level of analysis?
   a. Individual level
   b. Group level
   c. National level
   d. Industry level

ANSWER: D

10. In which of the generic strategies is expense control most important?
    a. Focus
    b. Low-cost leadership
    c. Differentiation
    d. Mass customization

ANSWER: B

11. Which of the following is (are) important to developing low-cost leadership?
    a. Experience curve
    b. Economies of scale
    c. Vertical integration
    d. All of the above

ANSWER: D

12. Differentiation is an effort to establish competitive advantage through:
    a. Product innovation
    b. Producing at lower costs than rivals do
    c. Focusing on a market segment
    d. None of the above

ANSWER: A

13. Vertical integration is the process by which:
    a. A firms starts buying their competitors
    b. A firm starts selling units to competitors
    c. A firm develops a new strategic alliance
    d. A firm buys either their customers or their suppliers

ANSWER: D

14. Focus strategies do *not* have which of the following characteristics?
    a. A small market segment
    b. A specified solution to a particular problem
    c. A wide distribution pattern
    d. Extensive use of intensive promotional methods

ANSWER: C

15. Advanced manufacturing technologies have begun to:
    a. Blur the lines between generic strategies
    b. Increase costs
    c. Hold strategies constant
    d. Decrease strategic instability

ANSWER: A

16. The maturity stage of the product life cycle is most often associated with:
    a. Rapid growth
    b. Uncertainty in the market
    c. Improvements in manufacturing processes
    d. High exit barriers

ANSWER: C

17. Cost drivers are especially important to which of the following strategies:
    a. Differentiation
    b. Focus
    c. Low-cost
    d. Mixed

ANSWER: C

18. Which of the following is *not* an example of distinctive competence?
    a. Exceptional quality
    b. High technical skill
    c. Engineering design
    d. Differentiation

ANSWER: D

19. Focus strategies enable a firm to avoid which of the following?
    a. Direct competition
    b. Financial losses
    c. High profits
    d. None of the above

ANSWER: A

20. One of the main disadvantages of the low-cost leadership strategy is:
    a. It is easily copied
    b. It implies poor quality to customers
    c. It is vulnerable to "commoditization"
    d. It is too complex for most employees to understand

ANSWER: A

21. Which of the following is a response to technological changes?
    a. Prospecting
    b. Defending
    c. Harvesting
    d. All of the above

ANSWER: D

22. Defending is a strategy that involves the preservation of a company's current:
    a. Mission
    b. Value chain
    c. Market share
    d. Pricing structure

ANSWER: C

23. A firm with a strong ability to change that faces a low magnitude of threat from changes in the environment should choose which type of response?
    a. Prospecting
    b. Harvesting
    c. Investing
    d. Defending

ANSWER: D

24. The biggest reason that firms have a hard time adjusting to changes in the external environment is:
    a. An entrenched strategy
    b. Large size
    c. Strong culture
    d. All of the above

ANSWER: D

25. Which of the following is *not* an example of an industry change trigger?
    a. A new technology
    b. A shift in the industry's economics
    c. New distribution channels
    d. Addition of new top management team personnel in a competing firm

ANSWER: D

26. The firm successfully implementing the cost leadership strategy would expect:

    a. competitors to compete against it primarily on the basis of prices charged.
    b. to constantly face challenges from a steady stream of new entrants to the industry.
    c. to be able to fend off the challenge of product substitutes.
    d. to focus on its own cost structure, but not its competitors' cost structures.

ANSWER: C

27. The firm successfully implementing a differentiation strategy would expect all of the following EXCEPT:

    a. customers to be more sensitive to price increases.
    b. to be able to charge a premium price for its product.
    c. to be able to pass additional costs of supplies to the customer.
    d. to be partially insulated from competitive rivalry.

ANSWER: A

28. A firm successfully implementing a differentiation strategy would expect:

    a. customers to be sensitive to price increases.
    b. to charge premium prices.
    c. customers to perceive the product as standard.
    d. to automatically have high levels of power over suppliers.

ANSWER: B

29. Companies successfully implementing an integrated cost leadership/differentiation strategy are better positioned to do all of the following EXCEPT:

    a. learn new skills.
    b. adapt quickly to a changing environment.
    c. continue using current technology.
    d. leverage core competencies across business units.

ANSWER: C

30. It is unethical to do which of the following to a competitor's products?

    a. Buy information from employees
    b. Examine the products bought at the store
    c. Question employees about the products
    d. Develop comprehensive testing facilities for competitor's products

ANSWER: A

Competing on the Net: Building Virtual Advantage

CMBA Objective Correlations

- Describe network effects.

- Describe what factors were ignored by dot.coms in developing their strategies.

Sample Questions

1. The Internet is a potential source of _____ for many companies.
   a. Customers
   b. Competitive advantage
   c. Employees
   d. Distributors

ANSWER: B

2. The idea of virtual advantage is based on:
   a. Financial resources
   b. Disintermediation
   c. Network effects
   d. Speed

ANSWER: D

3. Sources of virtual advantage include:
   a. Speed of competitive response
   b. Knowledge of customers
   c. Consistency of customer service
   d. All of the above

ANSWER: D

4. Key drivers of Internet-Based business models include:
   a. High information intensity
   b. Lower levels of competition
   c. Less price sensitivity
   d. Low price elasticity

ANSWER: A

5. Prices have become _____ since the Internet was developed.
   a. Higher
   b. More transparent
   c. Less variable
   d. Less important to customers

ANSWER: B

6. Disintermediation is characterized by which of the following?
    a. Shorter value chains
    b. Less contact between manufacture and end consumer
    c. Increased use of distributors and wholesalers
    d. None of the above

ANSWER: A

7. One of the key advantages for customers of e-businesses is:
    a. Extreme convenience
    b. Product testing
    c. Shorter product development time
    d. None of the above

ANSWER: A

8. Product life cycles become _____ with the advent of the Internet.
    a. Longer
    b. Cyclical
    c. Shorter
    d. None of the above

ANSWER: C

9. The failure of many of the Business-to-Consumer websites was based on:
    a. Poor website design
    b. Weak customer relationships
    c. Technological advances
    d. Price variation

ANSWER: B

10. In the Internet age the customer will have:
    a. Less power
    b. The same power
    c. More power
    d. No power

ANSWER: C

11. One of the bases for the development of competitive advantage using the Internet is:
    a. Increased exposure
    b. Immediacy of competitive response
    c. Long-term value of the Internet
    d. The innovation of early stage companies

ANSWER: B

12. One of the biggest strengths of Internet-based strategies is that they:
   a. Impact only the local area
   b. Develop slowly
   c. Create minimal impact
   d. Have no geographic boundaries

ANSWER: D

13. The product mix of Internet firms is:
   a. Wider than traditional firms
   b. More narrow than traditional firms
   c. No different than traditional firms
   d. None of the above

ANSWER: A

14. The easy availability of pricing data to consumers creates:
   a. Less competition
   b. More competition
   c. The same level of competition
   d. Little competition

ANSWER: B

15. Network effects refer to the extent to which:
   a. Networks make communication easier
   b. Networks make communication harder
   c. The value of the network goes up the higher the number of people who use it
   d. The value of the network goes up the lower the number of people who use it

ANSWER: C

16. An example of a Consumer-to-Consumer platform includes:
   a. EBay
   b. Amazon
   c. Bluelight.com
   d. Yahoo

ANSWER: A

17. Business-to-Business platforms were designed to create a portal through which:
   a. Industry goods would be traded
   b. Exchange of information between buyers and suppliers would be easier
   c. Development of new products would be easier
   d. All of the above

ANSWER: D

18. An example of a Business-to-Consumer portal includes which one of the following?
    a. EBay
    b. Amazon.com
    c. MetalSite.com
    d. Chemconnect.com

ANSWER: B

19. The primary motive for developing Business-to-Business platforms is to:
    a. Expand a firm's sales territory
    b. Reduce transaction costs
    c. Lengthen a firm's value chain
    d. Bypass the middleman to reach consumers directly

ANSWER: B

20. Mass customization is _____ possible because of the Internet.
    a. Less
    b. Not
    c. More
    d. None of the above

ANSWER: C

21. One of the biggest bases for competitive advantage that could be developed from the Internet is:
    a. Information overload
    b. Tracking consumer tastes in real time
    c. Tracking sales in real time
    d. None of the above

ANSWER: B

22. Providers of highly standardized products face:
    a. Little competition in the future
    b. The same amount of competition in the future
    c. No competition in the future
    d. High levels of competition in the future

ANSWER: D

Corporate Strategy: Leveraging Resources to Extend Advantage

CMBA Objective Correlations

- Describe synergy and identify examples of it.

- Distinguish between vertical and horizontal integration.

- Describe the key components of a business model.

- Distinguish between integration and diversification.

- Describe corporate motives for mergers and acquisitions.

- Describe the process for evaluating mergers and acquisitions.

- Describe what is meant by "stuck in the middle."

- Describe the typical factors that cause an organization to go into decline.

- Describe the process involved in the strategic transformation of an organization in decline.

Sample Questions

1. Full integration is the concept of controlling:
    a. The value chain
    b. The market
    c. The product mix
    d. Competitors

ANSWER: A

2. Related diversification involves merger or acquisition activities with companies that:
    a. Have different products
    b. Are direct competitors
    c. Employ similar technologies
    d. Have similar distinctive competencies

ANSWER: D

3. The resource-based view of the firm says that strategies should be developed that maximize the effect of a firms resources on:
    a. Profit
    b. ROE
    c. Competitive advantage
    d. Competitors

ANSWER: C

4. Synergy is a concept that argues that when combining business units it is possible for:
   a. The sum to be greater than the parts
   b. Gaining profits
   c. Increasing ROI
   d. All of the above

ANSWER: A

5. Sharing activities is an important concept in:
   a. Related diversification
   b. Unrelated diversification
   c. The development of synergies
   d. All of the above

ANSWER: A

6. Unrelated diversification is an attempt to limit:
   a. Risk
   b. Profit
   c. ROI
   d. ROE

ANSWER: A

7. Partial diversification is diversification that:
   a. Is selective about which activities the firm will perform
   b. Is all inclusive
   c. Attempts to minimize competitiveness
   d. All of the above

ANSWER: A

8. Related diversification seeks to create:
   a. Profits
   b. Synergy
   c. ROE
   d. All of the above

ANSWER: B

9. Costs of cooperation include:
   a. Communication
   b. Accountability
   c. Compromise
   d. All of the above

ANSWER: D

10. Corporate restructuring is the process of:
    a. Organizational redesign
    b. Cost cutting
    c. Spinning units off
    d. All of the above

ANSWER: D

11. Dangers of conglomerate diversification include:
    a. Loss of focus
    b. Neglect of main business
    c. Loss of competitive advantage
    d. All of the above

ANSWER: D

12. Access to resources for competitive advantage is a key aspect of:
    a. Integration
    b. Merger and acquisitions
    c. Relatedness
    d. None of the above

ANSWER: B

13. Which of the following is a potential reason or benefit for diversification?
    a. Growth
    b. Profitability
    c. Stability
    d. All of the above

ANSWER: D

14. Resources should be of prime consideration in corporate strategy because:
    a. Resources are the basis for competitive advantage
    b. We need resources to compete
    c. Resources are the basis for operations
    d. We need resources for strategic planning

ANSWER: A

15. A firm's scope of operations refers to the:
    a. Diversity of industries in which it operates
    b. The extent to which it has a corporate strategy
    c. The extent to which it has research and development
    d. How many plants it has

ANSWER: A

16. Types of vertical integration include:
    a. Forward
    b. Sideways
    c. Extended
    d. Developed

ANSWER: A

17. The concept of "fit" in corporate strategy refers to the extent the firm's _____ fit together.
    a. Functions
    b. Service and products
    c. Business units
    d. Outsourcing

ANSWER: C

18. The most important reason to diversify is to reduce risk by:
    a. Creating value
    b. Creating inimitable resources and abilities
    c. Developing a new firm
    d. Creating competitive advantage

ANSWER: B

19. Unrelated diversification is basically focused on:
    a. Creating value
    b. Increasing profitability
    c. Increasing returns
    d. Decreasing risk

ANSWER: D

20. Diversification is attractive to companies because it can:
    a. Lead to faster growth
    b. Lead to higher profitability
    c. Lead to higher stability
    d. All of the above

ANSWER: D

21. Which of the following is *not* a common motive to diversify?
    a. Access to expertise
    b. Access to human resources
    c. Access to technology
    d. Access to physical assets

ANSWER: B

22. Which of the following does *not* characterize sharing activities?
    a. Common research and development group
    b. Different accounting groups
    c. Common distribution systems
    d. Common marketing departments

ANSWER: B

Global Strategy: Harnessing New Markets to Extend Advantage

CMBA Objective Correlations

- Describe forces driving globalization.

- Distinguish between multinational, global and transnational strategies

- Describe key organizational challenges in globalization.

Sample Questions

1. Expanding across international borders is increasing because of:
    a. Narrowing of demand characteristics
    b. Escalating costs of R & D
    c. Reduction of factor costs
    d. All of the above

ANSWER: D

2. A firm spent $600 million to develop a new product, and realizes that it will need to sell the product in markets all over the world in order to recoup its costs. Which environmental factor accelerating globalization does this represent?
    a. Narrowing of demand characteristics
    b. Role of government policy
    c. Escalating costs of R & D
    d. New distribution channels

ANSWER: C

3. Using a global strategy, a firm seeks to operate with:
    a. Operational consistency
    b. Different products
    c. In many international markets
    d. All of the above

ANSWER: A

4. A multi-domestic strategy is a strategy of:
    a. Global consistency
    b. National segmentation
    c. One product line and mix
    d. None of the above

ANSWER: B

5. The key benefit to international expansion is:
    a. Revenue growth
    b. Access to additional markets
    c. Increased ROE
    d. All of the above

ANSWER: D

6. Most strategists tend to argue for the benefits of internationalization without understanding which of the following:
    a. Costs
    b. Improved ROI
    c. A larger value chain
    d. All of the above

ANSWER: A

7. Competitive advantages can be developed from internationalization by:
    a. Access to non-domestic technology
    b. Increased resources
    c. Purchase of non-domestic technologies
    d. All of the above

ANSWER: D

8. Information technology and media proliferation have caused which of the following:
    a. Population homogeneity
    b. Market homogeneity
    c. Cultural striations
    d. None of the above

ANSWER: B

9. The costs of globalization around the world are being offset by:
    a. Lower foreign labor costs
    b. Higher material costs
    c. Competitive national markets
    d. None of the above

ANSWER: A

10. In a global strategy business units are considered to be:
   a. Highly interdependent
   b. Having less ROE impact
   c. To have little effect on other business units
   d. All of the above

ANSWER: A

11. The multi-domestic strategy argues that business units should be:
   a. Highly interdependent
   b. Equally important
   c. Independent and entrepreneurial
   d. None of the above

ANSWER: C

12. Benefits of global expansion do *not* include:
   a. Market growth
   b. Recovery of R & D costs
   c. Image creation
   d. Increased strategic flexibility

ANSWER: D

13. Which of the following is among the costs of an international strategy?
   a. Costs of cooperation
   b. Costs of flexibility
   c. Costs of strategic leverage
   d. All of the above

ANSWER: D

14. Heterogeneity of demand is most often characterized by:
   a. The sale of component products
   b. Basic research and development
   c. Only products
   d. Only services

ANSWER: A

15. Globalization has allowed firms to utilize _____ in multiple markets.
   a. A common currency
   b. Common ethical standards
   c. Research and development
   d. A common language

ANSWER: C

16. The major attraction(s) for U.S. companies in moving companies abroad include:
    a. Lower cost labor
    b. Taxes
    c. Government regulation
    d. Superior infrastructure

ANSWER: A

17. Which of the following factors has encouraged global business development?
    a. Decreasing communications costs
    b. New distribution channels
    c. Improvements in inventory control systems
    d. All of the above

ANSWER: D

18. Strategies to expand globally should include an examination of:
    a. The firm's strategic resource base
    b. The ability of their current employees to speak foreign languages
    c. Owning foreign lands and properties
    d. A developed strategic alliance with a foreign company

ANSWER: A

19. Which of the following is a part of a global strategy?
    a. Standardization
    b. Plant location
    c. Leveraging resources
    d. All of the above

ANSWER: D

20. Which of the following is *not* a benefit of globalization?
    a. Increased demand for products
    b. Decreased complexity of business decisions
    c. Creates a strong image of the business
    d. Full recovery of the firm's investment

ANSWER: B

21. Which of the following is *not* a cost of globalization?
    a. Increased market exposure
    b. Increased management coordination
    c. Increased exposure to economic cycles
    d. Loss of strategic flexibility

ANSWER: A

Strategic Alliances: Teaming and Allying for Advantage

CMBA Objective Correlations

- Describe different types of alliances.

- Identify the advantages and disadvantages of alliances.

Sample Questions

1. Strategic alliances are:
    a. Strategically valuable relationships
    b. Links between business units within a single firm
    c. By definition, in violation of anti-trust laws
    d. None of the above

ANSWER: A

2. The reasons for forming strategic alliances include:
    a. Extension of product line
    b. Organizational learning
    c. New market entry
    d. All of the above

ANSWER: D

3. Joint ventures are potential cooperative relationships that can help develop:
    a. Synergies
    b. Organizational learning
    c. Industry standards
    d. All of the above

ANSWER: D

4. Firms often enter joint ventures to learn and understand the market applications of:
    a. New technology
    b. Research
    c. Corporate culture
    d. Management

ANSWER: A

5. The most complex form of strategic alliances is:
   a. Consortia
   b. Licensing
   c. Joint ventures
   d. Cooperation

ANSWER: A

6. Joint ventures allow firms to benefit from:
   a. Vertical integration
   b. New skills
   c. New technologies
   d. All of the above

ANSWER: D

7. Key risks of strategic alliances include:
   a. Financial loss
   b. Loss of proprietary knowledge
   c. Lower ROI
   d. Decrease in cash flow

ANSWER: B

8. Which of the following is *not* a cost of alliance control or operation?
   a. Legal costs
   b. Coordination costs
   c. Learning costs
   d. Inflexibility costs

ANSWER: A

9. Inflexibility can develop from strategic alliances because of an inability to:
   a. Utilize skills
   b. Utilize technologies
   c. Get permission from partners
   d. None of the above

ANSWER: C

10. One of the major predictors of joint venture failure is an incompatibility with:
    a. Technology base
    b. Skill base
    c. Organizational cultures
    d. All of the above

ANSWER: C

11. The steps that help firms develop an effective alliance strategy include:
    a. Understanding skills
    b. Choosing complementary partners
    c. Keeping alliance personnel long-term
    d. All of the above

ANSWER: D

12. Which of the following is a type of strategic alliance?
    a. Teaming up
    b. Cooperation
    c. Multi-partner consortia
    d. Exchange

ANSWER: C

13. Most firms use strategic alliances as an effort to:
    a. Test new markets without full commitment of resources
    b. Develop a new relationship
    c. Build better relationships with suppliers
    d. Develop the firm's network

ANSWER: A

14. Many firms use joint ventures as a way to gain access to the latest:
    a. Stars in the industry
    b. Technologies
    c. Products
    d. Brands

ANSWER: B

15. Companies will often develop strategic alliances in an effort to:
    a. Improve the level of strategic learning
    b. Improve older relationships
    c. Gain access to people
    d. Augment the firm's current understanding of what is new

ANSWER: A

16. Strategic alliances between two competitors can be used to:
    a. Develop a competing product
    b. Develop a new technology
    c. Round out the product line
    d. None of the above

ANSWER: C

17. Using a strategic alliance for global expansion improves a firm's:
    a. Market penetration
    b. Number of new products
    c. Advertising coverage
    d. Quick market access

ANSWER: D

18. Vertical integration generally occurs using which type of strategic alliance?
    a. Joint venture
    b. License arrangement
    c. Technology development
    d. None of the above

ANSWER: A

19. A potential risk of strategic alliances includes:
    a. Incompatibility of partners
    b. Dependence on the partner
    c. Risk of knowledge drain
    d. All of the above

ANSWER: D

20. The risk of dependence refers to:
    a. Drug and alcohol addiction
    b. The need for continued market expansion
    c. Over-reliance on a partner's skill set
    d. A need for continued capital contributions

ANSWER: B

21. Strategic alliances can paradoxically become a source of strategic:
    a. Flexibility
    b. Inertia
    c. Inflexibility
    d. Advantage

ANSWER: C

Strategy Implementation: Organizing for Advantage

CMBA Objective Correlations

- Describe the structure-conduct-performance paradigm.

- Describe the two-dimensional growth vector matrix.

Sample Questions

1. Matrix structures have which of the following as an advantage?
    a. Slow decision-making
    b. High cost
    c. High levels of collaboration
    d. High stress levels

ANSWER: C

2. Specialization is especially conducive in which of the following structures?
    a. Functional
    b. Geographic
    c. Matrix
    d. All of the above

ANSWER: D

3. The strategic business unit structure is a variation of which of the following broad categories of industry structures?
    a. Product
    b. Geographic
    c. Matrix
    d. Functional

ANSWER: A

4. Which of the following is *not* a basic form of organizational structure?
    a. Product
    b. Matrix
    c. Practice
    d. Functional

ANSWER: C

5. The benefits of a simple structure include all of the following <u>EXCEPT</u>:
    a. providing ease of coordination within the organization.
    b. permitting direct communication.
    c. active involvement by the owner-manager.
    d. allowing quick commercialization of products.

ANSWER: C

6. The functional structure allows for effective:
    a. control of strategic issues by functional managers.
    b. control of potentially time-consuming activities by the chief executive.
    c. control of any myopic vision.
    d. development of professional expertise in functional areas.

ANSWER: D

7. Functional structures work best for firms with:
    a. diversified products.
    b. diversified markets.
    c. single and dominant business strategies.
    d. conglomerate strategies.

ANSWER: C

8. One disadvantage of the functional structure is that:
    a. career paths and professional development are not facilitated.
    b. it does not allow for functional specialization.
    c. the CEO cannot coordinate and control the efforts of functional level employees.
    d. communication is hindered among organizational functions.

ANSWER: D

9. Which of the following does <u>NOT</u> cause a firm to move from a functional structure to a multidivisional structure?
    a. Increasing diversification
    b. Coordination and control issues
    c. Decreasing sales revenues
    d. Greater amounts of data and information to process

ANSWER: C

10. The functional structure works well in large firms implementing a _____ strategy.
    a. differentiation
    b. highly diversified
    c. backward vertical integration
    d. horizontal integration

ANSWER: A

11. Which of the following is a true statement about organizational structures for implementing business-level strategies?
    a. A cost leadership strategy requires a simple structure emphasizing high specialization, centralization, and structured job roles.
    b. A differentiation strategy requires a functional structure with limited formalization, broad job descriptions, and an emphasis on the R&D and marketing functions.
    c. An integrated cost leadership/differentiation strategy requires a multidivisional structure using high formalization, decentralized decision-making, and vertical coordination.
    d. A focused strategy requires a functional structure featuring high levels of both specialization and formalization.

ANSWER: B

12. Which of the following is a true statement about implementing corporate-level strategies and effective organizational structures?
    a. Firms pursuing a related-linked strategy should implement a competitive structure with a competitive culture and centralized strategic planning activities.
    b. Firms pursuing an unrelated diversification strategy should use an SBU structure with a small corporate staff, emphasize the R&D function, and integrate divisions to achieve synergies.
    c. Firms pursuing a related-linked strategy should use an SBU structure, emphasize independence among divisions, and manage the strategic planning function from the central office.
    d. Firms pursuing a related-constrained strategy should implement a cooperative structure, use integrative devices to link divisions, centralize the R&D function, and emphasize sharing.

ANSWER: D

13. A matrix organization is characterized by:
    a. hierarchy of authority.
    b. decentralized decision making.
    c. a dual organization combining both functional specialization and business product or project specialization.
    d. a dual organization featuring both multidivisional and simple organizational structures.

ANSWER: C

14. A firm pursuing an unrelated diversification strategy will utilize a _____ structure.
    a. matrix
    b. cooperative form multidivisional
    c. competitive form multidivisional
    d. functional

ANSWER: C